Away for the WEEKEND™

Away for the WEEKEND™

Eleanor Berman

Great Getaways Less Than 200 Miles from
NEW YORK CITY
for Every Season of the Year

CLARKSON N. POTTER, INC./Publishers • New York
Distributed by Crown Publishers, Inc.

Copyright © 1982 by Eleanor Berman

Inquiries should be addressed to Clarkson N. Potter, Inc., One Park Avenue, New York, New York 10016

Away for the Weekend is a trademark of Clarkson N. Potter, Inc.

Printed in the United States of America

Published simultaneously in Canada by General Publishing Company Limited

Library of Congress Cataloging in Publication Data

Berman, Eleanor, 1934–
   Away for the weekend, New York.

   1. Middle States—Description and travel—Guide-books.
2. New England—Description and travel—1982–   —Guide-books. 3. New York region—Description and travel—Guide-books. I. Title.
F106.B47   1982   917.4′0443   82-5233
ISBN 0-517-54647-7   AACR2

Designed by Dennis J. Grastorf
Maps by Susan Hunt Yule

10 9 8 7 6 5 4 3

Contents

FALL

WINTER

MAPS

Acknowledgments

A SINCERE WORD of thanks is in order here to Steve Schatt, travel editor of *Newsday*, and Eileen Swift for whom I began contributing articles to the newspaper's "Weekenders" series more than six years ago. They provided the format that inspired this book and their assignments have introduced me to many of the destinations that are included here.

Thanks, too, to Tony Davenport of the Connecticut Department of Economic Development for the use of the cover photo, as well as for the unfailing help provided for so many years by the department and its travel director, Barney Laschever, as well as their representatives, Dick Hazlett and Robert Grode of Sontheimer and Company, and Lisa Rhodes.

Others who have provided invaluable assistance in the preparation of this book are Len Panaggio of the State of Rhode Island Department of Economic Development, Wendy Lindquist of the Delaware State Travel Service, Tony Patterson of the State of New Jersey Division of Travel and Tourism and the many helpful county chambers of commerce in the state, Sam Rogers of the Philadelphia Convention and Visitors Bureau, Marilyn Kane of the Pocono Mountains Vacation Bureau, Daniel Kamal of Hershey Entertainment and Resort Company, Norene K. Lahr of the Pennsylvania Dutch Visitors Bureau, Don Whitney of the Central Bucks County Chamber of Commerce, Pat Redmond of the Chester County Tourist Promotion Bureau, Alan Ray of the New York State Museum, Michele Vennart of the Albany Convention and Visitors Bureau, Bill North of Mystic Seaport, and Peter Hopper of the Saratoga Performing Arts Center. The material and in many cases the personal guidance they provided made my visits far more informative as well as far pleasanter.

My appreciation should be expressed, too, to the many friends and strangers who pointed me to the restaurants, inns, special towns, museums, little known events, and wonderful scenery that made the researching of this book so rewarding.

Before You Begin . . .

WEEKEND GETAWAYS—a change of scene, refreshment for mind and spirit—that's what this book is all about. In the pages ahead you'll find suggestions for trips for every season of the year; jaunts with and without children; visits to country fairs and music festivals, Colonial towns and seaport villages, gardens and galleries . . . with parks, beaches, rivers, lakes, and mountains all along the way.

Some of these destinations may be familiar to you, but I hope that *Away for the Weekend* will prove to be for you, as it was for me in the writing, a source of discoveries and unexpected pleasures even in places you may have visited before.

Human nature being what it is, it is the faraway places that beckon most alluringly, often causing us to overlook attractions nearer at hand. We travel thousands of miles to look at scenery, monuments, mansions, and museums and ignore many equally fine places just a few hours from home. Nature's bounty, 300 years of history, and the many talented residents of our region, past and present, have combined to bless us in the New York area with an abundance of treasures for exploring. I've tried to highlight some of the special places that are easy to miss, particularly the unusual once-private collections that now comprise unique and pleasurable small museums. Wherever possible, I've also provided just a bit of background on the colorful people who have amassed these treasures for us.

All of the trips outlined here are less than 200 miles from New York and its environs, most within three hours of driving time (minus traffic jams), in order to be easily manageable for a weekend sojourn. Their proximity offers still another bonus. Not only are these places easy to get to, but once having found them it's easy to go back!

There are a few things you should know before you start reading. This is, of necessity, a somewhat personal and selective guide to places I have visited and enjoyed. It does not include many large resorts or amusement parks for two reasons: I usually don't like them, and you usually don't need a book to find them.

Nor will you necessarily find every single sightseeing attraction or lodging available in the areas covered. I've tried to stick to places I've either been to myself or had personally recommended by local sources or frequent visitors to the destination, people whose judgment I consider reliable.

This is a guide to destinations, not to country inns. Sometimes motels are the only accommodations available in a particular area. When inns are mentioned, it is because they are the best in the vicinity, not the pick of all possible inns as you find in books devoted to this subject. Keep that in mind if occasionally you find some place a little disappointing compared to the dream inns you've visited elsewhere. When they are special, however, I've tried to say so.

BASIC INFORMATION

As for the basic format of the trips, they are laid out assuming you are spending a normal two-day weekend, arriving on Friday night and departing late on Sunday. There usually is a recommended itinerary, with added suggestions to accommodate varying tastes and time schedules. Sometimes there is more than enough to do for a long weekend, and a symbol at the start will indicate trips that fit that category.

If you want to spend more time in any area, check also for trips listed under other seasons for the territory near where you are going. Bucks County, for example, could fill several days if itineraries for both the lower and upper portions were combined. The same is true of the Hudson Valley, much of Connecticut, the Massachusetts Berkshires, and the Brandywine Valley.

The trips are arranged by season not only because activities change around the calendar but to give you time to read about upcoming special events and reserve rooms before it is too late. Advance notice may also enable you to plan a whole weekend around a special show or open house, rather than see it as a last-minute daytrip and miss all the sights and activities in the area nearby.

Since attractions do vary from season to season, you will find some areas mentioned more than once, or, as in the case of Philadelphia, recommended in different ways depending on whether children are along.

Don't, however, feel bound by the calendar. Many of these destinations are equally pleasant and less crowded when nothing special is going on, and they are appealing both in and out of season. Think especially about the seashore in the fall, when you can enjoy the scenery and the best accommodations in the Hamptons or Cape May without the summer crowds—and sometimes at bargain rates.

Symbols will indicate which trips seem most appropriate with children, though you are the best judge of your own family's interests and may find others that sound right for you. There are also symbols for trips that are manageable without a car. Unfortunately, such trips are few. One possibility is to take public transportation to a central point and rent a car for a day for the sights you can't see without one.

The symbols to watch for indicating these varying categories are these:

🧸 = recommended for children

🚌 = can be done at least in part via public transportation

🧳 = recommended for long weekends

As for prices, dollar signs indicate the range, as follows, for a double room:

$ = under $40

$$ = $45 to $65

$$$ = $70 to $90

$$$$ = $90 and up

and for restaurants:

$ = entrées mostly under $10

$$ = entrées averaging $10 to $15

$$$ = entrées mostly over $15

$$$$ = expect to pay $25 or more per person

Some accommodations may also include some meals in their rates, and letter symbols following prices will indicate these. CP (Continental Plan) provides both bed and breakfast; MAP (Modified American Plan) includes breakfast and dinner; and AP (American Plan), all three meals.

Since there is always a lapse of several months between the writing and the publication of a book, I have used general price categories rather than specific figures, knowing that rates change rapidly in these inflationary times. Even so, it is possible that a few of the places listed will raise prices in the future, placing them into the next category. So use the book as a guide—I hope you will find it an accurate one on the whole—but *always* check for specific prices when you plan your trip.

The information here was as accurate as could be determined as of January 1982. However, innkeepers and chefs change, as do hours and fees for attractions, so do use the telephone numbers that are listed to check for current information.

If you find information that has become seriously inaccurate—that a place has closed or gone way downhill—I hope you will let me know care of the publisher so that it can be corrected in the future. If you discover places that I have missed, I hope you'll share them as well.

As for maps, there was just no way to provide maps detailed enough to take in every attraction or accommodation mentioned. There are basic area maps here to give you your bearings and one map showing ways out of the city, but don't make the mistake of starting off without a really good road map of your destination. One way to get a detailed map free is by writing to the travel or tourism offices in the states included here. These offices offer not only maps but also informative brochures on their states. Note on the list following that many offer toll-free numbers for travelers.

In most cases, there is a source listed for further information at the end of each itinerary. Do write away, for the more you know about your destination ahead of time, the more pleasurable your trip will be.

Anyone who has ever tried to leave the city on a Friday knows that departing as well as returning at peak weekend traffic hours can be a frustrating experience, and can add an hour or more to your driving time. If you can't get away before 4 P.M. on Friday, particularly in the summer, consider having an early dinner in town and depart after 7 P.M., when the roads are more likely to be clear. If your destination is a particularly popular place, such as the Hamptons, you might find it more pleasant to take a train or bus, hop a local cab to your lodgings, and then pick up a car (or maybe a bike) the next day. Just remember to ask about the availability of local car rentals when you make your room reservations and be sure to reserve a car in advance.

In many locations in Connecticut, car rental offices are conveniently located at train stations. Again, inquire when you make arrangements for lodgings.

Public transportation is subject to its own delays, of course, but sometimes it can be less aggravating to let someone else do the driving and fretting rather than begin or end a relaxing weekend stuck in a traffic jam.

One last word: When it comes to inn reservations, plan ahead if you don't want to be disappointed. If you want to visit popular places at peak summer or fall seasons, three to four months ahead isn't too soon. Most places do offer refunds on deposits with reasonable notice, so remember that old adage and be safe rather than sorry.

With that out of the way, the only thing left to say is read on—and have a wonderful time!

INFORMATION

Any of the state offices listed here will provide maps as well as information and literature on attractions throughout their state:

Tourism Division
Connecticut Department of Economic Development
210 Washington Street
Hartford, Connecticut 06106
Toll free: (800) 243-1685 [in Connecticut, (800) 842-7492]

Delaware State Travel Service
630 State College Road
Dover, Delaware 19901
Toll free: (800) 441-8846

Division of Travel and Tourism
State of New Jersey
P. O. Box 400
Trenton, New Jersey 08625
(609) 292-2470

Division of Tourism
New York State Department of Commerce
99 Washington Street
Albany, New York 12245
(518) 474-2121

Division of Tourism
State of Massachusetts
100 Cambridge Street
Boston, Massachusetts 02202
Toll free: (800) 343-9072
or (617) 727-3201

Bureau of Travel Development
Department of Commerce, State of Pennsylvania
Forum Building
Harrisburg, Pennsylvania 17120
Toll free: (800) 323-1717

Tourist Information
Department of Economic Development, State of Rhode Island
7 Jackson Walkway
Providence, Rhode Island 02903
(401) 277-2601

Spring

Arts and Flowers in Pennsylvania

The paintings are overwhelming, floor to ceiling and wall to wall.

There are more than 1,000 of them, including nearly 200 Renoirs; masterpieces by Matisse, Picasso, van Gogh, and Rousseau; more Cézannes than you'll find in any one place outside the Louvre; Modiglianis, Klees, and Mirós. And just so the older masters won't feel slighted, there are a smattering of names like El Greco, Daumier, Titian, and Tintoretto.

The Barnes Foundation in Merion, Pennsylvania, just five miles outside Philadelphia, is recognized as the most notable private art collection of this century. But for 24 years almost nobody was allowed to see it.

You'll still need an advance reservation to be sure of admittance—and a pair of field glasses may come in handy for viewing the paintings nearest the ceiling—but if you care about art, this museum is a not-to-be-missed experience. Taken in combination with some nearby plea-sures—dogwoods in bloom at Valley Forge, tulips and azaleas at Longwood Gardens, and Wyeth paintings plus the riverside panorama from the glass walls of the Brandywine River Museum—the Barnes can be the starting point for a spectacular spring weekend.

It wasn't that Albert Coombs Barnes didn't intend to share his treasures. A Philadelphian who made a mint developing a medical potion called Argyrol, Barnes became one of the first patrons of modern art, sparked by the encouragement of his childhood friend, William Glackens, who had become one of the painters of the Ashcan School.

Barnes traveled to Europe to study art then began buying up canvases wholesale—50 Renoirs at a time, the first major purchases of Modigliani's work, 60 Soutines at $50 per canvas.

In 1923 he loaned 75 canvases to the Pennsylvania Academy of Art to introduce to Philadelphia the latest in European art. But Barnes's artistic judgment was ahead of his time. The critical reception of his paintings was so vicious that it caused Barnes to withdraw completely from the art establishment. When he built his 24-room museum the next year, only handpicked art students and a few individuals who had nothing to do with museums or art collectors were allowed to call. Barnes's will saw to it that his foundation remained all but inaccessible to the public until the state of Pennsylvania stepped in in 1961, ten years after his death, to insist that a tax-free educational foundation had to allow people in to be educated.

The hours remain limited, as do the number of visitors allowed. Nor have the curators made it easy to appreciate the paintings fully. There are no titles or dates on the works, just the artists' names, and some believe that Barnes deliberately placed the best paintings highest on the walls. Still, this remains a museum you could visit over and over without exhausting the abundance of fine art to be seen—and it will probably leave you too glutted to be interested in further viewing that day, even though Philadelphia's museums are just a short drive away.

Instead, make this an out-of-the-city weekend. Stay at the perfectly pleasant motel-hotels on Philadelphia's nearby City Line Avenue; enjoy their indoor pools and the shopping malls down the road in Bala-Cynwyd; take a stroll in the arboretum on the campus of Haverford College, not far away on Route 30; or take a 15-minute drive to Valley Forge National Park, off Route 76, where the spring dogwood display across the park's beautiful 2,200 acres brings visitors from miles around between mid-April and mid-May each year.

The park itself is an interesting one, with restorations of Washington's headquarters, the quarters of General Varnum, and the encampments of the enlisted men at this important Revolutionary War site. A marked tour route shows you the historical sights as well as the outstanding scenery on the grounds. If you'd rather not make the drive back, there are ample accommodations in this area for the night.

Come Sunday, south of Valley Forge, the first stop is Chadds Ford and the Brandywine River Museum, a century-old gristmill beautifully restored to make the most of its riverside setting, with a dramatic glass silo tower and brick terraces overlooking the Brandywine. In galleries with handhewn beams, pine floors, and plastered walls, you'll find the works of artists who were inspired by this scenic valley. The museum is a showplace for art by three generations of Wyeths, including the Andrew Wyeth landscapes that have immortalized the area and Jamie Wyeth's famous portrait of a pink pig, as well as work by famous illustrators from the region, including Howard Pyle, Maxfield Parrish, and Frank Schoonover.

Farther west on Route 1 is Kennett Square and one of the most exquisite public gardens in the United States. You don't have to be a flower lover to appreciate Longwood Gardens. The privately endowed former estate of Pierre S. du Pont on 1,200 acres with 12,000 kinds of plants is a visual delight for everyone.

Walk into the conservatory and just breathe in the perfume of early spring and take in the colors of the artfully grouped tulips and lilies and flowering shrubs. The ivy-covered trees stand as straight as the building's marble columns, a counterpoint to the colors of the blooms, and the ferns and orchids are an exotic contrast to the rest of the display. The four-acre conservatory is a pleasure rain or shine, but hope for sun so that you can walk on the magnificent grounds; listen to the fountains at play in the Italian water garden; enjoy the formal patterns of the show gardens, the meandering cherry trees along the lake, and the splashing of the waterfall near the chimes tower. No detail has been overlooked to make the gardens a treat for all the senses.

When you've had your fill of flowers, you can switch to antiquing all along Route 1 between Chadds Ford and Kennett Square. In Kennett Square itself a stop at The Mushroom Place will let you come home with a souvenir, a box of the pearly white giants grown in this mushroom farming center. There's even a little museum to explain the mystique of growing mushrooms.

At dinnertime take your pick of several atmospheric old inns within a few minutes drive, any one a fitting end to a memorable weekend.

Philadelphia Area Code: 215

DRIVING DIRECTIONS New Jersey Turnpike to Route 276 (Pennsylvania Turnpike exit) to Route 76 (Schuylkill Expressway). Take City Line exit, about 6 miles west of Philadelphia. Barnes Foundation is about ½ mile off US 1 at North Latch's Lane in Merion.
Total distance: just over 100 miles.

BY PUBLIC TRANSPORTATION Amtrak to Philadelphia; Paoli local to Merion Station and walk to the Barnes Foundation. Phone Barnes Foundation for exact directions.

ACCOMMODATIONS *Ramada Inn,* City Line Avenue, Philadelphia. Just opening at presstime, so check information for phone number • *Marriott,* City Line Avenue and Monument Road, Philadelphia, 667-0200; with indoor pool and lighted paddle tennis; $$$ • *Sheraton-Valley Forge,* one mile off US 76, exit 35, Valley Forge, 337-2000; $$ • *Stouffer's Valley Forge Hotel,* 480 North Gulph Road, Valley Forge, 337-1800; $$–$$$.

DINING *Marriott* (see above) • *King's Wharf* (seafood) • *Kona Kau* (Polynesian-Chinese) • *Sirloin & Saddle* (charcoal pit, steak) • (none memorable but all adequate); $–$$ • *General Wayne Inn,* 625 Montgomery Avenue, Merion Station, 667-3330 (atmospheric, dates back to 1704; best to reserve ahead); $–$$ • *Bull Tavern,* Valley Forge Road, Phoenixville, 935-2855; $$–$$$ • *Seven Stars Inn,* Route 23, Phoenixville, 495-5205; $$ • *Brandywine Inn,* Route 202 at Delaware State Line, 459-0995; $$ • *Chadds Ford Inn,* Route 1, Chadds Ford, 388-7361; $$ • *Mendenhall Inn,* Route 52, Mendenhall, 388-1181; $$ (The last four are all country inns.)

SIGHTSEEING *Barnes Foundation,* 300 North Latch's Lane, Merion, 667-0290. (Ask for explicit driving directions.) Hours: Friday, Saturday, 9:30 A.M. to 4:30 P.M., Sunday, 1 to 4:30 P.M.; two hundred visitors admitted, half by appointment, half first-come (total of one hundred on Sunday); call or write for reservation. Adults $1, no children under 12 admitted • *Brandywine River Museum,* US 1, Chadds Ford, 388-7601. Hours: daily 9:30 A.M. to 4:30 P.M. Adults $1.75, senior citizens $1, children age 7–12 75¢ • *Longwood Gardens,* US 1, Kennett Square, 388-6741. Hours: April to October, 9 A.M. to 6 P.M. Adults $4, children age 6–12 75¢ • *Valley Forge National Historical Park,* Route 23 at Route 363, Valley Forge, 783-7700. Hours: daily 8:30 A.M. to 5 P.M. Free. Bus tours April to October from Visitor Center with narrated 1½ hour circuit of historic sites. Adults $3, children age 6–16 $2.

The Quiet Side of the Delaware: Discoveries in New Jersey

Over in Bucks County the tourists are teeming, but on the New Jersey side of the Delaware all is serene.

In sleepy Lambertville, with its rows of unself-conscious tiny Victorian homes, there are only a few antique shops located near the New Hope Bridge to lure stray shoppers across. The one and only inn in town dates back to 1812.

Next door in Stockton, it's even quieter—nary a visitor in sight until you take a right hairpin turn up the hill to discover a 1793 manor that is now the Woolverton Inn. "A lot of our guests don't even want to go out after they get here," the pleasant assistant at the desk told us. "They're so happy to find a place like this, so private and away from it all."

Indeed, for a weekend retreat, this bit of southern New Jersey can't be beat, away from it all yet within easy striking distance of Bucks County shops, Flemington outlet stores, the many attractions of Princeton, and the lesser known pleasures on the backroads where some of the state's historic past still lives on in towns blessedly oblivious to tourists.

Lambertville House, which has hosted presidents Andrew Jackson and Ulysses Grant, as well as Colonel Tom Thumb, still has lots of authentic Early American atmosphere, but ask for a main floor room here as the upstairs accommodations are far less appealing.

As for the Woolverton, if you could build your own country manor, you might want it to look just like this one. The original mellowed stone core of the house has been adorned with Victorian froufrous from an 1850 remodeling that added columns, grillwork, and a mansard roof. Whitney North Seymour bought the place in 1939, then gave it another restoration and planted the formal gardens. In 1957 it was acquired by St. John Terrell, and it housed many of the celebrities who played at Terrell's famous "Music Circus." On Thanksgiving in 1980, it opened as a bed-and-breakfast inn, where you are sincerely invited to make yourself at home.

Sleep late in your antique-filled bedroom. Home-baked goodies will be waiting when you come down for breakfast. Take a walk around the grounds, or head for the antiques in Lambertville and Bucks County, or better yet, follow Route 523 north from Stockton, past the covered bridge outside of Sergeantsville to connect with Route 31 north to Clinton.

Just at the point where the south branch of the Raritan River joins Spruce Run Creek, Clinton's main street begins with a 200-foot-wide waterfall anchored at either end by an old mill. The red mill with the waterwheel is the Clinton Historical Museum. From April through October you can visit its exhibits of Americana—typewriters, bicycles, lighting devices, butter churns, spinning wheels, and the like. But it's almost enough to wander outside down the path along the river, past the blacksmith and the old country store, savoring the unmistakable air of the past and watching the ducks and geese go by.

The mill across the way, an old stone building with a gambrel roof, was still a working gristmill into the 1950s. Now it's an active community center with changing exhibitions of art and crafts.

Clinton's Main Street couldn't be a more charming representation of a nineteenth-century town. But unlike some vintage towns the shops along the way have not a touristy souvenir among them. The pleasant book shop, the clothing stores, The Attic with "antiques and nice old things," the Clinton Furniture Emporium that sells good used furniture, the weaving and spinning supplies at Fibre Craft, and the homemade food at the little café called Seasonings are all there for the people who live in Clinton and just take pride in keeping up appearances in their hometown. Clinton House, now a restaurant, outwardly at least still looks like what it was originally—a stagecoach stop, circa 1742.

Stop for lunch in Clinton, then head back by way of Route 31 again to Flemington. In spite of all the outlet stores, this town, parts of which date back to 1712, retains a quaint look. The 1828 Greek Revival courthouse in the center of town was the scene of the famous Lindbergh kidnapping trial.

What brings all the shoppers to Flemington? Primarily the factory outlets for Dansk, Stangl Pottery, Revereware, Corningware, George Briard, and Flemington Cut Glass. They've been joined by a couple dozen other stores that claim to discount almost every kind of ware, including luggage and furs and clothing.

Many of the outlets are clustered around Turntable Junction, where the Black River and Western Railroad still runs steam trains on hour-long trips to Ringoes from mid-April through November each year. Other nearby attractions are the Raggedy Ann Antique Doll and Toy Museum, and Liberty Village, a re-created eighteenth-century shopping village with working craftsmen.

When you've picked up your buys and returned to the Woolverton, you'll find afternoon tea being served to refresh you as you contemplate plans for dinner. Gerards and Café Renni in Lambertville and Le Bistro in Stockton are all recommended choices. The Stockton Inn, another possibility, was the inspiration for that old song, "There's a Small Hotel . . ."

On Sunday, once again you can pick and choose your destinations. Stop off if you like at the area flea market known as Governor's, held every Saturday and Sunday from 8 A.M. to 5 P.M., on Route 179, 1½ miles north of Lambertville. Then perhaps a stop at Washington Crossing State Park on Route 29, which commemorates the famous river crossing that was a turning point in the Revolutionary War. The park runs on both sides of the Delaware. On the New Jersey side you can visit the Ferry House, a restored Colonial inn where Washington and his men once spent the night, and a Flag Museum showing the evolution of the nation's flag.

Then it's back roads time, taking 546 to Route 31, then off the main road to Pennington, which has many Federalist and Georgian buildings dating back to Revolutionary times. From Pennington go west, then north on 579 to Harbourton where the historic district is typical of a crossroads farm settlement of the eighteenth and nineteenth centuries.

Continue north to Route 518 and east past Hopewell, then detour south on 206 to Kingston, once an old stagecoach stop and a town where the Delaware and Raritan Canal (now a state park) was a vital transportation link. Near the canal you can still see the mill house used at various times during the last 200 years to produce lumber, flour, and woolen fabrics. Many other old buildings also still stand amid the small shops and antique stores that dot the village.

Stay on Route 206 south to Princeton, which could fill a weekend on its own with its magnificent campus and historic homes. Sign up for the free one-hour campus walking tours offered by the Orange Key Guide Service in Maclean House to the right of the main campus gate at 1:30 P.M. and 3:30 P.M., or pick up literature in their office for a do-it-yourself tour. At Bainbridge House, the headquarters of the Princeton Historical Society at 158 Nassau Street, you can buy a little map guide to other historic places and interesting architecture in town.

On campus visit Nassau Hall, which was the country's capital back in 1783, the beautiful Gothic University Chapel with its collection of stained glass by American artists, the University Art Museum, and the enormous outdoor sculpture collection that dots the entire idyllic campus with works by Calder, Epstein, Lachaise, Lipchitz, Moore, Nevelson, Noguchi, and many others.

Off campus there are historic sites like Rockingham, Washington's one-time headquarters; Morven, the official residence of the governor of New Jersey; Thomas Clark House; the Quaker Meeting House; the homes of Woodrow Wilson, Albert Einstein, and Aaron Burr, and literally hundreds of fine eighteenth- and nineteenth-century homes in either direction on Nassau Street and the side streets around it. Alexander, Mercer, and Stockton are some of the many streets it is a pleasure to drive down or stroll on.

You could easily and happily spend the day in Princeton and have dinner at the Nassau Inn on Palmer Square. But there's yet another choice, one you'll have to make in advance. Duke Gardens on Route 206 in Somerville is right on the way home. Reservations are needed to tour these 11 classic world gardens under glass, and they are worth a visit anytime you are in the area since the blooms change according to the season.

Campus or gardens, route yourself home by way of 287 north and 24 east to Chatham and you can have dinner at The Tarragon Tree, the restaurant *New Jersey Monthly*'s dining critic picks as his personal favorite in the whole state. What nicer way to end the weekend?

New Jersey Area Code: 609 (except Chatham: 201)

DRIVING DIRECTIONS New Jersey Turnpike south to exit 10, then Route 287 north again to exit 10, Route 22 west for 2½ miles, take exit marked Flemington-Princeton, follow 202 south for about 25 miles, get off at Lambertville exit before Delaware River Bridge and follow Route 29 north to Lambertville and Stockton.

Total distance: Roughly 75 miles.

ACCOMMODATIONS   *The Woolverton Inn,* R.D. 3, Box 233-A, Stockton, 397-0802; $$ including continental breakfast and afternoon tea (no private baths) ● *The Lambertville House,* 32 Bridge Street, Lambertville, 397-0202; $–$$ with continental breakfast (rooms vary greatly, less expensive ones share baths).

DINING   *Cafe Renni,* 9 Kline's Court, Lambertville, 397-2631; $$ ● *Gerards,* 8½ Coryell Street, Lambertville, 397-8035; $$ ● *Le Bistro,* Bridge Street, Stockton, 397-2330; $$ ● *Nassau Inn,* Palmer Square, Princeton, 921-7500; $$–$$$ ● *The Tarragon Tree,* 225 Main Street, Chatham, 635-7333; prix fixe at $28.00 per person.

SIGHTSEEING   *Clinton Historical Museum,* 56 Main Street, Clinton, 735-4101. Hours: April to October, Monday to Friday, 1 to 5 P.M.; Saturday, Sunday, noon to 6 P.M. Adults $2; children age 6–12 $1, under 6 free ● *Hunterdon Art Center,* 7 Center Street (off Main), Clinton. Hours: Tuesday to Friday, 1 to 4 P.M.; Saturday, Sunday, 1 to 5 P.M. Free ● *Washington Crossing State Park,* Visitor Center, Route 29. Hours: Wednesday to Sunday, 9 A.M. to 4:30 P.M.; Summer daily till 5 P.M.; picnicking, arboretum, Ferry House and Flag Museum. Free ● *Princeton University,* guided tours from Maclean House. Hours: Monday to Saturday, 10, 11 A.M., 1:30 and 3:30 P.M.; Sunday 1:30 and 3:30 P.M. Free ● *Bainbridge House,* 158 Nassau Street, Princeton, 921-6748. Hours: Tuesday to Friday 10 A.M. to 4 P.M.; Saturday, Sunday 2 to 4 P.M. Donation requested ● For list of Flemington outlet stores and map, write to M.T.A., P.O. Box 686, Flemington, NJ 08822. ● *Duke Gardens* US 206, Somerville, 722-3700. Hours: October to June 1, daily noon to 4 P.M.; reservations required by mail or phone. Adults $2.50; children age 6–12 $1.50, under 6 free. No high heels allowed.

Spring Spectacular: The Dogwoods of Fairfield

Isaac Bronson would hardly believe his eyes.

A retired Revolutionary War surgeon turned farmer, Bronson decided back in 1795 that his Fairfield, Connecticut, property could be enhanced if he transplanted some of the native wild dogwood trees blooming so prodigiously in the nearby woods.

Bronson propagated, and so did his trees. By 1895 the blooms nurtured by the family were so outstanding that the neighborhood Greenfield Hill Village Improvement Society took on care of the dogwoods as an official project, adding many new plantings, including pink varieties that were not native to Connecticut. Today Greenfield Hill boasts 30,000 dogwood trees, and if you drive up early in May, you can enjoy a view of the steepled church, village green and Colonial homes enveloped in clouds of pink and white blossoms. Bronson's original trees, carefully tagged, are still an integral part of the show.

Thousands turn out each year to revel in this spring spectacular and to attend the annual Dogwood Festival sponsored by the women of the Greenfield Hill Congregational Church. Usually held for seven days the second week in May, the festival offers daily guided walking tours, concerts, an art show, handmade gifts, and homemade food so legendary that many diners make lunch reservations on the spot for the following year. Phone the church for this year's dates and reservations.

The town of Fairfield, named literally for the "fair fields" that attracted settlers from Hartford, was founded in 1639, just 19 years after the Pilgrims landed in this country. The 55 families who chose to settle in Greenfield Hill, two miles from the town center, made a lucky move, since it was the only part of the town not burned by the British during the Revolutionary War. Now designated as a historic district, it was a prime source of food for the American army, and the steeple of the original Congregational Church on the green served as a lookout for the British fleet.

Dogwood Festival concerts are presented in the present church sanctuary, allowing visitors to see its handsome Early American interior, with just 23 pews in a room of white with red velvet cushions and carpet and chandeliers of Colonial blue wood.

The 45-minute Heritage Walking Tour goes past many surviving Colonial homes as well as later Federal and Greek Revival houses. Down dogwood-festooned Bronson Road, the old windmill that once pumped water for Bronson's farm has been restored in his memory. Also on this road is Ogden House, a saltbox farm restored by the Fairfield Historical Society. Most of its authentic eighteenth-century furnishings have a history of local ownership. The lean-to kitchen and traditional English herb garden here make it well worth a visit, dogwoods or not.

The actual Historical Society headquarters, a red brick building, is located near the town center in one of Fairfield's two other historical districts. For a small museum, it offers an unusually large collection of early Americana. Dolls, dollhouses, and children's toys fill an entire top floor, and the lower level features an old country store and a country kitchen as well as every conceivable tool for every kind of Colonial craft, from candle- to carriage-making. Many of the wooden tools on the wall are almost works of art in themselves.

The corner of the Historical Society block, Beach and Old Post roads, was the central point of the original "four squares" of the town laid out in 1639. You can while away a pleasant hour exploring these two roads on foot. Though only four of the original homes survived the British fires, there are many beautiful post-Revolutionary homes to see, as well as historic churches and the town hall, whose central section remains as it was when it was rebuilt in 1790. It was on the town hall green that residents refused to submit to a royal proclamation, an act that led to the town's burning.

Save some foot power for Southport, the picturesque harbor area, which also has been named a historic district. Boats laden with onions from the Greenfield Hill farms used to sail out of this harbor. Now it is the home of the Pequot Yacht Club and the Fairfield Country Club; the hilly surrounding residential area, with water views at every turn, is one of the most exclusive and attractive along the Connecticut shore.

Southport's tiny village is an antiques center. There are four shops within about two blocks on Pequot Avenue, as well as the Fairfield Women's Exchange, which combines antiques and gifts with many original articles. You can have a number plaque handpainted for your front door here, or commission a pen-and-ink drawing of your home, or buy homemade items ranging from booties to braided rugs. Rare-book buffs will want to visit the Museum Gallery Book Shop, 246 Old Post Road, and Laurence Witten Rare Books, 181 Old Post Road.

For a lunchtime snack, check out Allinton's Ice Cream Manufactory, 70 Reef Road, for delicious homemade hot soups and hot fudge sundaes. And Larry's Diner, on the Post Road, which looks like a throwback to the 1920s, has an owner who whips up terrific Greek specialties for under $5.

An even nicer lunch suggestion: Pack a picnic and eat on the Greenfield Hills green or by the shore on the sandy Fairfield beaches that stretch for seven miles on and off along Long Island Sound.

Except for Dogwood Festival days, Fairfield's charms draw surprisingly few visitors, and it remains a peaceful and nontouristy place. The main shopping area on the "new" Post Road, US 1, is typically small-town, and the shopping centers on Black Rock Turnpike are fairly standard. There's an interesting little gallery of limited-edition art prints at the Greenwich Workshop just off the Post Road at 61 Unquowa Road, but for serious shopping, boutiques and the like, follow the Post Road a few miles west into more sophisticated Westport.

It's possible that the beautifully wooded residential sections of Westport boast more celebrity residents than any other single Connecticut town (Paul Newman and Joanne Woodward among the more prominent), but the town itself is hardly a country village. There is a Main Street about two blocks long, with pleasant small shops and a bookstore that is something of a local landmark. The rest of the shopping area stretches along State Street, which is actually busy US 1, and is divided into little modern shopping centers. There's plenty of browsing potential, but by car rather than on foot.

If you continue farther west on US 1 into Norwalk and bear left to West Avenue, you'll come upon two Fairfield County shopping standbys. On one corner is a branch of Loehmanns, well known to bargain-conscious fashionably dressed women, and across the street and down a few doors is Decker's, a haven for the men. Gant shirts here sell for half the price as at New York stores, there are many other quality labels such as Polo or Robert Bruce that vary from visit to visit, and the side wall is stacked with classic Shetland or cashmere sweaters at excellent prices. There are women's sweaters, too, and a few women's shirts, but this is primarily a man's world. On the same block as Decker's are outlet stores for silver and for sheets and towels. If you want to spend a lot of time shopping, better plan it for Saturday and save Sunday for the dogwoods.

If you're more interested in the out-of-doors than the inside of stores, back in Fairfield the Connecticut Audubon Society and Larsen Sanctuary has more than six miles of trails along 168 wooded acres. The sanctuary is a managed wildlife area where you will find not only woods but meadows, streams, marshes, and ponds. An annual birdcarvers' show here usually coincides with the Dogwood Festival.

The closest lodgings to the dogwoods are motels, but there are two far more interesting places to stay a short drive away. The Inn at Longshore, a former estate on Long Island Sound, was acquired a few years back by the town of Westport as a recreational facility for its residents. The renovation included 14 guest rooms, done in attractive prints with period reproduction furniture. Some of the rooms have water views. The surroundings here are super—golf course, beach, beautiful grounds—and there is nightly entertainment in the lounge, sometimes by name jazz musicians.

On the more traditional New England side is Silvermine Tavern, a 200-year-old inn on a millpond with ten simple Colonial rooms upstairs. The food here is only average, but the low-ceilinged dining room filled with old tools and the deck overlooking the ducks and geese on the pond are so pleasant that you may want to eat here anyway, at least for the generous Sunday brunch buffet.

The Silvermine Guild of Artists is just across the way (though the official address is New Canaan). It's an art school housed in barns that has changing exhibits and a gift shop of paintings and handcrafts.

For dinner Fairfield offers two possibilities, a little spot appropriately called The Dogwoods that specializes in steaks and hot sandwiches, and a most unusual and elegant Colonial enclave known as Fredericksburg, an indoor "village" around a garden, where the Garden Room, Gazebo, Farm House, Counting House, and Governor's Palace all turn out to be dining rooms, each with a different decor. The most elaborate, the Governor's Palace, also has a different menu, a seven-course prix fixe French feast.

Westport restaurants often seem to change with the seasons, but a few that have been around and popular for a long time are Le Chambord (French), Café de la Plage (Creole), Allen's (seafood), and the Mansion Clam House (noisy and no atmosphere, just terrific clams).

If you want to end your weekend with a Sunday dinner that makes the most of the Connecticut countryside, head home on the Merritt Parkway and detour at exit 42, go about four miles north on route 57 to Cobb's Mill Inn. It's the perfect country hideaway, full of antiques and with a view of trees, waterfall, and stream that is picture-perfect.

Fairfield Area Code: 203

DRIVING DIRECTIONS   Via New England Thruway to Connecticut Turnpike, take exit 21 to Fairfield, go left on Mill Plain Road, left on Sturgess, right on Bronson to Congregational Church and the Dogwood Festival. Via the Merritt Parkway, take exit 44, make immediate right on Congress Street to Hillside, left on Hillside to Old Academy Road and the church.

Total distance: 52 miles.

ACCOMMODATIONS   *The Inn at Longshore,* 260 Compo Road South, Westport, 226-3316; $$–$$$ • *Silvermine Tavern,* Silvermine and Perry Avenues, Norwalk, 847-4558; $–$$ • *Fairfield Motor Inn,* 417 Post Road, Fairfield, 255-0491; $$ • *Westport New Englander Motor Hotel,* 1595 Post Road East, Westport, 259-5236; $$.

DINING   *The Dogwoods,* 2070 Post Road, Fairfield, 255-2683; entrées $–$$, hot sandwiches $ • *Fredericksburg,* 1201 Kings Highway, Fairfield, 333-1201; $$–$$$ • *Café de la Plage,* 239 Hills Point Road, Westport, 227-7208; $$ • *Allen's Clam & Lobster House,* 191 Hills Point Road, 226-4411; $$–$$$ • *Le Chambord,* 1572 Post Road East,

Westport, 255-2654; complete dinner $$$ • *Mansion Clam House*, 541 Riverside Avenue, Westport, 227-9661; $–$$$ • *Cobb's Mill Inn*, Weston Road, Weston, 227-7221; $$ • *Silvermine Tavern* (see above); $$–$$$.

SIGHTSEEING *The Dogwood Festival*, Greenfield Hill Congregational Church, 1045 Old Academy Road, Fairfield, 259-5596. Write or phone for information and brochure giving current dates and schedule, rates for walking tours and sit-down luncheon, and reservations • *Silvermine Guild of Artists*, 1073 Silvermine Road, New Canaan, 966-5617. Hours: Tuesday to Sunday 12:30 P.M. to 5 P.M. • *Connecticut Audubon Society and Larsen Sanctuary*, 2325 Burr Street, Fairfield, 259-6305. Hours: Tuesday to Saturday 10 A.M. to 5 P.M.; Sunday noon to 5 P.M.

"The Mercer Mile" and Other Bucks County Byways

We stepped inside the doorway, looked up six stories to the ceiling— and stopped in our tracks. Almost everyone who came behind us did the same.

Hanging above us, suspended at various levels from a vast central core, were Early American objects of every conceivable size and shape—chairs, barrels, cradles, whaleboats, baskets, bellows, sleds, cigar-store Indians, a full-size buckboard, even a Conestoga wagon.

Circling the room in a spiral ramp were display cubbies jammed and crammed with the hand tools that made these items and scores of others—tools used by butchers, dairymen, cooks and coopers, carpenters, weavers, leathermakers and printers; tools for doctors, clockmakers, surveyors, and seamstresses—130 crafts represented in all and a total of almost 60,000 objects.

It is an eye-boggling display that greets visitors to the Mercer Museum, the largest collection of early hand tools and their finished products ever assembled. But the museum, located in Doylestown, the county seat of scenic Bucks County, Pennsylvania, is only the first of three extravaganzas in an area that has come to be called the Mercer Mile.

And the Mercer Mile is just the start of the many attractions in this county along the Delaware River, a setting of rolling hills, covered bridges, and distinctive stone houses that serve as country retreats for some of the nation's best known authors and entertainers. Shopping and shunpiking are two major activities here, and though there's history galore, it comes in lively form—riding on a steam train, gliding downstream on a mule-drawn canal barge, watching an antique printing press or a water-powered gristmill in action, or seeing Mr. Mercer's dream houses, monuments to a man who was an authentic American genius—and eccentric.

Henry Chapman Mercer was one of the nation's leading archaeologists when his personal passion for collecting Early American tools led to a surprising mid-life career change. Mercer became so intrigued with the tools used by the old Pennsylvania German pottery and tile makers that he determined to perpetuate the dying craft. He apprenticed himself to an old German potter, rented a decrepit kiln, and by 1898 exhibited a talent that brought him a new kind of fame. Mercer tiles can be seen today from the casino at Monte Carlo to the Gardner Museum in Boston, from a high school in Havana to the King Ranch in Texas. His largest work is the tile floor in the Pennsylvania state capitol at Harrisburg.

Mercer called his enterprise the Moravian Pottery and Tile Works. The factory is now a living museum, part of the Mercer Mile, still turning out his original patterns according to his formulas and methods. You can pick up a few as souvenirs in the Museum gift shop, which also has a fine selection of early Pennsylvania crafts—boxes of Pennsylvania Dutch design, tinware, unusual weathervanes, and the like. If you are searching for books on early American art or antiques, you'll find 400 titles here.

The most incredible display of tiles, however, awaits in Mercer's own home, Fonthill, a castlelike concrete fantasy that took 106 men more than two years to build. Mercer's mansion is a fantastic mélange of columns, balconies, beams, towers and arches, and winding stairs. Tiles are everywhere—on columns and beams, serving as headboards, tabletops, and ceilings, even lining the stairs. There is a copy of an English tapestry in tile, the story of the discovery of the New World told in tile—and in addition to Mercer's own creations, he gathered fine specimens of historic tiles from every part of the world.

Fonthill and the museum that Mercer built in 1913 to house his enormous collection of tools and artifacts established Mercer as an eccentric prophet of modern architecture. The October 1960 issue of *Progressive Architecture* says: "Though the effect is often weird and theatrical . . . [Fonthill] with its unique spatial plan and its frank and bold techniques . . . [is] one of the important forerunners of the modern movement." The museum's ramp arrangement is believed to be the inspiration for New York's Guggenheim Museum.

The Mercer Mile can take a good half day, but there should be enough time left to enjoy some of the many other pleasures of Bucks County.

You might start with a short walking tour of Doylestown center, reached by driving west from the Mercer Mile on Court Street. Main Street, State Street (Route 202), and Oakland Avenue are the main streets in town and are lined with interesting homes dating from early to late nineteenth century.

Heading back east on 202 you'll come to Buckingham, a tiny village that maintains the early flavor of Bucks County and that is also the site of Buckingham Farmer's Market on 202 held on Saturdays from 9 A.M. until the farm produce is sold. (Bountiful Acres, a little farther east on 202, has fresh-picked produce all the time.)

Another famous Saturday event in Buckingham is Brown Brothers auction on Route 413 just south of 263. It begins at 9:00 A.M. with box lots and moves on to bigger and better things as the day progresses, including all kinds of antiques, furniture, and accessories that change by the week.

Lahaska, a little farther east on 202, is for shoppers. Peddlers Village, a nicely landscaped Colonial-style complex (so nice it has been designated as one of the few "All-American Selections") has 42 shops crammed with clothes, crafts, jewelry and gifts. More shops adjoin in The Yard, a Victorian mélange of 14 boutiques. The café in The Yard is a good place for lunch.

Afterward, cross the street to an antiquer's haven, the Lahaska Antique Courte, with 14 shops featuring all kinds of collectibles.

All of Bucks County is an antiquer's paradise. The last printed guide listed 60 stores. There are three big annual shows in and around Doylestown, the last usually held in mid-October. Write to the Bucks County Antique Dealers Association for this year's dates and locations.

Finally, follow Route 202 north to where all roads in Bucks County lead eventually—New Hope, the picturesque artists' colony on the banks of the Delaware. Take a nostalgic river ride here on the last operating mule-drawn canal barge in the country. You can also hop a huffing, puffing steam train beginning in May for an 8½-mile loop through the countryside that includes the famous trestle from the rescue scene in *Perils of Pauline*.

New Hope's labyrinth of paths and alleyways offers lovely old homes, almost 100 shops, and lots and lots of shoppers, a good reason to avoid the busiest summer months.

Two favorite attractions in town are the Parry Mansion, which displays in ten rooms the furnishings and decor that might have been used by the one family who lived here for 182 years from the late eighteenth to early twentieth centuries, and the Bucks County Playhouse, the famous old summer theater in a restored gristmill that now has a season almost year round.

Take time to mingle with that mass of shoppers in New Hope. The shops have interesting wares, particularly the Old Franklin Print Shop, which not only sells reproductions of rare documents but demonstrates the techniques of early hand printing.

Save a good chunk of your Sunday for a backroads tour to see the rural countryside and the stone farms and barns that are the special trademark of Bucks County. Part of the fascination is that no two of the houses are alike. Even the color and texture of the homes varies according to the native stones that were used for construction. You'll see mostly limestone and shale in central Bucks and craggier granite in the upper regions. Notice the double houses with twin doors, the big trilevel barns, and the "bride and groom" trees that flank many doorways. The trees were planted long ago for good luck by newlyweds who hoped their love would flourish along with the saplings.

The main roads are the River Road (Route 32), 611, and 413, and you can't go wrong making your own way back and forth. One possible route is to follow the River Road north. The thin strip of land running alongside the canal is officially called Theodore Roosevelt Park but generally just referred to as the tow path, named for its historical use as a path for the mules who pulled barges down the canal. Now you'll see hikers and bikers using it.

The drive takes you through the sleepy town of Lumberville and to Point Pleasant, where you may be tempted to take an hour out to see the river from one of its nicest perspectives—by canoe. Point Pleasant Canoe can provide all the necessary equipment, and even novices need not worry about this placid stretch of water.

In Ralph Stover State Park near Point Pleasant you can see the Big Red Bridge, and there are other covered bridges farther north in Erwinna and Uhlerstown. Stover Mill in Erwinna still has its old machinery intact but is used now by the Tinicum Civic Association as a gallery for local art. There's also a restored Federal-style home in Tinicum Park on River Road, as well as picnic facilities if you want to take a break.

Two and a half miles west of River Road in Upper Black Eddy is a strange 3½ acres of huge boulders known as Ringing Rocks because many of the rocks, when struck, do actually ring.

From Upper Black Eddy continue west on 32 to the connection with 611 and proceed south once again through more charming towns such as Pipersville (site of Cabin Run and Loux covered bridges and another restored mill) and Plumsteadville. Not far away in Dublin is a home with a special kind of history. It is Green Hills Farm, where Pulitzer and Nobel prize-winning author Pearl Buck lived and worked for 40 years. Mrs. Buck's 1835 stone house is filled with Oriental antiques in a rustic setting of Pennsylvania beams, wideboard oak floors, and big stone fireplaces. It is, unfortunately, open only on weekdays.

There are many other sights to see: contemporary art at the Arts Alliance in Lahaska, the Fred Clark Museum on Aquetong Road in Carversville (fine art in a restored church in another of the area's particularly attractive towns), winery tours at the Bucks County Vineyards near New Hope. And there are more covered bridges (13 in all) and more historic sights all over the place. For a more comprehensive listing, write for the "Highways of History" folder before you make your trip.

The final bonus is from the large number of stone houses that have been converted to atmospheric inns and restaurants. Suggestions around New Hope are listed, but don't overlook two stops during your tour of the upper part of the county, Ferndale Inn for French food, and The Inn of the Sorrel Horse, not only for fine dining but for one of the area's most delightful small places to stay.

Bucks County Area Code: 215

DRIVING DIRECTIONS   Take New Jersey Turnpike south to exit 10, then north on US 287 15 miles to another exit 10 (287 widens to five lanes just before the exit, so stay left), west on Route 22 for about 3½ miles, then right at sign marked Flemington-Princeton, Route 202 south to Doylestown.

Total distance: about 85 miles.

ACCOMMODATIONS   *Sign of the Sorrel Horse Inn,* Old Bethlehem Road, Quakertown, 536-4651; $–$$ including continental breakfast (higher with private bath); dinner entrées $$ • *The 1740 House,* River Road (Route 32), Lumberville, 297-5661; $$ with private bath and buffet breakfast; dinner $$$, bring own wine • *Centre Bridge Inn,* River Road, New Hope, 862-2048; $–$$ with bath; dinner entrées $$, breakfast $ • *The Inn at Phillips Mill,* North River Road, New Hope, 862-9919; $–$$; dinner entrées $–$$ • *Holiday Inn,* Route 202, New Hope, 862-5221; $$. (Inns are small and fill fast, so reserve far ahead or call to check on last-minute cancellations.)

DINING   All of the above plus: *Ferndale Inn* (French) Route 611 and Church Road, Ferndale, 847-2662; $$ • *Candida Ristorante Italian,*

Route 611, Kintnersville, 847-2332; $$ • *Cock 'n Bull,* Colonial restaurant in Peddler's Village, Doylestown, 794-7051; $–$$.

SIGHTSEEING *Mercer Mile* open March 1 to December 31. *Mercer Museum,* Green and Ashland Street, Doylestown, 345-0210; Hours: Saturday, 10 A.M. to 5 P.M., Sunday, 1 to 5 P.M. Adults $2; senior citizens, students, children $1; families (two adults, plus under-18s) $4.50 • *Fonthill,* East Court Street, Doylestown, 348-9461 • *Moravian Pottery and Tile Works,* Swamp Road (Route 313), Doylestown, 345-6722. Hours: Wednesday to Sunday, 10 A.M. to 5 P.M. Adults $1.75; senior citizens, students, children $1; families $3.50 • *Green Hill Farm,* 520 Dublin Road, Dublin, 249-0100. Guided tours Monday to Friday, 10:30 A.M. and 2 P.M. Adults $3.50; senior citizens $2; students and children $1; families $4.50 • *Peddler's Village,* Route 222, Lahaska, 794-7055. Shops open Friday, 10 A.M. to 9 P.M.; Saturday, 10 A.M. to 5 P.M.; Sunday, noon to 5 P.M. • *Parry Mansion,* Main Street, New Hope, 862-2194. Hours: May to October, Friday to Sunday, 1 to 4 P.M. Adults $1.50, children age 6–12 50¢ • *Mule-drawn barge rides,* New Street at southern end of New Hope, 862-2842. Hours: daily, April 15 to October, 11:30 A.M. and 1, 2, 3, 4:30 P.M. Adults $3.75, children age 2–11 $1.75 • *New Hope Steam Railway,* Bridge Street (Route 179) near the center of New Hope, 345-0292. Hours: May to October, Saturday, Sunday, 1, 2:30, 4 P.M.; June to September weekends 12:50, 2, 3:15, 4:30 P.M. Adults $4, children $2 • *Point Pleasant Canoe Rental & Sales,* Point Pleasant, 297-8400. Canoe rates $2.50 per hour, $10 daily.

FOR FURTHER INFORMATION Contact (New Hope information) Chamber of Commerce, South Main and Mechanic Streets, New Hope, PA 18938, 862-5880 • (antique show information) Bucks County Antique Dealers Association, Inc., c/o Geraldine Limpan, 5 Byron Lane, Yardley, PA 19067, 295-6142 • (Bucks County guide "Highways of History") Bucks County Historical-Tourist Commissions, One Oxford Valley, Suite 410, Langhorne, PA 19047, 752-2203.

Stony Brook and the North Shore: A Springtime Ramble

A set designer couldn't have done better. Old white Colonial homes, a peaceful harbor, tiny tots toddling down the sloping green to feed the ducks on the pond. Even the shopping center of Stony Brook is built in Federal style so as not to spoil the picture.

This little North Shore village, so atypical of most people's visions of Long Island, is in one of the island's most historic enclaves—and it provides the perfect inn to suit the atmosphere.

Three Village Inn, a 1785 Colonial home at the end of the village green, where even the desk clerks wear Early American garb, is a must for its dining room as well as its old-fashioned accommodations. Start planning your trip by making your reservation here for dinner as well as for one of the seven Colonial rooms upstairs. There are more motel rooms in cottages around back, but the main building is much more atmospheric.

Early June is the best time for a visit, after the attractions are open but before the summer crowds descend.

After filling yourself on Friday night with New England clam cakes or Long Island bay scallops or roast turkey with chestnut stuffing, get a good night's sleep and after breakfast head straight for the Stony Brook Museums, a sampler of the past.

The clang of blacksmith hammers and the ring of a nineteenth-century recess bell greet you at a complex of buildings that includes a nineteenth-century schoolhouse complete with potbellied stove; a collection of more than 100 horsedrawn carriages from farm wagons to European stage coaches; costumes, textiles, decoys, toys, and 15 exquisite miniature rooms in a history museum; a working blacksmith shop; and an art museum featuring the works of "the foremost nineteenth-century American genre painter," William Sidney Mount. Mount's paintings, appropriately, focus on everyday life on rural Long Island.

After a stop at the Victorian-style Dark House Museum Shop, you're ready for further exploring of the real historic settlement known as the Three Villages. Setauket, East Setauket, and Stony Brook were among Long Island's earliest settlements, and their Historical Society brochure is accurate when it states that the years have been kind to them.

Pick up your copy of this brochure guide at the Three Village Garden Club Exchange right across the street from the Inn, but be prepared to spend a few minutes browsing among the tempting china, glassware, and antiques for sale there.

You might want to head for the farthest point, the village of East Setauket, since Benjamins Restaurant here, a former 1880s saloon, is a perfect spot for lunch. Use the brochure map to guide you through a few of the back roads of East Setauket, where the shingled farmhouses in their wooded settings probably reflect better than any other part of the area the original rural character of these communities. The oldest house in the villages is the 1655 Brewster House here.

On to Setauket and the Thompson House, the interesting headquarters of the Three Village Historical Society. Built in 1720, it is unique for its high ceilings and the decorative details on the exposed beams. Guides will take you through the house and answer your questions about the original inhabitants and the early Long Island furnishings inside.

An herb garden and the Thompson family cemetery are on the grounds of the house, as are the 1800s headquarters building for the Society for the Preservation of Long Island Antiquities, a barn, an icehouse, and a corncrib.

Not far away is Gallery North, a showplace for contemporary art housed in an 1870s structure, and the Tucker-Jones House, a former ship captain's residence, which has a working blacksmith shop open to the public.

Follow the pamphlet map past other historic churches and homes, then head back to Stony Brook for the night. If you want to try another dining place in town, the Country House restaurant, a 1710 farmhouse, is a good choice.

On Sunday, after a final walk through the village and a look at the old gristmill, you can spend a pleasant afternoon winding your way back home with a choice of attractions along the North Shore.

Route 25A will bring you to Northport and just past the town, the Vanderbilt Museum, or Eagle's Nest, a natural science museum and planetarium in a 24-room mansion on 43 wooded acres.

Go along on 25A until you come to Cold Spring Harbor, just south of Huntington, a perfectly delightful old whaling village that has been declared a National Historic District. Sunday brunch at the Whaler's Inn on Harbor Road goes on until 4 P.M., and there are several appealing shops here, as well as a small whaling museum that is one of the best of its kind.

A little farther on, in Oyster Bay, follow the signs in town to Theodore Roosevelt's "bully" home at Sagamore Hill, a huge Victorian affair with a big shaded porch where Teddy used to sit and rock and look at the sunset.

There's no mistaking whose home this is. Teddy's huge hunting trophies—buffalo heads, elephant tusks, bearskins, and the like—are all over the place. Even the inkwell is made from a rhinoceros foot.

The great north room where the President entertained foreign dignitaries contains some of their gifts—samurai swords, ivory, paintings, and photographs. Roosevelt's masculine touch dominates all of the home's three stories and 22 rooms except for Mrs. Roosevelt's parlor, where the First Lady was allowed her own patterned brocade armchairs and flowered lampshades.

Aside from bringing the spirit of the late president to life, Sagamore Hill offers a glorious view of Oyster Bay and Long Island Sound.

If the weather is warm and you haven't eaten by now, you can walk down past the windmill to a cafeteria and enjoy your snack at a picnic table with a view. Or if you prefer to end your weekend with a proper fresh seafood dinner with a view, Steve's Pier One on the water in nearby Bayville is just the spot.

Long Island Area Code: 516

DRIVING DIRECTIONS   Long Island Expressway (Route 495) to exit 62. Proceed north on Nichols Road and turn left on 25A. Follow 25A into the village.

Total distance: about 58 miles.

PUBLIC TRANSPORTATION BY TRAIN   Long Island Railroad service is available from New York Penn Station to Stony Brook. You can walk around the village sights, take a cab or a ¾-mile walk from the station to the museums, then also taxi or walk to the inn.

ACCOMMODATIONS   *Three Village Inn,* 150 Main Street, Stony Brook, 11790, 751-0555; $$ ● If the inn is filled there are no alternatives in Stony Brook, few even nearby. Two other possibilities: *Holiday Inn,* 1740 Express Drive, South Hauppauge, 234-3030; $$–$$$ ● *Bert Bacharach's East Norwich Inn,* 25A and Route 106 (near Oyster Bay), 922-1500. Somewhat motelish but plush with gardens, heated pool, sauna, and game room; $$$.

DINING   *Three Village Inn* (see above); dinner $$–$$$, lunch $–$$$ ● *Country House,* New York 25A, Stony Brook, 751-3332; dinner $$, lunch $–$$ ● *Whaler's Inn,* 105 Harbor Road, Cold Spring Harbor, 367-3166; dinner $–$$, lunch $ ● *Steve's Pier One,* 33 Bayville Avenue, Bayville, 628-2431; complete dinner $$–$$$$.

SIGHTSEEING   *The Museums at Stony Brook,* Route 25A, 751-0066. Hours: Wednesday to Sunday 10 A.M. to 5 P.M. Adults $2, students and senior citizens $1.50, children over 6 $1 ● *Thompson House,* North Country Road, Setauket. Hours: late May to mid-October, Saturday, Sunday 1 to 5 P.M. Adults $1, children age 7–14 25¢ ● *Vanderbilt Museum,* Little Neck Road, Centerport (watch for signs on 25A). Hours: May to October, Tuesday to Saturday, 10 A.M. to 4 P.M.; Sunday noon to 5 P.M. Adults $1.75, senior citizens and children age 6–12 $1, under 6 not admitted • *Cold Spring Whaling Museum*, Main Street (Route 25A), Cold Spring Harbor, 367-3418. Hours: Memorial Day to September, daily, 11 A.M. to 5 P.M.; rest of year, Tuesday, Thursday, Saturday, Sunday only. Adults $1, children age 6–14 25¢ • *Sagamore Hill*, Cove Neck Road, Oyster Bay, 922-6808. Daily, June to August 9:30 A.M. to 6 P.M.; spring and fall, to 5 P.M., winter to 4:30 P.M. Adults 50¢, children under 12 free.

Down to the Sea at Mystic Seaport

Wait for the weather forecast. Make sure it's going to be the kind of perfect spring day when breezes billow the square sails, masts and rigging stand out against the blue sky, and the sun warms you while you listen to sea chanteys being sung on the green.

That's the kind of day to save for Mystic Seaport Museum, not only a place for ships but a 17-acre total re-creation of a nineteenth-century maritime village. You can only pick your weekend at the last minute if you go to visit the northeast's major maritime attraction before summer tourists fill the local motels. And you'll enjoy your visit even more without summer humidity and crowds.

Mystic's shipbuilding history dates back to the 1600s. When wooden shipbuilding was at its peak in the 1800s, Mystic yards produced some of the fastest clippers on the seas, many built at the George Greenman and Company Shipyard, the site of the present Seaport Museum. Three town residents formed a Marine Historical Association back in 1929 to preserve some of the objects of the town's maritime past, and sea-minded friends from all over soon became involved, helping the Museum grow to more than 60 historic buildings, four major vessels and more than 200 smaller boats, important collections of maritime artifacts and paintings, and a planetarium to teach the secrets of celestial navigation.

No question that for most visitors the most exciting part of Mystic is the ships, especially the big three: the *Charles W. Morgan*, America's last surviving wooden whaling ship; the full-rigged training ship *Joseph Conrad*, and the fishing schooner *L. A. Dunton*.

You can come right aboard, pace the decks, examine the intricate rigging and enormous masts, go down below to see the crew's cramped quarters and the officers' cabins, even take an imaginary turn at the wheel. On the *Morgan,* the whaleboats, tryworks, sails, and rigging are all in place. Aboard the *Dunton,* crew members show another kind of fishing expertise in action—the cleaning, splitting, and salting of cod for drying. Fishermen's skills like trawling, net weaving, and lobster-pot building are also demonstrated.

Smaller boats once used for oystering, lobstering, salmon fishing, clamming, and other kinds of fishing are moored near the *Dunton,* and you can see the fishing gear used by three generations of one family at the Robie Ames Fishing Shack nearby.

Almost as interesting as seeing the boats is learning how they were built. Mystic's Henry B. DuPont preservation shipyard is a unique facility with the equipment and craftsmen to perform almost any task in the restoration and preservation of wooden boats. A visitor's gallery overlooks the carpenter's shops, rigging loft, and other areas where older vessels are maintained and new ones are built.

In the Small Craft Shop, boat builders are at work crafting small wooden sailboats or rowboats. Some are sold to finance the seaport's boat-building apprenticeship program, which keeps the old craft alive. Others are part of a fleet of nineteenth-century dories, wherries, canoes, split-sail boats, and catboats that are sailed and rowed on the river, enlivening the waterfront.

All of this goes on against the backdrop of a nineteenth-century seafaring village with more than 20 authentic structures—grocery store, printer's shop, school, chapel, ship chandlery, sail loft, shipsmith, cooperage, and other necessary services. Some of these shops and houses are on their original sites; others were moved here from the town of Mystic or from other New England communities. All are furnished with authentic period items, and in many costumed craftsmen are on hand to explain and demonstrate their trades.

There are several museums on the grounds displaying maritime art and artifacts, ship models, paintings, and scrimshaw. One exhibit traces the development of the maritime industry from the seventeenth to nineteenth centuries; another tells the story of fishing, America's oldest industry. One of the most delightful displays for adults is the collection of ships' figureheads and wood carvings in the Wendell Building. Children are invariably charmed by the Children's Museum, done up like the interior of the ship's quarters for a captain's family. Young visitors can climb up in the bunks to peer out of portholes at a mock sea and play with reproductions of toys that might have been used to amuse children on a sea voyage long ago.

It's all educational, but they also keep things lively here with demonstrations, sail setting and furling, whaleboat rowing and sailing, a breeches buoy rescue drill. And there are "sailors" all around the grounds ready to break into a sea chantey at the drop of a sea breeze.

It's almost impossible to absorb it all in a single visit. You can opt for a two-day ticket that allows you to rest up and come back for more. At least take a long break for a clamburger at the Galley snack bar and a cruise down the river on the jaunty little steamboat *Sabino* to rest between bouts of seeing the sights.

And don't think the sights of Mystic are finished when you leave the seaport. The Mystic Marinelife Aquarium is almost as popular with youngsters as the museum itself for its dolphins and seals; the Memory Lane Doll and Toy Museum has more than 1,500 dolls from all over the world; and there's the Denison Nature Center if you want to take a spring walk in the woods.

The town of Mystic is also appealing, with many fine old homes (ask for the walking tour at the information center in Olde Mistick Village). A nautical flavor remains downtown with the river running through; check out the riverside art gallery and the railroad station that was the model for millions of toy train sets for years.

There are shops galore—Olde Mistick Village, a pseudo-Colonial shopping mall with shops selling pewter, Early American furniture, kites, and much more; and all manner of stores in town selling everything, including antiques. One of the most interesting complexes is Factory Square, a century-old brick mill transformed into stores, a crafts workshop, a bakery, restaurants, and apartments. And don't overlook the seaport store, headquarters for nautical paraphernalia and memorabilia and also an old-time country store and bakeshop.

Just outside Mystic you can visit Whitehall, a 1770 country mansion that has been restored and authentically furnished by the Historical Society of neighboring Stonington.

As if all that isn't enough, there is Stonington village just four miles away. This is one of the most picturesque towns on the Connecticut shore, filled with eighteenth- and nineteenth-century homes that belonged to sea captains of another age, a Greek Revival town center, village green with requisite white churches, and a lighthouse that dates back to 1823. Should you be here in summer, don't miss the little museum in that lighthouse or the view of the Sound from its tower.

If you are totally taken with Stonington (and lots of people are), ask at Whitehall for a walking tour pamphlet and while away some time getting a closer look at the town's charming homes. There are a couple of excellent antique shops for browsing on Main Street and two good places to eat, informal Noah's or the very elegant Harborview. Yesterday's Manner, back toward Mystic, is another good choice.

Dining in Mystic is also varied and good. Visit the Seaport's

Seamen's Inne or try the Steamboat Cafe in town. For lobster, Abbot's in nearby Noank, a no-frills establishment with outdoor-picnic-tables, has been famous for years. And there are lots of little places for less formal meals. Two Sisters Deli, 13 Water Street, Kitchen Little, and the Mischievous Carrot are among those local residents recommend.

Where to stay? There are scads of motels. And surprisingly, tucked on a hilltop behind one of the motels, the Mystic Inn is a true inn that is one of the most elegant to be found. It's a former private estate with beautiful gardens, the place where legend says Humphrey Bogart and Lauren Bacall spent their honeymoon. It has recently been renovated in exquisite taste. The unbeatable views of the harbor needed no improvement. If you want to forget about children and make Mystic a romantic nautical getaway for two, this is definitely the place.

Connecticut Area Code: 203

DRIVING DIRECTIONS   Take US 95 to exit 90. Mystic Seaport is about one mile south of the exit on Route 27.
   Total distance: about 127 miles.

BY PUBLIC TRANSPORTATION   Amtrak trains and Greyhound buses serve Mystic daily, and the town of Mystic runs free mini-bus service to all major points daily except Tuesdays, May to September, 10 A.M. to 6 P.M.

ACCOMMODATIONS   *Mystic Motor Inn* (motel and real inn), Route 1 at Route 27, 536-9604; $$$–$$$$ • *Ramada Inn,* Route 27 just off I-95, 536-9604; $$–$$$ • *Howard Johnson's,* Route 27 at I-95, 536-2654; $$ • *Days Inn,* off I-95, 572-0574; $.

DINING   *Seamen's Inne,* Greenmanville Avenue, 536-9649; (seafood specialties) lunch $, dinner $–$$ • *Steamboat Cafe,* 73 Steamboat Wharf, 536-1975; $ • *Yesterday's Manner* (moving to new location— phone for address and prices), *Old Mystic,* 536-1228 • *Harbour View,* 60 Water Street, Stonington, 535-2720; $$ • *Noah's,* 113 Water Street, Stonington, 535-3925; $.

SIGHTSEEING   *Mystic Seaport Museum,* Route 27, Mystic, 536-2631. Hours: May 1 to October 31, daily, 9 A.M. to 5 P.M., grounds open evening from mid-May till 8 P.M. Steamboat *Sabino* rides, adults $2, children $1.25 • Adults $8, children $4, under 5 free (less in winter); two-day tickets, $10 and $5. (Many special weekends are scheduled for photographers: sea music festival, dory races, fish frys, etc.; phone for specific dates.) ● *Mystic Marinelife Aquarium,* Route 27, Mystic, 536-3323. Hours: daily, 9 A.M. to 5 P.M., hourly dolphin, sea lion, and whale demonstrations from 10 A.M. Adults $4.50, children $2 ● *Memory Lane Doll and Toy Museum,* Route 27, Mystic 536-3450. Hours: Monday to Saturday, 10 A.M. to 6 P.M.; Sunday, noon to 6 P.M. Adults 50¢, children 25¢, under 5 free ● *Dennison Pequotsepos Nature Center,* Pequotsepos Road, Mystic 536-1216. Hours: Tuesday to Saturday, 9 A.M. to 5 P.M., Sunday from 1 P.M. Adults 75¢, children under age 12 50¢.

Winterthur and Other Delaware Delights

Who could have foreseen what lay ahead in 1923 when Henry Francis du Pont acquired his first American-made antique, a simple Pennsylvania chest dated 1737?

A man of extraordinary taste as well as wealth, du Pont recognized the distinctive work of early American craftsmen before collecting native antiques had become fashionable. He saw the nation's early culture reflected in its decorative arts and was soon amassing not only the finest furniture from the period between 1640 and 1840 but also curtains, bed hangings, rugs, lighting fixtures, silver pieces, and ceramics.

Even that wasn't enough to satisfy him. It wasn't long before du Pont was combing the eastern seaboard for paneling, fireplace walls, doors, and ceilings from the finest homes of the period, dismantling and reinstalling them at Winterthur as proper background for his collections.

Eventually there were almost 200 room settings, and after living pleasurably with his antiques for almost 30 years, du Pont turned his home into a museum and educational facility in 1951 so that the rest of the world could appreciate it with him.

Winterthur is now one of the outstanding attractions in the Northeast. There is no better place to see the very best of America's early arts. Nor is there a pleasanter place to visit in spring during the annual open house from mid-April to early June, since the du Pont gardens are also a showplace, a 64-acre woodland wonderland of rare azaleas, rhododendrons, and other prize plants.

During most of the year visitors without special appointments see only 18 rooms, the "American Sampler" tour showing the chronological development of American crafts. During the spring open house another 16 rooms are open. All along the way there are specially trained guides to point out the treasures in each setting.

If anything stands out after touring so many rooms, it is the very variety of the settings and the progression of styles. Among the memorable re-creations are a simple seventeenth-century dining room with tables and benches before an open hearth; the Readbourne Parlor with woodwork and appropriate accompanying furnishings from a 1733 Maryland home; a drawing room with New England Queen Anne furniture and an equally elegant parlor from Port Royal, with yellow carved sofas and wing chairs, Chippendale side chairs and highboy, Oriental rugs, marble fireplace, and crystal chandeliers.

The gardens, like the rooms, were created under du Pont's personal direction, with meticulous care to make them appear as natural growth among the native trees and shrubs that have been preserved around them.

Tanbark and turf paths wind through shaded woodland and over rolling hillsides, bringing spectacular vistas into view at every turn. The Azalea Woods for which the gardens are most noted reach their peak in the first half of May, a mist of white, pink, and salmon as far as the eye can see, under a canopy of flowering dogwood and tall tulip trees. Be sure to see the quarry area as well, in full bloom in May with Asiatic primroses in jewel colors.

There is no nicer way to welcome spring than to visit Winterthur, and one pleasant way to do it is to arrive late morning, spend about two hours in the house, have lunch in the cafeteria-style Garden Pavillion, and then wander the gardens in the afternoon. You can make your own path or follow the arrows posted to give you the best route for seeing the peak of the blooms. The paths cover two and a half miles and can be covered in a leisurely hour and a half.

Although Wilmington isn't thought of as a tourist city, it is an interesting one. If you want to live like a du Pont, choose the Hotel du Pont with its carved ceilings, marble stairs, and antiques. The Christina Room has a million dollars' worth of Wyeths on its walls. The new Hotel Radisson is contemporary in decor but is also quite attractive and offers an indoor pool.

Take a walk from either hotel down the Market Street Mall to see the Grand Opera House, a cast-iron, highly decorative Neo-Classical building recently restored to become Delaware's Center for the Performing Arts. Willingtown Square, the 500 block on the mall, is a historic complex of six eighteenth-century houses. The Old Town Hall, dating back to 1798, has displays of decorative arts and a restored jail inside.

At dinnertime, try to sample some of the crabmeat dishes that are local specialties at places like the Columbus Inn or Leoune's at the Mansion.

On Sunday there are more diversions to choose from. The small but very interesting Delaware Art Museum in Wilmington is dedicated to Howard Pyle, whose Brandywine School turned out illustrators like N. C. Wyeth and Frank Schoonover, whose distinct works of art enlivened countless magazines and books early in this century. Pyle's own works are generously included in the exhibits. The museum's other specialty is Pre-Raphaelite art, a London school of the mid-1800s represented here by Rossetti, Millais, and Ford Madox Brown, the gift of a Wilmington industrialist and art collector, Samuel Bancroft, Jr.

The evolution of industry in the Brandywine Valley and in the nation as a whole is shown at the Hagley Museum on Route 141 in Greenville. The history of the du Pont Company, which dominates the valley, is prominent. The buildings include the original du Pont "black powder" mills, an 1814 cotton spinning mill, an operating waterwheel, and a water turbine. The first office of the du Pont Company is also part of the exhibits, as is the company founder E. I. du Pont's first home, Eleutherian Mills. Not the last of the attractions of the Hagley is its lush setting along the banks of the Brandywine River, which powered these and many other mills.

If you want to appreciate the fruits of the first Mr. du Pont's labors, pay a visit to Nemours, the Louis XVI chateau built by descendant Alfred I. du Pont in the early 1900s. The 77-room house and formal gardens do full credit to the French chateau country that inspired them.

A more down-to-earth way to pass the time is to take a ride on the old steam train at the Wilmington and Western Railroad in Greenbank, a huffing, puffing hour's excursion into the countryside.

An even more delightful visit to the past is the easy six-mile drive south along I-95 to New Castle, where you walk cobbled streets into Colonial times. Historic New Castle was Delaware's first capital and a meeting place for the Colonial assemblies. Later overshadowed by Wilmington and Philadelphia, it fell out of the mainstream of commerce, and its lack of prosperity kept architectural changes to a minimum. Today the old town with its mellow red brick townhouses and public green, seems hardly changed by the passing of time. Many of the old homes are exquisitely furnished and open to the public, as is the Old Court House that once housed the state assembly. The handsome cupola atop the Court House is distinguished by being the center of the 12-mile circle surveyed by Mason and Dixon, which formed Delaware's northern boundary with Pennsylvania.

The tiny William Penn Guest House just across from the Court House is the perfect historic hostelry for the town, and there's even an appropriately atmospheric dining place, the New Castle Inn, in an old arsenal behind Delaware Street.

The third Saturday in mid-May each year is designated as "A Day in Old New Castle," and many of the private homes and gardens in town are open to the public. If you can time your trip to coincide, set aside the day and save Sunday for Winterthur.

Also note that the first Saturday in May each year is Wilmington Garden Day, a once-a-year opportunity to visit some of the city's finest houses and gardens, and another reason to postpone Winterthur until the next day.

Either event, plus Winterthur in the spring, makes for an unbeatable combination.

Delaware Area Code: 302

DRIVING DIRECTIONS   Take the New Jersey Turnpike to the end, cross the Delaware Memorial Bridge to 295, turn north on I-95 into Wilmington. From Wilmington to Winterthur, take Route 52; entrance is on the right about two miles past the railroad tracks at Greenville Shopping Center. From Wilmington to New Castle, follow I-95 south to Route 41 east.

Total distance: about 125 miles.

BY PUBLIC TRANSPORTATION   Amtrak serves Wilmington; Bus No. 14 (Kennett Pike line) goes from the train station past Winterthur three times daily. Check for current schedule.

ACCOMMODATIONS   *Hotel du Pont,* 11th and Market Street, Wilmington, 656-8121; $$$–$$$$; ask about other special weekend package plans ● *Radisson Wilmington,* 700 King Street, Wilmington, 655-0400; $$$; weekend packages as low as $$ per night with breakfast—check for current packages ● *Holiday Inn—North,* 4000 Concord Pike, Wilmington, 478-2222; $ ● *William Penn Guest House,* 206 Delaware Street, New Castle, 328-7736; $; no private baths.

DINING   *Hotel du Pont* (see above), Brandywine Room and Christina Room, both elegant; lunches $–$$, dinners $$–$$$ ● *Columbus Inn,* 2216 Pennsylvania Avenue (Route 52), 571-1492; regional seafood specialties, especially crab; $$ • *Leoune's at the Mansion,* Bancroft Estate Road, 658-5266, atmospheric old home near Delaware Art Museum; $$–$$$ • *New Castle Inn* (behind the courthouse), New Castle, 328-1798; historic arsenal buildings with specialty chicken and oyster pot pie; dinner $$, Sunday brunch served 11 A.M. to 2 P.M., $ • *Greenery Too,* Route 52, Greenville Center; lunches $, dinner $–$$, brunch $.

SIGHTSEEING *Winterthur Museum,* Winterthur, 654-1548. "Winterthur in Spring," 16 rooms normally seen by reservation only, plus the 18-room American Sampler tour and self-guided garden tour, mid-April to early June. Hours: Tuesday to Saturday, 10 A.M. to 4 P.M.; Sunday, Monday, holidays, noon to 4 P.M. Adults $5, children over age 12 only $3.75 • *Delaware Art Museum,* 2301 Kentmere Parkway, Wilmington, 571-9590. Hours: Monday to Saturday, 10 A.M. to 5 P.M.; Sunday, 1 to 5 P.M. Adults $1, children age 12–18 50¢, under 12 free • *Old Town Hall,* 512 Market Street Mall. Hours: Tuesday to Friday, noon to 4 P.M.; Saturday, 10 A.M. to 4 P.M. Free • *Hagley Museum,* Route 141, Greenville, 658-2400. Hours: Tuesday to Saturday, 9:30 A.M. to 4:30 P.M.; Sunday, 1 to 5 P.M. Adults $2.50, senior citizens $1.25, students $1, children under age 14 free • *Wilmington & Western Railroad,* Routes 2 and 41, Greenbank Station, one-hour steam train ride from Greenbank to Mount Cuba Picnic Grove. Hours: May to October, Sundays only, 12:30, 2, 3:30 P.M. Adults $3, children $1.50, under 6 free • *Wilmington Town Hall,* 512 Market Street Mall, Wilmington, 655-7161. Hours: Tuesday to Friday, noon to 4 P.M.; Saturday 10 A.M. to 4 P.M. Free • *Amstel House Museum,* 2 East 4th at Delaware Street, New Castle, 322-2794. Hours: Wednesday to Saturday, 11 A.M. to 4 P.M.; Sunday, 1 to 4 P.M. Adults $1, children age 5–12 50¢, under 5 free • *Old Court House,* 2nd and Delaware, 571-3059. Hours: Tuesday to Saturday, 10 A.M. to 4:30 P.M.; Sunday, noon to 5 P.M. Free • *Old Dutch House,* 32 East 3rd Street, 322-9168. Oldest dwelling in state, early eighteenth-century furnishings. Hours: April to October, Tuesday to Saturday, 11 A.M. to 4 P.M. Adults 50¢, children age 5–12 25¢. Sunday, noon to 5 P.M. • *George Read II House,* 42 The Strand, 322-8411. Georgian home with period antiques, formal garden. Tours Tuesday to Saturday, 10 A.M. to 4 P.M.; Sunday, noon to 4 P.M. Adults $2; senior citizens, children 75¢.

On the Back Roads in Connecticut Laurel Country

All of Connecticut may be known as the Laurel State, but it is the northwest corner that seems to have cornered the most magnificent displays of the state flower—and a little known spot near Torrington that has the most spectacular show of all.

Known as Indian Lookout, it's actually the private property of the Paul Freedmans, who some 35 years ago began clearing their six acres of mountainside to allow the wild laurels to spread and gradually landscaped the area to provide a balanced natural setting. The six acres grew to 100 and the pale pink clouds of laurel enveloping the mountain grew more beautiful with the seasons until, in 1958, the owners decided it was too beautiful to keep to themselves.

So visitors are now welcome to Indian Lookout for laurel season only, from mid to late June. Come dressed for the occasion—you'll have to climb the hill on foot unless you are one of the senior citizens who are allowed to drive through on weekdays from 5:30 to 6 P.M. But the view is worth every step of the climb.

Having literally scaled the heights when it comes to laurel watching, you're now all set for further excursions into the countryside, a rural ramble through little towns where the residents still patronize the general store, past historic homes and unexpected museums, in and out of antique stores. You'll have plenty of opportunity to get back to nature, to hike, or possibly even to paddle your way down the Housatonic River.

All along the way, the laurels lend a pastel glow to the scenery.

Just a few miles north of Torrington along Route 8 is Winsted, a tiny town that calls itself the Laurel City. Until the late 1960s, Winsted celebrated the appearance of its bountiful blossoms every year with a weekend festival. Recently they've tried to revive the custom, staging a true bit of small-town Americana with bands and a homemade float parade, the crowning of a Laurel Queen, booths of homemade goodies set around the village green, and an old-fashioned square dance on Saturday night. Phone the town clerk (379-4646) to check on this year's dates—and to be sure that inflation hasn't deflated the town's enthusiasm.

Festival or no, Winsted usually posts markers to send visitors on self-guided auto tours of the most scenic laurel views. While you're in town stop at the corner of Lake and Prospect streets to see the Solomon Rockwell House, an antebellum mansion that is a national historic landmark, furnished with Hitchcock chairs, Thomas and Whiting clocks, and memorabilia dating back to the Revolutionary War.

Take Route 20 north from Winsted to Riverton for a closer look at Mr. Hitchcock's famous chairs in a museum building that was once an old church meetinghouse. The Hitchcock Museum has an extensive collection of the originals; the modern factory nearby makes reproductions, using some of the traditional hand procedures, and you can visit a showroom and a gift shop there.

Also in the village is a Seth Thomas factory outlet where you can get good buys on mantel, wall, and grandfather clocks from America's oldest clockmaker.

There are a couple of antique shops in Riverton (Elizabeth Winsor McIntyre claims the largest collection of fine dolls in New England), an herb shop, a contemporary crafts gallery that specializes in pewter, and a gift shop that has many Appalachian and Blue Ridge Mountain craftwares. For lunch the Catnip Mouse Tearoom will serve your sandwich on homemade bread, and the Village Sweet Shoppe has tempting chocolates and ice cream for dessert.

From Riverton, plot your course according to your inclinations. If you want to get out and hike, there are two possibilities. The People's State Forest on Route 44 in Barkhamsted offers miles of well-marked trails. Or, since it's laurel season, you might want to go back toward Winsted and follow Route 44 northwest to Haystack Mountain State Park or Dennis Hill State Park, both in Norfolk. Each park has summit buildings with magnificent views, but Dennis Hill is a particularly good choice if you are looking for laurel vistas.

If you prefer to continue traveling the backroads by car, take 183 out of Winsted to Colebrook, where you'll find a genuine one-room schoolhouse and a general store that has been in operation since 1812. The town hall here also dates back to 1816. You couldn't have found a more authentic nontouristy New England village. And there's also a haven for book buffs, the Book Barn, with more than 5,000 selections, some rare, some just secondhand.

Catching up with the hikers in Norfolk, you'll find a drive through the local parks an enjoyable outing. Beginning in late June, this is also the site of the Yale Summer School of Music and some excellent summer concerts. It may be a bit early, but check locally to see if the season has begun.

Your country inn headquarters for the weekend should be either the Mountain View Inn in Norfolk, a Victorian house on a hill, or the more Colonial-style Old Riverton Inn, which has been entertaining travelers since 1796. Both have good food as well as charm. One other alternative if these are full is the Yankee Pedlar in Torrington.

On Sunday you can continue shunpiking on Route 44 to Canaan, where the old railroad station houses quaint shops and restaurants and where you'll find a curiosity—a museum devoted to postcards. Follow 44 west to Salisbury, Lakeville, and Sharon and you'll be passing through three of the loveliest northwest Connecticut towns. In Sharon the Audubon Center on Route 4 offers self-guided nature trails over 684 acres of sanctuary.

Don't be afraid to venture off on your own onto the sideroads. One of the real pleasures of this kind of weekend is discovering your own memories—a white steepled church, a picture-book Colonial farmhouse, or a babbling brook. And don't forget the camera.

But to really make the most of the Connecticut springtime, there's nothing to compare with the quiet and the country scenery on a cruise down the Housatonic River by canoe. Follow Route 7 south out of Canaan to Falls Village, and a place called Riverrunning Expeditions will provide everything you need. Don't be frightened by the name— the portion of the river from Falls Village to West Cornwall is almost all placid flatwater, and if you remember your strokes from those long-gone days at summer camp, you'll have no trouble at all. They'll give you a quick refresher or a whole day of instruction if you really want to prepare for running a river, even the whitewater. And if you don't trust yourself at all, you can splurge and hire a guide who'll lead you safely down the river, filling you in on the history and the wildlife and vegetation of the area as you float by.

If you debark at Cornwall Bridge, you're in just the right place for a last bit of picturesque scenery—the covered bridge that gives the town its name. Proceed across the bridge into town to The Deck, and you can have a drink or a meal with a waterfall view, the perfect end to a country ramble, whether by land or by canoe.

Connecticut Area Code: 203

DRIVING DIRECTIONS Hutchinson River Parkway to Merritt Parkway. Follow the Merritt past Bridgeport, then take Route 8 north to Torrington. Follow Route 4 west through Torrington and past town to Mountain Road and Indian Lookout.

Total distance: about 109 miles to Torrington.

ACCOMMODATIONS AND DINING *Mountain View Inn,* Litchfield Road, Norfolk, 542-5595; $$$$ MAP; dinner $$ ● *Old*

Riverton Inn, Route 20, Riverton, 379-8678; \$\$; dinner \$\$, lunch \$
• *Yankee Pedlar Inn,* 93 Main Street, Torrington, 489-9226; \$\$; dinner
entrées \$\$, lunch \$.

SIGHTSEEING *Indian Lookout,* Mountain Road, Torrington.
Hours: weekdays, 1:30 P.M. to 6 P.M.; weekends, 11 A.M. to 6 P.M.
Free, but donations accepted • *Solomon Rockwell House,* Lake and
Prospect streets, Winsted. Hours: June 15 to September 15, Thursday
to Sunday, 2 to 4 P.M. (Hours are extended for laurel festival
weekend.) Donation • *Hitchcock Museum,* Route 20, Riverton,
379-1003. Hours: June to October, Tuesday to Saturday, 10 A.M. to 5
P.M. Free • *Sharon Audubon Center,* Route 4, Sharon, 364-5909.
Hours: Wednesday to Saturday, 9 A.M. to noon, 1 to 5 P.M.; Sunday, 1
to 5 P.M. Adults \$1, children 50¢ • *Riverrunning Expeditions, Ltd.,*
Main Street, Falls Village, CT 06031, 824-5579. Write or call for
brochure and current rates.

Big Bird to Ben Franklin: Family Fun near Philadelphia

There goes little Susan, diving and paddling her way through a spongy-
bottomed "pool" filled with 80,000 little plastic balls. And there's
brother Mark, pushing through a forest of giant punching bags. And
who's that coming right behind them? None other than Mom and Dad,
both with grins every bit as wide as the kids'.

Sesame Place, a "family play park," in Langhorne, Pennsylvania,
just south of Trenton and north of Philadelphia, began as a place where
3- to 13-year-olds could exercise mind and muscles cavorting on one of
the nation's most innovative playgrounds, trying out do-it-yourself
science experiments, and having a go at some six dozen specially
designed educational computer games.

Parents, however, knew a good thing when they saw one. So many
adults asked to join the tempting fun during the park's first season in
1980 that the following winter was spent renovating things to give the
grown-ups their wish.

Now all ages can, and do, take part in most of the park's activities.
But, although it's also a treat for parents who want to feel young again,
the park remains a special paradise for young children, the only
amusement park planned with their special abilities, interests, and
attention span in mind.

Sesame Place was the brainchild of Children's Television Workshop, who had already proved with "Sesame Street" that education and entertainment can be mixed. In partnership with Busch Entertainment, old pros at amusement parks, they created a totally "kid-powered" park, run on the energy of the eager youngsters who come to play.

Indeed, there's enough energy flying around to light a small city. The kids gliding, tumbling, climbing, sliding, and bouncing around the playground never stop to miss the passive roller coasters and rides that have no place in this park. Nor do they realize that all that fun is teaching them things. The idea here is to encourage children to try new activities and master new skills.

When and if children tire of the outdoor equipment, they can move on to experiment with a stationary bicycle that will produce enough power to light a bulb if young legs pedal hard enough, or with the optical illusions that teach about sight and sound.

And then there are all those computer games. This is the first real encounter with computers for many of the children (not to mention their parents), and the games are designed to be appealing rather than intimidating. The cabinets are as colorful as a game arcade, the special keyboards are in alphabetical order to accommodate young fingers that can't follow a typewriter keyboard, and the hosts for many of the programs are the likes of Oscar the Grouch, Bert and Ernie, and other "Sesame Street" favorites.

These are very personal computers. They praise and encourage and some even make jokes, like the space game that tells a talented player, "Far out. You are true star quality."

To make sure there is enough room for little people to have fun without excessive crowding, Sesame Place actually shuts its gates temporarily when the place fills up. So it is a good idea to make it your first destination in the morning, enjoying a few hours of fun and then lunching in the restaurant where a see-through kitchen and a two-way microphone to the cooks makes even food preparation a learning experience for the kids.

When you can convince the family to leave, go back through Big Bird's Beak (the park entrance) and you're ready to proceed to Philadelphia and some other kinds of pleasurable education that are kids' perennial favorites in the city.

Everyone seems to get a special kick from seeing the real Liberty Bell, crack and all. The bell is just one of the sights in a complex called Independence National Historical Park, which is billed rightly as America's most historic square mile. Start at the visitors center at 3rd and Chestnut streets to see a thirty-minute film to put it all in perspective, then take the walking tour map and see the sights. These include Independence Hall, where the Declaration of Independence was adopted; Congress Hall, the home of the legislature in the late eighteenth century; Franklin Court, the site of Benjamin Franklin's home and of a lively underground museum; Old City Hall; Carpenter's Hall, where the first Continental Congress met; the First and Second U.S. Banks (literally); City Tavern; and any number of other historic homes, churches, and businesses. It's all free, and you can take in as much or as little as your family can absorb, a neat little American history lesson to close out the day.

On Sunday, after a good night's rest, you're ready for a return to the old city and a nautical change of scene at Penn's Landing on the waterfront, where the U.S.S. *Olympia,* Commodore Dewey's flagship during the Civil War, can be boarded, along with the U.S.S. *Becuna,* a World War II submarine, a Portuguese square rigger called the *Gazela Primero* and the *Moshulu,* a four-masted marque that is the largest all-steel sailing ship in the world. Seeing the cramped quarters where the crew lived for months underwater on the submarine and walking the decks of the tall ships is interesting whatever your age.

Within walking distance is the Perelman Toy Museum with over 2,000 items on display.

Next it's on to the Franklin Institute Science Museum on Benjamin Franklin Parkway, another place filled with hands-on, highly educational fun. Some of the highlights of the imaginative science exhibits are manmade lightning, a simulated flight in a 707, and a walk through a human heart. There's a planetarium here, too, and a Benjamin Franklin Memorial, but by now you may have had as much edification as anyone can handle in one weekend.

So it's on to South Philadelphia and a final fling at the outdoor food malls of the city's Italian Market, a colorful and totally satisfying end to the weekend. It's about a 15-minute drive straight down Market Street—when you come to Catherine or Fitzwater or Christian Street, park wherever you can and walk into the heart of things.

If you prefer a sit-down Italian dinner, Dante's and Luigi's, Cous's Little Italy, or Strolli are recommended. You can afford the calories; think of all the energy you've just expended!

Philadelphia Area Code: 215

DRIVING DIRECTIONS Take US I-95 into Lower Bucks County, Pennsylvania, to the Levittown exit (25-E). Follow signs for the Oxford Valley Mall on the US 1 Bypass and you'll see signs for Sesame Place. To get to Philadelphia continue on I-95 south.

Total distance: about 100 miles to Philadelphia, 80 to Sesame Place.

ACCOMMODATIONS Most convenient when driving in from Sesame Place are lodgings northeast of the city, such as: *Holiday Inn Northeast,* 3499 Street Road, Bensalem (near US 1) 638-1500; $$, children under 18 free in same room • *Sheraton Inn Northeast,* 9461 Roosevelt Boulevard, Philadelphia, 671-9700; $$, under 18 free in same room • *Holiday Inn Independence Mall,* 4th and Arch street, 923-8660; $$, under 18 free • Don't overlook special weekend family packages in some of the top city hotels: *Bellevue Stratford,* Walnut and Broad, Philadelphia, 893-1776; normally $90 to $110, but sometimes offers *two* rooms on weekends for $50. For current available packages write to Philadelphia Convention and Visitors Bureau, 1525 John F. Kennedy Boulevard, Philadelphia, PA 19102, 568-1976.

DINING The following Philadelphia restaurants are suitable for families, mostly moderate: *Cheese Cellar,* 120 Lombard Street, 923-6112, fondue and moderate entrées; $ • *City Tavern,* 2nd and Walnut, 923-6059; historic and very special, $$; lunch $ • *Fiddler,* 1515 Locust, 546-7373; deli with extensive menu including pastas, mostly $–$$ • *Dante's and Luigi's,* 762 South 10th Street, 922-9501; Italian, $ • *Old Original Bookbinders,* 125 Walnut, 925-7027; landmark, not cheap but they have a children's menu, $$–$$$ • *Strolli,* 1528 Dickinson, 336-3390; Italian, $ • *Cous's Little Italy,* 11th and Christian, 627-9753; $–$$.

SIGHTSEEING *Sesame Place,* Oxford Valley Mall off US 1 Bypass, Langhorne, 752-7070. Hours: daily, April to Labor Day, 10 A.M. to 7 P.M.; September, October, to 6 P.M.; rest of year indoors only, 10 A.M. to 10 P.M. All ages $4.95 • *Independence National Historical Park,* 3rd and Chestnut, Philadelphia, 597-7132. Hours: daily, 9 A.M. to 5 P.M. Free • *Penn's Landing,* Delaware and Spruce streets, Philadelphia, 922-1898. Hours: daily, 10 A.M. to 4:30 P.M.; summer till 6 P.M. U.S.S. *Olympia* adults $2, children under 12 $1; *Gazela Primero,* Wednesday to Sunday, 9:30 A.M. to 4:30 P.M., adults $1, children 50¢; *Moshulu,* 11 A.M. to 8 P.M., Sunday from 1 P.M., adults $1, children 50¢ • *Perelman Toy Museum,* 270 South 2nd, Philadelphia, 922-1070. Hours: Monday to Saturday. 9:30 A.M. to 5 P.M.; Sunday, 9:30 A.M. to 4 P.M. Adults $1, children 55¢ • *Franklin Institute Science Museum,* 20th and Franklin Parkway, Philadelphia, 448-1000. Hours: Monday to Saturday, 10 A.M. to 5 P.M.; Sunday, noon to 5 P.M. Adults $2.75, children and students $2, under 5 free.

FOR FURTHER INFORMATION Contact Philadelphia Convention and Visitors Bureau, 1525 JFK Boulevard, Philadelphia, PA 19102, 568-1976.

Mansion-Hopping Along the Hudson

For years the spectacular views of the Hudson River Valley and the gentle juxtaposition of the river and mountains seen from the river's east bank have fascinated artists—and millionaires. The area's beauty inspired the first cohesive group of American artists, aptly known as the "Hudson River School," and also attracted people like the Vanderbilts, Roosevelts, and Livingstons, who built their mansions on sites overlooking the majestic river.

Today, many of those magnificent estates are open to the public, offering both a living lesson in American history and a firsthand look at the life-style of a more opulent era. A weekend of mansion-hopping also provides an ample helping of scenery, with special towns, antiques, and unexpected pleasures to be found all along the way.

Ideal headquarters for a Hudson River ramble is the pretty little town of Rhinebeck, home of the hotel that proudly calls itself the oldest in America. The Beekman Arms, a stagecoach stop dating back to 1700, fascinates modern visitors with its venerable guest books. Washington, Lafayette, and Aaron Burr stayed here, along with later notables like Horace Greeley, William Jennings Bryan, and many of our presidents. Franklin Roosevelt, who lived nearby at Hyde Park, wound up every campaign with an informal talk on the inn's front porch.

Early travelers used to curl up on sheepskins before the fireplace, and although the mellow beams and planks and old-fashioned charm remain, today's accommodations are up to date and even include private baths. The inn is a charmer and it's worth planning far ahead to make sure of getting a room.

Once settled into Rhinebeck, you can plan a first day of touring to the north and your second day making mansion stops downriver, on the way home. In between, there are lovely old homes and shops to explore in Rhinebeck (be forewarned that most shops close on Sunday), plus the Old Rhinebeck Aerodrome, a one-of-a-kind place with antique airplanes both on display and in the air for shows held every weekend. Everything's in the spirit of the old glory days, including the pilots who wear uniforms dating back to World War I.

Start your mansion tour driving north on scenic route 9G to Hudson. Make a stop along the way at Clermont, the former estate of the Livingston family and now a museum home and state park with grounds that are among the most beautiful of any along the river. They're open free for picnicking or just looking.

About four miles below Hudson you'll come to Olana, the Persian castle built by painter Frederic Lewis Church, well-known member of the Hudson River School.

Whether your interest is art, gardens, decorating, or architecture, you'll find much to see in the domain of the well-traveled Mr. Church. The unusual structure and decor of the house and the meticulously planned grounds are strongly personal expressions of his taste, and outside the windows there is virtually a finished Hudson River School painting, with sweeping views of the river and the mountains beyond.

The city of Hudson offers its own perspective of the river from the Parade Walk, and its restored and revitalized Warren Street is almost a miniature Georgetown. The American Museum of Fire Fighting in Hudson tells its own special history from bucket brigade to horse-drawn pumps to contemporary gear. There are also some fancy antique fire engines used by volunteer brigades more for show than fighting fires, and they are fun to see.

There are still more mansions awaiting to the south. One of the lesser known is the Mills Mansion in Staatsburg, an 1895 Neoclassical 65-room affair designed by Stanford White and furnished in fancy Louis XV and Louis XVI styles.

Far less elaborate and more famous is Franklin Roosevelt's home and library in Hyde Park. This is not so much a showplace as a warm testament to an exceptional family who left the home stamped with their own personalities. Franklin Roosevelt grew up here, and he and his wife, Eleanor, spent a great deal of time in Hyde Park with his mother, Sara. Though the house was damaged by a fire recently, repairs should be complete by now.

The family memorabilia ranges from FDR's boyhood pony cart to papers that shaped world history. The collection is arranged chronologically, and seeing it is a wonderful way to learn or remember what happened here and abroad between the years of 1932 and 1945. There are also records of Eleanor's humanitarian activities extending to 1962. On the tape tour of the house, you can hear Eleanor describe life at Hyde Park in her own distinctive voice.

Admission to Hyde Park includes a visit to the opulent mansion down the road built by Frederick Vanderbilt, grandson of "The Commodore." Designed by the famous firm of McKim, Mead, and White in the late 1890s, it is a lavish Beaux Arts structure where hundreds of guests could be, and were, entertained. The landscaping of the grounds and the views of the Hudson and the Catskills are magnificent.

If the Beekman Arms is filled, you'll have to settle for a meal there, and for the motel rooms to be found around Hyde Park and Poughkeepsie a few miles south. You might make a note to stop in Poughkeepsie, anyway, to see the unusual Shakespeare Garden on the handsome campus of Vassar College. It's made up of plants that were mentioned by the bard in his works.

But if inns are not plentiful, the bounty of good restaurants makes up for it. Across the Rip Van Winkle Bridge from Hudson in Catskill is La Rive, the kind of French country restaurant you would be pleased to find in France. The Beekman Arms serves good traditional American fare, and in Hyde Park you can sample haute cuisine produced by the soon-to-be-greats at the nation's top school for chefs, the Culinary Institute of America. If you want dinner or luncheon in the formal Escoffier Room, you'll have to make reservations as much as three months ahead for weekends. But if you come for an informal lunch, the coffeeshop serves excellent soups and sandwiches and a fresh-baked tart and flaky apple pie.

Continuing south, the Treasure Chest in Poughkeepsie dates back to 1741 and still maintains a bit of Colonial ambience. Farther west in Patterson, there is another classic French inn, L'Auberge Bretonne.

Better get explicit driving directions for country retreats like La Rive when you make your absolutely essential reservation for dinner.

But you'll need no help finding the antique shops in the area. They're plentiful on Route 9 and on the main street of Rhinebeck and almost anywhere you go in the Hudson Valley.

Rhinebeck, Hyde Park, Poughkeepsie, Patterson Area Code: 914; Catskill Area Code: 518

DRIVING DIRECTIONS New York Thruway to exit 19, across the Rhinecliff Bridge to Route 9G south, then a right turn onto Route 9 south. Or take the Saw Mill onto the Taconic Parkway and get off at Route 199, following 308 left to Route 9 Rhinebeck.

Total distance: about 100 miles.

ACCOMMODATIONS *Beekman Arms,* Route 9, Rhinebeck,

876-7077; $ ● *Golden Manor Motel,* Route 9, Hyde Park, 229-2157; $ ●
Hyde Park Motel, Route 9, Hyde Park, 229-9161; $ ● *Holiday Inn,*
Sharon Drive, Poughkeepsie, 473-1151; $$ ● *Best Western Red Bull
Motor Inn,* 576 South Road, Poughkeepsie, 462-4400; $–$$.

DINING   *Beekman Arms,* Rhinebeck (see above); $–$$ ● *La Rive,*
Catskill, 943-4888, $$$ ● *Culinary Institute of America,* Route 9, Hyde
Park, 471-6608; Escoffier Room, complete dinner $27.50 per person,
complete lunch $13.50 per person; coffeeshop $ ● *Treasure Chest,* 568
South Road, Poughkeepsie, 462-4545; lunch $, dinner $$ ● *L'Auberge
Bretonne,* Route 22, Patterson, 878-7882; $$$.

SIGHTSEEING   *Old Rhinebeck Aerodrome,* Stone Church Road, off
Route 9, Rhinebeck, 758-8610. Hours: displays daily, mid-May to
October, 10 A.M. to 5 P.M., air shows Sunday, 2:30 P.M., and on
Saturday and Sunday, July and August. Adults $5.00, children $2.50 ●
Clermont State Historic Park, Route 6 (off 9G), Hudson, 537-4240.
Hours: late May to October, Wednesday to Sunday, 9 A.M. to 5 P.M. Free
● *Olana State Historic Site,* Route 9G, Hudson, 828-7695. Hours: late
May to October, Wednesday to Sunday, 9 A.M. to 4:30 P.M. Adults 50¢,
children under 12 free ● *American Museum of Fire Fighting,* Harry
Howard Avenue, Hudson, 828-7695. Hours: daily, April to November,
9 A.M. to 5 P.M. Free ● *Mills Mansion and State Park,* US 9, Staatsburg,
889-4100. Hours: June to October, Wednesday to Sunday, 9 A.M. to 5
P.M. Free ● *Roosevelt-Vanderbilt National Historic Site,* US 9, Hyde
Park, 229-9115. Hours: daily, Memorial Day to Labor Day, 9 A.M. to 6
P.M.; rest of year, 5 P.M. Combination ticket adults $1.50, under 16 and
over 62 free.

Horsing Around in New Jersey

"We raise 'em, we ride 'em, we race 'em."

Way out west in New Jersey, the subject was horses and a gentleman
was explaining to us that in this state, which is better known for
turnpike traffic than green pastures, there probably are more cowboys
to be found than anywhere else east of Texas. The reason is that raising

horses is one of the state's principal industries, particularly in Monmouth County, not far from the Jersey shore.

The horse farms are in full view along the roads, concentrated in a triangle between Holmdel, Freehold, and Colt's Neck—a particularly pleasant sight in spring when the colts are in the fields grazing beside their mothers. The trotters run at Freehold and the thoroughbreds at Monmouth Park, and just south of the county in Lakewood you can watch the cowboys in action at a rip-roaring, old-fashioned rodeo every Saturday night beginning in late May.

With all of that within easy reach of some interesting historic sights and prime antiquing territory, and just a breeze from the shore, what better plan for a late May to early June weekend than a sampling of horse country?

The best base is the Molly Pitcher Inn in Red Bank, not your cozy country inn by any means, but an imposing red Colonial structure with a beautiful view of the Navesink River out the dining room windows. There are rooms in the inn as well as a motel unit in back and an outdoor pool in season. An alternate might be the Sheraton Gardens in Freehold or Hilton Inn in Tinton Falls.

Since you are only heading about 45 miles out of the city, it should be easy to make it for Friday night dinner. A highly recommended restaurant for French food is the Fromagerie in nearby Rumson. In Red Bank itself there is the Olde Union House on the river, a good bet for seafood.

Save Saturday morning for a look around Red Bank. Masted schooners once plied the river here, carrying shellfish, farm produce, and other goods from the area to the world markets in New York. Later on romantic paddlewheel steamers brought vacationers from the city to this quaint Victorian town perched on the red soil banks for which it was named. Carriages in Red Bank would take them to the races or the shore or out into the gentle countryside, much the same kind of things that attract visitors today. Red Bank grew as a shopping hub as well as a racing and boating center, but it never completely lost its Victorian feel. The shops along Front, Broad, Monmouth, and Maple have kept their old facades, making for a pleasant stroll on a spring morning.

But the real shopping attraction in Red Bank is its Antiques Center, a complex along West Front Street and Shrewsbury Avenue that just keeps growing. There are some 150 dealers congregated here, spread over four buildings, and there isn't much in the way of antiques that is not for sale there.

Marine Park at the foot of Wharf Avenue is the most popular recreation spot in town, and for history there is the Allen House in neighboring Shrewsbury. Its lower floor has been restored as a tavern and upstairs is a small museum.

If you're going to the races, you will have to schedule it for Saturday afternoon, since neither track operates on Sunday. Freehold runs all other days of the week at 1 P.M. January through May, resuming again in August, while Monmouth goes into action in late May and continues to early September, with races starting at 1:30 P.M.

Freehold's historic American Hotel, filled with racing memorabilia, is an atmospheric place for an early dinner, as is Winklemann's on River Avenue in Lakewood, where excellent German food is served in an old-world atmosphere. The rodeo begins at 8 P.M. and goes on as long as you remain interested in the procession of bareback bronco riders, steer wrestlers, calf ropers, and bull riders struggling to stay on their bucking mounts. The real entrants go first (this is an officially sanctioned rodeo); afterward lots of people take a turn, and activities often go on into the wee hours. It's all a lot of fun, especially if you've never seen a live rodeo. (If you've brought the kids along, come early for free hayrides on the grounds beginning around 6:30 P.M.)

Sunday, it's time for your horse farm tour. You needn't go far looking for farms in that Holmdel–Colt's Neck–Freehold triangle. Some of the roads to follow are Routes 537, 79, 520, 34, and 516. But feel free to turn off onto smaller lanes. You're not likely to get lost and even if you do for a bit, you'll have fine scenery as compensation.

You'll find a couple of interesting stops in Freehold, site of the Revolutionary War Battle of Monmouth, where Molly Hays took over for her wounded husband and brought water to the parched troops, earning her place in the history books as Molly Pitcher. The Monmouth County Historical Museum has many exhibits from Revolutionary to Civil War memorabilia, and rooms furnished in period furniture from the seventeenth to early nineteenth centuries. The kids love the attic, filled with toys, dolls, and dollhouses played with by children of another age.

An even more special kind of museum is the National Broadcasters Hall of Fame, a bit cramped in space but providing a lot of nostalgia when you pick up the phone and hear Phil Harris arguing with Alice Faye, Orson Welles announcing a Martian invasion, and the Lone Ranger galloping off into the sunset. An audio-visual program covers landmarks in broadcasting history such as the first commercial, the first coast-to-coast broadcast (the 1927 Rose Bowl game), and Franklin D. Roosevelt's inaugural speech. You'll also see collections of old radios, microphones, and photos from broadcasting's good old days.

From Freehold you can pick your destination. One of the biggest flea markets around takes place every weekend to the west in Englishtown—five buildings with everything from antiques to live chickens. To the south is the Deserted Village, a restored iron-working town in Allaire State Park. The site of an historic iron and brass foundry, Allaire was once a self-contained community, and it retains some of the furnaces, forges and casting houses that once turned out pots, kettles, pans, stoves, and screws. The old town bakery, a barn and carriage house, and a general store and post office also remain, giving an interesting and vivid picture of an industrial community of the past.

Or if the weather is fine, you may prefer to forget about sightseeing and just head for Route 33 east to the shore and the boardwalk. Spring Lake is the prettiest nearby shore town. Even Asbury Park, which can seem pretty shabby in season, has a nostalgic charm when you see the amusement area without summer crowds. Ocean Grove, a religious colony by the sea right next door, has a fascinating collection of Victorian houses.

Drive north right along the shore parallel to the water on Ocean Avenue, past the gracious old vacation houses in Deal, and you'll come into good eating territory. The Side Room restaurant in Elberon has many well-prepared and unusual dishes such as shrimp and snow peas with fresh ginger or chicken in raspberry vinegar. Farther up in Sea Bright the Quay has good seafood, and if it is still light you can cut over to River Road and follow the Navesink to Front Street and back to the Parkway home.

Red Bank Area Code: 201

DRIVING DIRECTIONS   Garden State Parkway southbound to Route 109 Red Bank. Route 34 runs into Rumson. Take 109 west and 50 south to 537 east to Freehold; and Route 9 south of Freehold brings you to Lakewood. Route 537 eastbound takes you to Monmouth Park; take it or Route 36 back to the Garden State south for Lakewood.

Total distance: about 50 miles.

ACCOMMODATIONS   *Molly Pitcher Inn,* State Highway 35, Red Bank, 747-2500; $ • *Hilton Inn,* Hope Road at Garden State Exit 105, Tinton Falls, 544-9300; $$–$$$ • *Sheraton Gardens,* Route 537 and Gibson Place, Freehold, 780-3870; $$.

DINING   *Fromagerie,* 26 Ridge Road, Rumson, 842-8088; $$ • *Shadowbrook,* off Route 35, Shrewsbury, 747-0200, Georgian mansion with gardens; $$ • *Olde Union House,* 11 Wharf Avenue, Red Bank, 842-7575; $$ • *American Hotel,* 18-26 Main Street, Freehold,

462-0819; $$ • *Winklemann's,* 945 River Road (Route 9), Lakewood, 363-6294; $$ • *The Side Room,* 1195 Lincoln Square, Elberon, 222-9558; $ • *The Quay,* Ocean Avenue, Sea Bright, 842-1994; $$.

SIGHTSEEING *Red Pony Rodeo, Red Pony Rodeo Ranch* (formerly South Jersey Horse Center), 436 Cross Street, Lakewood, 367-6222. Hours: rodeo Saturdays at 8 P.M.; hayrides at 6:30 P.M. Adults $6, children $4, family of four $15 • *Freehold Raceway,* Park Avenue at US 9 and Route 33, Freehold, 462-3800. Hours: daily except Sunday, January to May, August to December, 1 P.M. Admission $2 • *Monmouth Park,* Oceanport Avenue (Garden State exit 105), 222-5100. Hours: daily except Sunday, late May to early September, 1:30 P.M. Grandstand $2.25, clubhouse $4.25 • *Allaire Village,* 938-5524. Hours: April to September, 10 A.M. to 5 P.M. Adults, $2.50 weekends, $1.50 weekdays; train rides 75¢ • *Monmouth County Historical Museum,* 70 Court Street, Freehold, 462-1466. Hours: Tuesday to Saturday, 10 A.M. to 4 P.M., Sunday 1 to 4 P.M. Adults $1, senior citizens, children age 5–18 50¢ • *National Broadcasters Hall of Fame,* 19 West Main Street, Freehold, 431-4656. Hours: daily except Monday, noon to 5 P.M. Adults $2, senior citizens $1.60, children age 6–13 $1 • *Englishtown Auction Sales,* 90 Wilson Avenue (Route 527), Englishtown, 446-9644. Hours: Saturday 5 A.M. to 5 P.M.; Sunday 9 A.M. to 5 P.M. • *Allen House,* Route 35 at Sycamore Avenue, Shrewsbury, 462-1466. April to December, Tuesday, Thursday, Saturday, Sunday, 1 to 4 P.M. Adults $1, senior citizens 75¢, children age 6–18 50¢.

Chocolate and Roses in Hershey, Pennsylvania

The streetlights are chocolate kisses, the signs are chocolate color with candy-bar lettering, the main intersection of town is at Chocolate and Cocoa streets, and they give you a Hershey bar when you check into the hotel.

There's no mistaking the main attraction in Hershey, Pennsylvania, where even the grand hotel is placed to include the chocolate factory in its hilltop view. And there are few better places for a family weekend than this "company town," where chocolate really is only the beginning of the fun.

Magnificent gardens, a major amusement park, a zoo, a museum of American life, and sports facilities that include five golf courses are all waiting after the chocolate tour is over.

It's all a bit ironic since Milton Hershey, who made a fortune satisfying America's sweet tooth, probably never expected further profits from tourists. When the former farmboy came back to his hometown of Derry Township to build a chocolate factory in 1904, his main aim was to make the town a pleasant place for his workers to live. The first parks, gardens, museum, and zoo were strictly for their benefit.

But from the very start people wanted to see how this new confection called milk chocolate was made, and the factory began offering tours to meet the demand. Savoring the sweet smells, the free samples, and the pleasant atmosphere of this unusual small town, visitors sent their friends. In 1928 the count was 10,000; by 1970 it was pushing a million and the factory could no longer accommodate the crowds. Chocolate World was built to take the place of the old tour, and it is now almost everyone's first stop in Hershey.

The free 10-minute trip in a Disney-like automated car whisks you off to the tobacco plantations of Ghana. You watch the story of chocolate unfold from bean to candy bar, from picking and shipping the beans, grinding and blending them with milk in a simulated factory, to the wrapping of the bars. There's no more chocolate smell—or free samples—but well over a million and a half took the ride last year, anyway.

You exit from the tour into a tropical garden containing some 99 varieties of trees, including cacao, and hundreds of flowering plants and shrubs. You're also facing stands stacked high with Hershey bars and dozens of other souvenirs, chocolate and otherwise. And there's a refreshment pavilion specializing in you-know-what.

Opposite Chocolate World is Hershey Park, once a place where factory employees came to picnic, play ball, go boating, and be entertained at the pavilion. Mr. Hershey kept improving the facilities, adding a swimming pool and a convention hall that doubled as an ice-skating rink. Hershey Zoo was actually Hershey's own private animal collection, one of the country's largest, housed at the park for all to see. And for the kids he bought a carousel and, as a twentieth birthday present to the town, a roller coaster.

As the crowds grew the notion of an actual amusement park seemed a natural one, and in 1971 redevelopment began. Unless you have a total aversion to theme parks, it's hard not to like this clean and pretty one, where you stroll through a mock English town called Tudor Square, a Pennsylvania Dutch community known as Der Deitschplatz, and an eighteenth-century German village labeled Rhine Land. All come complete with appropriate costumes, music, shops, and restaurants. It's undeniably commercial, but the happy crowds don't seem to care.

The original 1919 carousel at the park now has a lot of company, including three roller coasters (scariest is the sooper-dooper Looper that literally turns you upside down), a flume ride, and a couple of dozen others, from "scream machines" to rides for tots. You can get a view of the whole 75-acre park from the kiss-shaped windows of the 330-foot Kissing Tower or take the Monorail for a scenic ride with an audio accompaniment. The Monorail will even take you into town.

There is also continuous live entertainment at four theaters scattered through the park, and the adjoining Arena hosts not only the Ice Capades and hockey games but also name entertainers such as Johnny Cash and John Denver.

Almost everyone's favorite souvenir of the park is a photo taken with the life-size candy-bar characters who greet visitors. Don't forget your camera.

The zoo, too, has come a long way. It now represents the major natural regions of North America—waters, desert, woodlands, plains, and forest, with native plants and animals of each zone in their native habitat. You'll see alligators in the swamps; pumas, bison, and eagles in Big Sky Country, black bear and timber wolves in the forest; wild turkeys, bobcats, otters, and raccoons at home in the woodlands.

There's more than enough to fill a Saturday here—but more still to fill your Sunday. All ages can appreciate the beauty of the Hershey Gardens, which have grown in 40 years from an old-fashioned rose garden into 23 acres featuring 700 varieties of roses, as well as six classic gardens—English, Oriental, Colonial, and Italian, a rock garden, and a fountain garden. Now maintained by the Ortho plant people, who use it as an experimental garden, this is an attraction too beautiful to miss.

Even the Hershey Museum proves to be more than you might expect. In addition to some fascinating collections of Indian artifacts, Pennsylvania Dutch crafts, and early clocks, you get a compact tour through the changing life-styles of America in terms of decorative styles and fashion, including the effect of inventions like the sewing machine. It's less overwhelming than a lot of museums and for that very reason makes its point unusually well. Try to time your visit to coincide with the noon performance of the Apostolic Clock, with moving carved figurines depicting the Last Supper.

You may also want to look in on the Reading China and Glass factory outlet, improbably placed just past the Museum entrance.

There are some good values here from top names such as Lenox, Arabia, and Wedgwood, and housewares of all kinds as well.

One other unique sight in Hershey has nothing to do with tourists. The Milton Hershey School was founded in 1909 by childless Milton and Catherine Hershey to provide a free home as well as an education for orphan boys. Now coed, the school tries to re-create the feel of family living for its residents with 92 campus homes spread across 10,000 acres of campus. Each house shelters 12 to 16 children with house parents. The schooling, which extends through high school, is unusual in many ways. It includes time working on community farms and the opportunity to learn a trade or prepare for college, according to each student's talents and inclinations.

Founders Hall, a striking domed limestone building that is a tribute to the Hersheys, is awesome architecturally, yet it serves well as church, theater, and concert hall for 1,300 very energetic orphaned children. Some of the profits from Hershey's current commercial ventures are used to supplement the endowment Milton Hershey left for his school. Founders Hall is well worth a visit—if you can only find the time with everything else there is to do.

Where to stay in Hershey? The natural choices are the excellent Hershey-run accommodations, not cheap but not as expensive as you might think when you figure all the admissions included in weekend packages. Hotel Hershey does seem a bit steep and elegant for a family jaunt, but it is a grand hotel in every sense, Mediterranean in style, with a lobby that looks a little like a small Spanish town with its tiled fountain and arcaded stucco walls. The circular dining room has windows all around that look out at gardens and grounds, and the food is a match for the setting. There are pools indoors and out, four tennis courts, and a golf course. You could happily spend a weekend here without ever venturing off the grounds.

The Lodge is motel-style and obviously more family-oriented, as you can tell when you drive up and spot the children feeding the ducks on the pond out front. There are pools here, too, a playground, tennis and paddle tennis, a golf course and a par-3 pitch and putt, a game room for the kids, and movies at night.

June is the perfect time for Hershey, when the roses are in evidence but the summer crowds are not. The only problem may be how to see it all in one weekend. You may decide to take it in parts. That way you can see the gardens with tulips or mums as well as roses in bloom.

Hershey Area Code: 717

DRIVING DIRECTIONS   Take I-80 or 78 to 81 west exit at Route 743 and follow signs to Hershey.
   Total distance: about 183 miles.

BY PUBLIC TRANSPORTATION   Amtrak service to Harrisburg. Hotel Hershey provides limousine service for guests; free shuttle service to all attractions June 13 to September 7. Bus service to Hershey via Capitol Trailways.

ACCOMMODATIONS   *Hershey Resorts,* Hershey, 533-3311, or toll-free, (800) 223-1588; in New York (212) 661-4540 ● *Hotel Hershey;* $$$$ MAP ● *Hershey Lodge;* $$$, children under 18 free. Both hotels offer summer package plans including meals, lodging, and admissions. Call for information and brochure.
   If you want less expensive lodging, try: *Best Western Inn,* 533-5665; $$, including movies in room and continental breakfast ● *Chocolate-town Motel,* 533-2330; $ ● *Milton Motel,* 533-4533; $ ● *Spinner's Motor Inn,* 533-9157; $.

DINING   Unless you want to settle for *Friendly's,* $, just opposite the Motor Lodge, or *Spinner's Restaurant* at that motor inn, $, it's a Hershey world once again: *Hotel Hershey*; $$–$$$ ● *Hershey Lodge*; choice of three dining rooms; $$. (Lots of restaurants at the park, all prices.)

SIGHTSEEING   *Hersheypark,* 534-3900. Hours: daily, Memorial Day to July 3, 10:30 A.M. to 8 P.M.; July 4 to Labor Day, 10:30 A.M. to 10 P.M.; usually weekends only early May and late September, phone to check dates and hours. All ages $11, July 4 to Labor Day, children under 4 free; rest of season $10. (Prices plus 50¢ local amusement tax.) ● *Hershey Museum of American Life.* Hours: daily, Memorial Day to Labor Day, 10 A.M. to 6 P.M.; rest of year 10 A.M. to 5 P.M. Adults $2, children age 5–18 $1 ● *ZooAmerica.* Hours: daily 10 A.M., closing varies with seasons. Adults $2, children ages 5–18 $1 ● *Hershey Gardens.* Hours: daily, June, July, August, 9 A.M. to 7 P.M.; April, May, September, October, 9 A.M. to 5 P.M. Adults $2, children age 5–18 $1 ● *Hershey Chocolate World.* Hours: daily, May to July 3, 9 A.M. to 4:45 P.M.; July 4 to Labor Day, 9 A.M. to 7:45 P.M.; September to October, 9 A.M. TO 4:45 P.M.; November to April, Monday to Saturday, 9 A.M. to 4:45 P.M.; Sunday, noon to 4:45 P.M. Free ● *Founder's Hall.* Hours: weekdays, May through October, 9 A.M. to 4

P.M., weekends 10 A.M. to 4 P.M.; November to April, weekdays, 9 A.M. to 4 P.M., weekends, 10 A.M. to 3 P.M. A film on the Milton Hershey School is shown hourly May to October beginning at 9:30 A.M. Free.

FOR FURTHER INFORMATION Contact Hershey Information, Hershey, PA 17033, 534-3005.

Summer

Summering with the Arts in Saratoga Springs

Horses and Health. The nation's oldest racetrack and the mineral-water baths were the drawing cards that brought the elite to Saratoga Springs in its 1870s heyday.

Both still entice visitors, but they share billing these days with music and dance, performed in an amphitheater in the middle of a 2,200-acre park. Since Saratoga Spa State Park opened in 1962 with swimming, tennis, golf, and hiking facilities in addition to the bathhouses, and since the addition of the Saratoga Performing Arts Center in 1966, only real racing aficionados need wait for the August racing season when the rates in town almost double. Saratoga now is a super destination for almost any summer weekend, particularly for ballet fans during the three-week residency of the New York City Ballet in July, and for jazz lovers over the Fourth of July weekend when the Newport Jazz Festival takes over. For those willing to pay the price for rooms, the Philadelphia Orchestra is the main attraction in August.

If you want to experience the flavor of old Saratoga, make your reservations early for the Adelphi Hotel, the only one of the old grand hotels remaining in town. It was built in 1877, when Saratoga was undisputed Queen of the Spas, and it still boasts a piazza overlooking Broadway, once a spot to see who was out taking a morning stroll. Breakfast is served on the piazza on sunny days.

The grand staircase, tall windows, and lofty ceilings of the lobby have been restored, and each of the 17 rooms has been done with period wall coverings and bedspreads and Victorian curlicue sofas and chairs. Some have fireplaces; all have their original woodwork and high ceilings.

Other than motels, the only attractive alternative for lodging is the slightly more sedate (and more expensive) Gideon Putnam Hotel, which does have the advantage of being right in the park. It matches the red-brick, white-columned architecture of the other park buildings and is gracious and old-world inside as well as out.

Having set your accommodations, there is one other absolutely necessary reservation to be made: for a mineral bath and massage at the spa that made Saratoga famous. The brochure says to call 24 hours in advance, but on a recent Fourth of July weekend there wasn't one spare hour for four straight days.

The state of New York acquired the rights to the mineral waters in 1910 in order to conserve this natural resource, and it began purchasing the land that has been gradually developed into the present park. Waters geyser up and are available for drinking in six locations in the park, and the "treatments," which have remained reasonable in price, are a real treat.

First you are shown to a private room where a tub is filled with naturally carbonated water at body temperature. After you've sat back and let the tiny bubbles bathe you into a relaxed state, you proceed to the massage table where a masseur takes away any tension the mineral water hasn't already dissolved. Then you're wrapped in hot sheets and put to bed to relax—most probably to fall into a divinely restful sleep. No wonder people used to flock here.

Also available in the park are both an 18- and a 9-hole golf course, 4 swimming pools, tennis courts, a dozen picnic areas, and the Ferndell Nature Trail—most everything you might need in the way of summer recreation.

At the Saratoga Performing Arts Center, known locally by its initials *SPAC,* something happens almost every night from late June through Labor Day. The attractions are uniformly top quality. The amphitheater, done in browns and greens to blend with its park setting, seats 5,100, and its outdoor "mezzanine" of sloping grounds has accommodated as many as 30,000.

The stage was designed to George Balanchine's specifications for the New York City Ballet, and it is also used by other dance companies such as the Nikolais Dance Theater and the José Limon dancers over the summer. In addition to dance companies and the Philadelphia Orchestra, there are top-name popular performers on the schedule. Recently these have included entertainers like John Denver, Liza Minnelli, Harry Belafonte, James Taylor, and Judy Collins.

The jazz greats over the Fourth of July weekend play from noon until night. Each year the list of performers changes, but it often includes such people as Woody Herman, Dizzy Gillespie, Carmen McRae, Dave Brubeck, and Mel Torme. There is often a crafts show on the grounds during this weekend.

At the adjoining John Houseman Theater, drama is a summerlong production featuring Houseman's own highly regarded Acting Company, as well as the Circle Repertory from New York and other groups that might range from the Empire State Youth Theater Institute to Ireland's Abbey Theater.

Write to SPAC for schedules and order blanks, but you'll never be shut out of a concert if you're willing to sit on the lawn.

To see the sights of Saratoga, go into town and stop at the

Information Center at Drink Hall, a former trolley station in the town center on Broadway, for free maps and a walking-driving tour. Cross the street on Broadway and stroll into Congress Park, a green oasis of fountains and gardens, and get some sense of Saratoga history at the Casino, a mid-Victorian structure with a ballroom and reception room that were once part of a flourishing gambling establishment during the town's grander days. Upstairs here the Hall of History shows Saratoga's development from a frontier village to flamboyant resort town with some of the country's grandest hotels. There is an elaborate re-created Victorian parlor taken from a town mansion and a period bedroom with a four-poster bed and a rocker in front of the fireplace.

Upstairs on the third floor the Walworth Museum is a sampling of the rooms from the home of Reuben Hyde Walworth, the last chancellor of the state of New York, whose family lived in Saratoga for 125 years.

Saratoga had gone downhill, but it is obviously on the way back up. With walking tour in hand, go back to Broadway to see the section of downtown shops being brought back to their charming original Victorian appearance, and the sidewalk cafes and boutiques that are beginning to flourish. On North Broadway, Circular Street, and Union Avenue, you can tour the architecture of the mansions that have survived since the 1800s, and at Franklin Square, examine the Doric columns and pediments of 1830s Greek Revival Houses currently being restored.

Wherever you go you'll see natural springs bubbling up the mineral water that made Saratoga—in Congress Park, in front of City Hall, even at the race track. Many of the spring sites offer samples of the none-too-tasty waters.

Saratoga's very attractive National Museum of Racing, a Colonial brick structure across from the track, is the only one of its kind in the world. You don't have to be a racing fan to appreciate the colorful silks of the sport's top stables, the magnificent silver trophies that have gone to prize winners like Man O' War, and the really fine collection of equestrian paintings on display here.

Outside Saratoga proper you can visit the campus of Skidmore College and the grounds and garden at Yaddo, the gray stone mansion that has been an inspirational refuge for writers and musicians such as Aaron Copland, Carson McCullers, and Saul Bellow.

On US 4 in Schuylerville, Saratoga National Historic Park marks the Battle of Saratoga, one of the critical encounters of the Revolutionary War. The Visitor Center offers a 20-minute film and the route for a nine-mile self-guided driving tour of the battlefield. Costumed hostesses will greet you at the residence of General Phillip Schuyler, who fought the battle, and demonstrate Colonial arts such as cooking and candlemaking.

If kids are along, you may want to head for Saratoga Lake, three miles east on Route 9P, which has two amusement parks on its shores, or the Petrified Gardens, three miles west on Route 29, to see reefs and other relics of the days when the area was covered by the ancient Cambrian Sea. The prehistoric specimens have been declared a National Landmark by the U.S. Department of the Interior.

If you are looking for further evening amusement, a festival of baroque music goes on in town, and there is harness racing every summer night except Sunday, regardless of whether the thoroughbreds are running.

If you do decide to come for the August activity at this beautiful track dating back to 1863, save a morning for one of its traditions, a buffet breakfast followed by a tour of the paddocks behind the scenes. The running of the big Travers Stake Race in the middle of the month touches off a whole week of festivities in town, including antique and art shows, a parade, and polo matches at the Saratoga Polo Grounds.

If you're after antique stores, you'll find them on Route 29 east and west of town, and there are more than enough restaurants in the area to provide good eating for a weekend. One of the best is a place you might overlook because of the name. It's Mrs. London's Bake Shop, which not only has superior pastries but homemade pasta for dinner that shouldn't be missed.

It's just one more of the arts that make Saratoga a special summer destination.

Saratoga Area Code: 518

DRIVING DIRECTIONS   New York State Thruway to exit 24 at Albany-Northway (#87) to exit 13N, Saratoga.
Total distance: 175 miles.

BY PUBLIC TRANSPORTATION   Take Amtrak or Greyhound to Saratoga. It's easy to get around town via town mini-bus (schedules at visitors center), or you can rent a bike from Springwater Bike Rentals, 454 Broadway, or the Gideon Putnam Hotel.

ACCOMMODATIONS   *Adelphi Hotel,* 365 Broadway, Saratoga 12866, 587-4688; $$ except August racing season, $$$ • *Gideon Putnam Hotel,* Saratoga Spa, 584-3000; $$$$ American plan, inquire for EP rates; higher in August • *Carriage House Motel,* 178 Broadway, Saratoga, 584-0352; $ • *Coachman's Motor Inn,* 231 Broadway,

Saratoga, 584-4220; $ • *Holiday Inn,* Broadway and Circular Street, Saratoga, 584-4550; $$. (All are higher in August.)

DINING   *Chez Sophie,* 69 Caroline Street, for French fare; be sure to make reservations, 587-0440; $$–$$$ • *Mrs. London's Bake Shop,* 33 Philadelphia Street, 584-6633; $–$$$ • *Ye Olde Wishing Well,* Route 9 north, Gansevoort, 584-7640, an 1823 farmhouse; $–$$ • *Gideon Putnam* (see above); $–$$$ • *Charles Restaurant,* with outdoor patio, 231 Broadway, 548-4111; $$ • *Caunterbury Restaurant,* Union Avenue and Route 9P, 587-9653, a converted barn; $$–$$$ • *Old Firehouse Restaurant,* 543 Broadway, 587-0047; $–$$$.

SIGHTSEEING   *Saratoga Performing Arts Center,* Saratoga Springs, 587-3330. Phone or write for schedule of concerts and John Houseman Theater; prices vary with attractions, run from $5.50 to $12; lawn tickets $5.50 to $7. Tickets are also available at Ticketron • *Saratoga Spa State Park Recreation Center,* South Broadway (Route 9), 584-2000. Hours: pools 11 A.M. to 7 P.M.; golf $4 to $7, par-29 course $3.50 to $4, parking fee $1.50 • *Saratoga Spa Mineral Bathhouses,* Saratoga Spa State Park, 584-2011. Phone for mineral-bath reservations. Bath with massage $8 to $13; available at extra charge: Turkish bath, steam room, hot packs • *National Museum of Racing,* Union Avenue and Ludlow Street, 584-5000. Hours: Monday to Friday, 9:30 A.M. to 5 P.M.; Saturday, Sunday, noon to 5 P.M.; daily, August, 9:30 A.M. to 7 P.M. Free • *The Casino, Walworth Museum, and Historical Society of Saratoga Springs,* Congress Park, Broadway, 584-6920. Hours: daily, July to August, 9:30 A.M. to 4:30 P.M.; June, September, October, Monday to Saturday, 10 A.M. to 4 P.M.; Sunday 1 to 4 P.M. Adults $1, students and senior citizens 50¢, children under 12 free with adults • *Saratoga Harness Track,* off Route 9, 584-2110. Hours: late April to late November, Monday to Saturday, 8:15 P.M., holiday matinees 2:15. Grandstand $1.75, clubhouse $3, parking $1 • *Petrified Gardens,* Route 29, 584-7102. Hours: daily, late May to late September, 9 A.M. to 5 P.M. Adults $2, children age 6–12 50¢ • *Saratoga National Historic Park,* US 4, 664-7821. Hours: daily, April 1 to November 30, 9 A.M. to 6 P.M. Free • *Schuyler House,* Hours: daily, mid-June to Labor Day, 10 A.M. to 5 P.M. Free • *Saratoga Circuit Tours,* P.O. Box 38, Saratoga Springs, 587-3656. Two-hour sightseeing tour with guide, daily, 10 A.M. to 1 P.M. All ages $8. Drink Hall, opposite Congress Park • *Saratoga Race Track Information:* 584-6200.

FOR FURTHER INFORMATION   Contact Chamber of Commerce, 494 Broadway, Saratoga, NY 12866, 584-3255, or Visitors Information, City Hall, Saratoga, NY 12866, 587-3550.

Litchfield and Lake Waramaug: A Connecticut Double Feature

Lake what? Even in Connecticut, lots of people haven't heard of this placid blue oasis just north of New Milford in the Litchfield Hills. Just over eight miles around, ringed by wooded hills and as smooth as a looking glass, Lake Waramaug has a small public beach at one end, and at the other a state park, with boating and swimming facilities as well as walking trails—and not a commercial facility in sight. All you'll find around the lake are summer homes and four fine small country inns.

Each of the inns is different and has something special to offer. The largest, the Inn at Lake Waramaug, is a mini-resort with its own beach and dock, sailboats and canoes, a little paddlewheel showboat to cruise you around the lake, tennis, and an indoor pool. There are a few rooms in the charming inn building, a 1795 Colonial house, but most are in motel-type modern lodges on the grounds. Hopkins Inn across the way is a pretty yellow house with a porch looking out at the lake, with 10 modest Colonial bedrooms upstairs, and the best dining room in the area. Make a reservation for dinner even if you don't stay here.

The Boulders Inn, literally built with boulders in its fieldstone walls, is well described as a rustic lodge. It used to be a dark, old-fashioned place until new owners recently brightened everything up, filled the inn rooms with antiques, and made it a totally appealing place. Boulders accommodates 45 people, a dozen in the pretty inn rooms and the rest in cottages on the grounds, and gives its guests 250 acres for roaming.

Finally, there is The Birches, the newest of the inns, located away from the others on the west shore of the lake, with just six rooms in the outbuildings and a dining room in the old white main house whose menu reflects the Austrian background of the owners.

A pleasant inn, good food, and plenty of outdoor activity could fill a weekend on its own, but an added attraction at Lake Waramaug is its proximity to some of Connecticut's loveliest Colonial towns. Prime among them is Litchfield, invariably on every list of the most beautiful Main Streets in America and considered by many experts to be the finest unrestored, unspoiled Colonial town in America.

One of the nicest things about visiting Litchfield is that its three dozen or so choicest homes, those comprising the center Historic

District around the village green, are easily strollable, concentrated on two long blocks, North and South Street, just off the green.

You may recognize the steepled Congregational Church on that green; it shows up in countless photographs of typical New England scenes. Next door is the 1787 parsonage where Harriet Beecher Stowe's father lived when she was born here in the 1800s.

Across the way on South Street are two homes that help to explain why Litchfield has remained unique and unchanged. The Moses Seymour House was completed in 1817 for Jane Seymour, who married Dr. Josiah G. Beckwith. The Beckwith family has remained in the house to this day. The Seymour House next door, one of the best examples of Federal architecture of this period, was built by Moses for his son Ozias; later occupied by Origen Seymour, chief justice of Connecticut; and remained in the Seymour family until 1950. Litchfield's families didn't move on to greener pastures; they stayed to tend to their green.

Tapping Reeve opened the nation's first law school in his superb 1773 home with his brother-in-law, Aaron Burr, as his first pupil. Eventually, the pupils outgrew the house and a school building was erected in 1784. Among its alumni were three Supreme Court justices, 28 senators, more than a hundred congressmen, two vice-presidents, 14 governors, and 16 chief justices of Connecticut.

John C. Calhoun was a student here, lodging in the rectory next door and planting some of the elms that remain along the street. Farther down the street is the 1736 home where Ethan Allen, Revolutionary War leader of the fabled Green Mountain Boys, is believed to have been born.

Beautiful white Colonials of the 1700s seem to go on and on, including the home of Oliver Wolcott, Jr., now the town library, and the obligatory structure boasting "George Washington slept here," in this case the Elisha Sheldon Tavern. With the exception of the law school and the town Historical Society, with exhibits of furniture, textiles, and clothing, almost all of these homes are private residences. Like so many towns, Litchfield has one day set aside for its annual open house of historic homes. It is usually the second Saturday in July (check with the Historical Society to be sure), and it is well worth timing your visit to coincide. Make it a Saturday visit in any case, as both the Reeve House and the Society are closed on Sunday.

There are a few shops in Litchfield, on the green and in Cobble Court (literally a nineteenth-century courtyard with cobble streets), but shopping is not a major attraction in town. Of more interest is the White Memorial Foundation Conservation Center, just west on Route 202. It is the state's largest nature center, with 4,000 acres and many appealing hiking trails into the hills and valleys. Bantam Lake is also part of the Center, offering swimming at Sandy Beach and boats for rent at the landing at Folly Point.

For anyone interested in flowers, particularly unusual perennials, White Flower Farm is a must. This is no ordinary nursery. Garden lovers make pilgrimages here to see the eight-acre formal display garden and to browse among the 1,200 varieties of unusual plants over 20 acres of growing fields. Delphiniums are a specialty, as are tuberous begonias.

It would be easy to spend a week, rather than a weekend, enjoying the out-of-doors and the other Colonial towns around Lake War- amaug—Washington, Kent, and Woodbury, to name just a few. At least mark this down for a return visit in the fall, when flaming foliage rings the lake in a blaze of color.

Connecticut Area Code: 203

DRIVING DIRECTIONS Henry Hudson Parkway to Sawmill River Parkway to 684N to Brewster, then 84E to Danbury, exit 7 to Route 7N to New Milford, then 202E to New Preston and Route 45 to Lake Waramaug.

Total distance: 85 miles.

ACCOMMODATIONS *The Inn on Lake Waramaug,* North Shore Road, New Preston, 868-0563 or also (212) 724-8775; $$$ MAP (three- day minimum in summer) • *Boulders Inn,* Route 45, New Preston, 868-7918; $$$ MAP • *Hopkins Inn,* Hopkins Road, New Preston, 868-7295; $$ EP (closed in winter) • *Birches Inn,* West Shore Road, 868-0229; $.

DINING *Inn on Lake Waramaug* (see above); $$ • *Hopkins Inn* (see above); $ • *Fife 'n Drum,* Route 7, Kent, 972-3243, owner Dolph Traymon's piano playing alone makes it worth the trip; $.

SIGHTSEEING *Litchfield Historical Society,* Litchfield Green, 567-5862. Hours: mid-April to mid-November, Tuesday to Saturday, 11 A.M. to 5 P.M. Donation. Phone for date of this year's open house tour • *Tapping Reeve House and Law School,* South Street, Litchfield, 567-5862. Hours: mid-May to mid-October, Tuesday to Saturday, 11 A.M. to 5 P.M. Adults $1.50, children 50¢ • *White Flower Farm,* Route 63 South, Litchfield, 567-0810. Hours: April to November, weekdays, 10 A.M. to 5 P.M., weekends, 9 A.M. to 5 P.M., closed Tuesday. Free

• *White Memorial Conservation Center,* Route 202, Litchfield, 567-0015. Hours: grounds open daily, museum open Tuesday to Saturday, 9 A.M. to 5 P.M.; Sunday 2 to 5 P.M. Free.

A Midsummer Escape to Shelter Island

Some say the name came from the Quakers who found refuge from religious persecution on the island. Others believe it comes from the Indians' term, *Manhansack-aha-quashawamock,* "an island sheltered by islands."

Whatever the origin of the name, here's a place for anyone saying "gimme shelter" from the usual commercial summer resorts.

Shelter Island's 12 square miles are tucked between the north and south forks of Long Island's east end, reachable only by ferryboat from Greenport to the north and Sag Harbor to the south. Though the population of 2,000 swells to about 8,000 in the summer, the effects of the influx are limited since most of the summer visitors have or rent homes—also limited in number, thanks to strict two-acre zoning. About a third of the island, 2,200 acres known as Mashomack Forest, remains unpopulated.

The current visitor's guide lists just over a dozen small hotels and/or restaurants, two antique shops, one gourmet and one gift shop, a couple of places to buy food, one gasoline station, and two ice cream parlors. The only local industry is fishing. The big summer event is the annual Firemen's Barbecue in August. That's it.

So what do you do on Shelter Island? You bike. Or hike. Sunbathe on crescent beaches. Rent a sailboat or go fishing. Play a little tennis or golf. Drive around to see the varied topography and homes. Mainly, you just plain relax and adjust to the calm pace of island life.

Despite its lack of commerciality today, Shelter Island was founded by four merchants. They were in the business of supplying sugar from Barbados and found the many white oak trees on the island could be used for making barrels. One of them, Nathanial Sylvester, built the first home here in 1652. The present manor house, the residence of a descendant, was constructed in 1773. It became a haven for Quakers who had been driven out of Boston and Friends groups still conduct services here regularly.

It's an interesting island to explore because the contours change so rapidly, from steep hills to flat valley to beach. If you arrive via the North Ferry from Greenport you are within walking distance of the Victorian homes in an area called The Heights. This is pretty much the center of activity, the site of the Chequit Inn, with its veranda for gazing out at the sailboats that often race in Dering Harbor. A walk down the hill brings you to Bridge Street and the town, such as it is, where you'll find the daytrippers over from the Hamptons.

If you keep to the right instead of going down Bridge Street from the Chequit, you pass a nine-hole public golf course and descend a steep hill to Crescent Beach, a major gathering spot for the island's resident tourists, with a motel and a couple of hotels in the vicinity. Back across town is the modern and expensive Dering Harbor Inn overlooking the harbor. It is on Winthrop Road, which leads to the village of Dering Harbor, the smallest but perhaps the richest per capita municipality in the state—200 acres and 30 homes. You can't come in unless you have an invitation from a resident. Adjoining is an area called Hay Beach, a subdivision of newer homes, and the Gardiner's Bay Country Club.

Two causeways lead to the more rugged terrain of big and little Ram Islands with Gardiner's Bay on one side and calm Coecles Harbor on the other. Mashomack Forest is to the south across the harbor. It is a game preserve and exclusive club, with only members allowed into the area. On the other side of Route 114 are two other residential areas, Shorewood, populated mostly by summer renters, and Silver Beach, a retirement colony. Adjacent to Silver Beach is Westmoreland Farms.

There is just one historic home to visit, the Haven House on Route 114 about a mile from the South Ferry, a 1743 Colonial with period furnishings, open Saturdays only from 10 A.M. to noon.

Though the number of hotels is not large, there is a choice of atmosphere. Chequit Inn is a gingerbread Victorian circa 1870 and puts you in the middle of what action there is in town. Dering Harbor is built motel-style with private terraces, a pool and tennis courts, and a busy harbor where many guests arrive by boat. The Pridwin is an old-time resort with a big porch, white wicker chairs in the lobby, and cabins for guests who prefer them. Senior citizens groups like to come here in the off season. There is a private beach plus pool, water skiing and sailing, and three tennis courts for guests, as well as such diversions as croquet, shuffleboard, and Ping-Pong. Then there is the Ram's Head Inn, the prototype country inn—16 rooms, way off by itself on one of the most scenic areas of the island with tennis, private beach, and sailing.

The Chequit has a piano bar, the Ram's Head Inn may have music on weekends, and there is entertainment in a converted barn called Inn Between on North Ferry Road. So much for Shelter Island nightlife.

Most vacationers on the island don't come expecting nighttime action and are perfectly happy being active by day and turning in early. The one peril is bad weather. But if the clouds do roll in, while Hamptons visitors get off the ferryboat looking for new diversion, you can board and head the other way to Sag Harbor. The old whaling center is nicer when you can really walk around, but it is a pleasant port in all but a real storm.

Wear a slicker if need be, and take the short walking tour beginning on Main Street that leads you past the town's exceptional architecture that goes from early Colonial saltbox to Greek Revival mansions that once belonged to wealthy sea captains. Go into one of the mansions, the home of the Suffolk County Whaling Museum, to see the big scrimshaw collection and many other relics of the town's early industry. Then visit the Old Custom House and the Whaler's Church with its hand-carved whaling motifs.

There are plenty of shops to browse through in town and the Romana Kramoris Gallery has shows by contemporary east end Long Island artists. The Long Wharf Restaurant on Bay Street right off Main will serve you informal meals with a harbor view. A stop at the information center off Main will provide a map and all the guidance you need to plot your way through the little village.

If this is the tail end of the weekend, you can drive directly home from Sag Harbor. Otherwise, you can take the four-minute ferry ride back to Shelter Island and leave the rest of the tourists behind.

Shelter Island Area Code: 516

DRIVING DIRECTIONS Midtown tunnel to I-495, Long Island Expressway to exit 73, Riverhead. Turn right and take Route 58, Old Country Road, east for about two miles to the traffic circle. Continue east past Central Suffolk Hospital for about two more miles on 58 until it turns into Route 25. Continue to Greenport and watch for a large sign, SHELTER IS FY, west of the shopping area to guide you off Front Street (Route 25) onto Fifth Street going south. Turn left at Wiggins Street (Route 114) to ferry landing. Service runs from 6 A.M. to midnight continuously, every 15 minutes. 749-0139 for information. Continual shuttle service to North Haven and Sag Harbor via South Ferry is from the southern end of Route 114, information 749-1200.
Total distance: 100 miles.

BY PUBLIC TRANSPORTATION Long Island Railroad to Greenport; no need for a car on Shelter Island if you stay near the

North Ferry station or ride a bike. You can also take the train to Babylon and a bus to Greenport, a combination called Ride-n-rail that usually takes less time. Information on current cost and schedules from L.I.R.R. (212) 739-4200.

ACCOMMODATIONS *Chequit Inn,* Shelter Island Heights, 749-0018; $$. Dinner entrées $$ • *Dering Harbor Resort,* P. O. Box AD, Shelter Island, 749-0900; $$$$ (more for villas); less on weekdays and off season, more on holiday weekends. Dinner entrées $$$ • *The Pridwin Hotel and Cottages,* Crescent Beach, Shelter Island, 749-0476; $$$$ MAP; also less weekdays, off season; more holiday weekends. Dinner entrées $$ • *Ram's Head Inn,* 108 Ram Island Drive, Shelter Island Heights, 749-0811; $–$$ with continental breakfast (more expensive rooms have private baths). Dinner entrées $$.

DINING All of the above plus *The Dory,* Bridge Road, 749-8871; $–$$.

FOR FURTHER INFORMATION Contact Shelter Island Chamber of Commerce, Box 577, Shelter Island Heights, NY 11965, 749-0399.

 # Concerts and Colonial Greens: Bedford and Caramoor

Bedford Village is a bit of New England transplanted to the New York suburbs—village green, white-steepled church, Colonial homes and all.

Caramoor is a bit of the Mediterranean, a villa filled with treasures from European palaces, with a Venetian theater that is the site of the most elegant kind of outdoor summer music festival.

Put them together and you have a gracious summer getaway not much more than an hour from home.

Those who liken Bedford to a New England village are not far wrong, for it was actually part of Connecticut when settled in 1680. A royal decree settled a border dispute by placing Bedford in Westchester County, where it prospered and became the county seat.

In the mid-1800s, when the railroad made the town more accessible to New York, Bedford's scenic beauty attracted wealthy families who built their country estates on the hilltops nearby and acquired the nickname of "hilltoppers." A local historian of the period noted kindly that the newcomers—many of them world-famous—were generally "unobjectionable." The estates still make for pleasant sightseeing along the country roads near town.

The buildings surrounding the village green were built after the Revolution, since most of the town was burned by the British in 1779. Bedford's early residents set out to replace each building on its original site. Most of the structures still stand, thanks to the unusually active Historical Society.

In 1916 when the Methodists stopped holding services in their aging church on the green, the church was bought at auction by someone who planned to convert it into apartments. An indignant band of citizens raised the money to buy the building back, repair it, and turn it into a community house. That was the beginning.

The 1787 Court House, the oldest public building in Westchester County, was restored to appear just as it did early in the last century when William Jay, son of the first chief justice, presided on the bench. On the second floor the Bedford Museum was built to trace 300 years of the town from its earliest Indian origins.

One ticket covers a visit to this building and the restored one-room schoolhouse across the green. The ticket also provides a printed walking tour of the village, a stroll that takes you past the Old Burying Ground (1681), the general store (1838), the post office (1838), the library (1807), and beautiful homes from the early 1800s.

One of the white-pillared structures once housed an A & P, which was an unusual link in the chain because the storefront was not painted red. The tradition-conscious owner made it a condition of the contract that the facade not be altered.

That building is now Bedford Green, a shop offering three floors of fine antiques. Turn off the main avenue to Court Road, and you'll find more shops in charming Colonial homes. Among them are the Richard Oliver House, for men's country clothes; Savoir Faire, a potpourri of porcelain, pewter, silver, and gifts; and Ida B.'s Stitchery, a haven for needlepoint enthusiasts.

Even trees are considered worth saving in preservation-minded Bedford. Take a drive just north of town on Route 22 to see a towering white oak estimated to be 500 years old. Somehow that tree became a symbol of the town's attachment to the past. The owner, Harold Whitman, deeded its ground to the town of Bedford in memory of his wife back in 1947, making it the Bedford Oak in truth as well as sentiment.

Of all our founding fathers, few filled so many high offices as John Jay. He served as president of the First Continental Congress, first chief justice, governor and chief justice of New York State, minister to

Spain, and author of the Jay Treaty. The Jay Homestead, located a few miles farther north on Route 22, has been designated a state historic site. An enlarged 1787 farmhouse, it is part clapboard, part shingle, and part stone, a blend of both Hudson Valley and New England building traditions. It was still occupied by the family as late as 1958. Their presence is tangible. Each of the generations added the conveniences and tastes of its own era, providing a dimension unusual in historic homes. Costumed hostesses will take you around, pointing out the fine furnishings and the periods represented by each of the rooms. The two kitchens are especially intriguing, each fully outfitted with fascinating paraphernalia.

Follow Route 22 south again and turn left onto Route 137 to reach Caramoor, a totally different kind of homestead. Best known for its Venetian Theater, Caramoor was the country home of Walter Tower Rosen, a lawyer and investment banker. Mr. and Mrs. Rosen built their pink stucco Mediterranean villa amid acres of woodland and formal gardens, then filled it with treasures from European palaces and villas. In fact, they installed whole rooms, complete down to wall panelings, molded ceilings, and priceless wall coverings. Down the narrow vaulted hallway, behind heavy carved wooden doorways, are rooms representing styles from sixteenth-century Renaissance to eighteenth-century Neoclassical. Many are hung with silk and wallpaper painted in China in the eighteenth century.

You visit an intimate library from a château in southern France, a small room from a palace in Turin, an English pine-paneled chamber from a home in Dorsetshire, a French Regency sitting room, or a Jacobean bedroom. You'll come upon Pope Urban VIII's bed and a chair owned by Spain's Ferdinand and Isabella, along with the most extensive collection of needlepoint upholstery in the Western Hemisphere. The needlework, both French and Italian, is displayed in almost overwhelming profusion in a 70-foot music room; the ceiling was carved for a palace in Italy 400 years ago.

To enter the theater area, you pass through great black and gold wrought-iron gates acquired by Mr. Rosen in Switzerland. The stage of the Venetian Theater is built around a set of Greek and Roman marble columns that once stood in a fifteenth-century garden near Venice. On a moonlit night this is a magical setting for music.

Caramoor is much too elegant a place for sprawling on blankets, but there are picnic tables in an apple grove near a grape arbor. Seating is on folding chairs, both in the main theater and in the Spanish courtyard where Sunday afternoon concerts are held. The music varies from opera to symphony to chamber music in the afternoons; the season runs from late June to late August.

If you don't want to hear music on Sunday, you can take a drive to North Salem to one of Westchester County's most unexpected attractions, the Oriental Stroll Gardens at the Hammond Museum. There's no more serene setting for a summer stroll than these 15 formal Oriental landscapes where weathered tree trunks, weeping willows, dwarf fruit trees, flowering shrubs, artfully placed stones, moss and pebbles, reflecting pools, and a mirror-still lake blend to form a setting of rare tranquillity.

The Hammond's other special claim to fame is an elegant three-course luncheon served in a shaded flagstone courtyard centered by a fountain and dotted with cheerful red geraniums. It has been aptly compared to lunching in the French countryside.

The museum building itself is attractive, with a soaring beamed great hall. It calls itself a museum of the humanities, and exhibits range widely, from religious artifacts to modern art to places of entertainment to Mexican tapestries.

Another excellent place for art is the Katonah Gallery, a new wing at the side of that town's library. It holds six major exhibitions a year borrowed from other museums, galleries, and private sources.

One final nearby attraction to note is Ward's Pound Ridge Reservation, a 4,600-acre park with some excellent hiking trails through the woods.

Though lodgings in this area are strictly motel variety, the dinner possibilities are atmospheric and varied. Some local favorites are Emily Shaw's Inn, in Pound Ridge near the Bedford line, a restored farmhouse; Nino's, a country home in Bedford; and The Arch in Brewster (tiny, so make reservations well in advance). If you want super-elegant four-star French cooking (and prices to match), La Cremaillere in Banksville isn't very far away.

Westchester Area Code: 914

DRIVING DIRECTIONS Take the Hutchinson River Parkway north to the intersection of I-684, then north on 684 to Route 35, Katonah. Turn right and follow Route 22 south into Bedford Village; Caramoor is at the intersection of Route 137, about half a mile east of 22.

Total distance: roughly 50 miles.

BY PUBLIC TRANSPORTATION Buses leave Lincoln Center at 6:30 P.M. for evening Venetian Theater concerts.

ACCOMMODATIONS   *Ramada Inn,* Route 22, Armonk (south of Bedford), 273-9090; $$$ ● *Holiday Inn,* Holiday Drive, Mount Kisco, 241-2600; $$.

DINING   *Emily Shaw's Inn,* Route 137, Pound Ridge, 764-5779; dinner $$–$$$, lunch $ ● *Nino's,* Route 121, Bedford Village, 234-3374; $$–$$$ ● *The Arch,* Route 22N, Brewster, 279-5011; $$$$ (complete dinner $30.00 per person) ● *Village Inn,* Route 22, Bedford, 234-9843; $–$$ ● *La Cremaillere,* 4 miles on righthand side off of exit 31, Merritt Parkway, Banksville, 234-3306; $$$$.

SIGHTSEEING   *Bedford Museum,* Bedford Village, 234-9328. Hours: Wednesday to Sunday, 2 to 5 P.M. Adults 75¢; children 25¢ ● *John Jay Homestead State Historic Site,* Route 22, Bedford Village 232-5651. Tours Wednesday to Sunday, 9 A.M. to 4:15 P.M. Free ● *Caramoor,* Route 137, Katonah, NY 10536, 232-4206. One hour guided tours mid-April to October, Wednesday to Saturday 10 A.M. to 4 P.M.; Sunday 1 to 4 P.M. Adults $3, children 50¢, under 10 not admitted. Write or call for summer music festival schedule and prices ● *Katonah Gallery,* Bedford Road, Katonah, 232-4988. Hours: Friday to Saturday, 10 A.M. to 5 P.M.; Sunday 1 to 5 P.M. Free ● *Ward Pound Ridge Reservation,* Route 121 at Route 35, Cross River, 763-3493. Hours: 9 A.M. to sunset. Parking, nonresidents $2, residents $1.

Crafts (Small and Otherwise) on the Connecticut Shore

Farm animals used to graze on the wide village green in Guilford, Connecticut. Colonial neighbors discussed the day's news under the shade of the trees, the local militia drilled here, and for a time the green even doubled as the local cemetery until someone decided such a central location really ought to be reserved for livelier residents of the town.

The green remains the hub of Guilford centuries later, surrounded these days by shops instead of sheep. And come the middle of July each year it is livelier than ever as it plays host to top craftsmen from all over New England: potters, weavers, glassblowers, smiths, carvers, and others who show their wares at the Guilford Handicrafts Exposition. Many are members of Guilford's excellent Handcraft Center.

Next to the big show held in Rhinebeck, New York, each June, this three-day affair is probably the area's biggest crafts exhibit. It is a perfect time to get acquainted with the quaint and historic towns that line the Connecticut shore from Guilford to Old Lyme.

Towns like Guilford, Madison, and Old Lyme owe their flavor more to their Colonial heritage than to their proximity to the Long Island Sound. They have long histories, many fine homes, some excellent small museums, and almost as an afterthought, proximity to the beach.

Most of the summer visitors here are people who own or rent the shingled cottages near the shore, so you won't find a lot in the way of tourist accommodations—or commercialism. The best move is to head straight for Old Lyme, where there are two excellent small inns, and work your way back gradually to Guilford and the crafts exposition on Sunday.

Whether you select the Bee and Thistle, an informal yellow Colonial house, or the Old Lyme Inn, an 1850s mansion with an elegant French menu in the dining room, you have a perfect home base for exploring a very special little town.

The wide shaded main street lined with Colonial homes has been declared an historic district; one residence housed one of the nation's first art colonies. The columned Georgian mansion is known as Florence Griswold House for "Miss Florence," who put up and fed a group of painters including Henry W. Ranger, Willard Metcalf, and Clark Voorhees. They eventually developed the "ideal Lyme landscapes" that brought national attention to the area. The house is now headquarters for the Lyme Historical Society and contains paintings and panels left by the artists, an extensive china collection, and completely furnished period rooms such as the front parlor, circa 1830s, and the lady's bedroom from the early 1900s.

Next door The Old Lyme Art Association was founded as a showcase for local artists back in 1914 and remains a prestigious gallery with changing exhibits of prominent current work.

Old Lyme's third attraction is a weird one, a Victorian house transformed into a Nut Museum. Curator Elizabeth Tashjian is tour guide in her own home for off-beat exhibits including the world's tallest nutcracker, and nut art, music, and lore. She also has a small sculpture garden outside.

Should you choose to spend Saturday afternoon at the beach, you can try the two small beaches here off Route 156 ($3 beach sticker required, available from the Town Hall on Lyme Street), or you can drive about 15 miles to Hammonasset, between Clinton and Madison (one mile south of exit 62), the largest Connecticut shoreline park.

You'll still have to put up with the pebbles that are unavoidable nuisances on Sound beaches, but the sand here stretches for two wide miles and the vistas of endless small boats offshore are a bonus.

If you want to see Madison's historic house, the Allis-Bushnell House and Museum, you'll have to squeeze it in on Saturday between 1 and 4 P.M. It's a bit unusual for its corner fireplaces and its reproduction of a doctor's office of the early 1900s. There are also children's toys and costumes from the late 1700s to 1900s.

If you do miss this house, take a drive instead down Madison's main and side streets and admire the handsome homes that are still private residences. This is also an ideal town for a shoreline drive to see those big rambling summer cottages.

Evenings are on the quiet side here—a long dinner, maybe a movie, or a local concert here and there. Ask at your inn what's happening currently.

Sunday, take a slow drive back to Guilford on US 1, detouring for the picturesque harbor at Saybrook Point in Old Saybrook and stopping at some of the antique stores along the way on US 1.

When you get to the Crafts Exposition, pick and choose carefully among the dozens and dozens of exhibitors. Buying hastily can be a mistake because you never know what's waiting in the next tent. When you've bought your ceramic pitcher, goblets, carvings, or whatever, take time to see the three historic sights of Guilford.

This town boasts the oldest stone house in the country, constructed by Reverend Henry Whitfield, founder of Guilford, around 1639. It was built like a manor house in the English midlands that its owner used to call home, with a steeply pitched roof, small windows, and a great hall 33 feet long with a huge fireplace at each end. A partition in the middle hinged to a second floor joist either turns the room into two or swings up to the ceiling out of the way. It's an unusually interesting house museum and offers some exhibits of early crafts such as weaving and metalworking.

The Hyland House is also an early home, a 1600 saltbox with a "new" lean-to added about 1660. It is completely furnished as though a family could be living in it still, and has beautiful paneling and original hardware. Thomas Griswold House, circa 1735, is pretty enough to have once adorned a commemorative stamp, and it is a repository for many of the historic artifacts of the town's long history.

One last possibility for the weekend finally does take you out to sea. Legend has it that Captain Kidd visited the Thimble Islands, offshore west of Guilford, and deposited his booty somewhere in the area when he fled the British in 1699. No one has found gold here yet, but a short cruise around the little known islands does make for a rewarding and scenic tour. Take exit 56 off I-95 and follow the signs to Stony Creek; ferryboats at the Stony Creek dock make the trip hourly during the summer.

Connecticut Area Code: 203

DRIVING DIRECTIONS   I-95 exit 70, Old Lyme; Guilford is at exits 57 to 59.
   Total distance: about 104 miles.

ACCOMMODATIONS   *Bee and Thistle Inn,* 100 Lyme Street, Old Lyme, 434-1667; $$ • *Old Lyme Inn,* 85 Lyme Street, Old Lyme, 434-2600; $ including continental breakfast • *Castle Inn* at Cornfield Point, Route 154, Old Saybrook, 388-4681 (sensational location on the Sound, pool, old mansion—but you'll have to put up with a somewhat musty atmosphere); $–$$$ including continental breakfast.

DINING   *Bee and Thistle Inn* (see above); $$ • *Old Lyme Inn* (see above); $$ • *Sachem Country House,* Goose Lane, Guilford, 453-5261, an eighteenth-century house; $$ • *Century House,* 2455 Boston Post Road, Guilford, 453-2216, for fine French food; $.

SIGHTSEEING   *Guilford Handicrafts Exposition:* For dates and this year's admission prices, contact the Chamber of Commerce, 669 Boston Post Road, Guilford, CT 06437, 453-9677, or the Guilford Handcraft Center, P. O. Box 221, Guilford, CT 06437, 453-5947.

Harmonious History in New Jersey

The Colonial dame, wearing a mop cap and a long homespun dress, was sweeping her front step. She smiled and nodded as we passed, as though this group in jeans and sneakers could have been just the Colonial family next door.

   The village around her, too, seemed perfectly natural in its surroundings, a clearing next to the Morris Canal. Despite the visitors strolling its paths, it might have still been the settlement known as Andover Forge during the Revolutionary War.

   Today it is called Waterloo Village and is a restoration consisting of

26 buildings along the canal in Stanhope, New Jersey. It isn't the biggest or most elaborate restoration you'll ever see, but there's something extraordinary about the place—a sense of entering a time warp and walking into the past.

There is a church, a stagecoach inn, several houses and barns, a working gristmill, a smithy's shop, an apothecary shop, and a general store, all seemingly occupied by people going about their daily affairs. A potter works at his wheel, the smithy's hammer clangs, herbs are hung on the racks in the drying room at the apothecary.

You watch them at work, maybe chat as they dip the candles, weave the cloth, or grind the grain, and there you are, back in the past. There are no guides to break the illusion. It's a self-guided tour at your own pace, with plenty of time to pause under a tree or have a snack of wine and cheese at a table beneath the low beams in the general store.

This is a pleasant experience anytime, but come summer there is double incentive to make the trip because the field in front of Waterloo Village turns into a music arena, presenting everyone from the Festival Symphony Orchestra to the State Opera to Charley Pride. Concerts are held some afternoons as well as evenings (some of the Sunday afternoons are free with admission to the village), so you'll want to check the schedule before you plan a final itinerary. Saturday will work better for you, though, for seeing other sights in the area.

You won't have to worry about dinner Saturday night; alongside the music tent local caterers dispense quiche, salad, chicken, and other perfectly fine outdoor fare.

Accommodations aren't the greatest in the immediate Stanhope area, but there are two possibilities not far away. One is the Chester Inn, an 1810 tavern recently restored to its authentic appearance, with period guestrooms on the upper floors and a restaurant downstairs. In Bernardsville, the Old Mill Inn is another Colonial establishment, this time in a 1768 barn, but only a restaurant is situated here; you'll have to settle for the motel across the parking lot. Best Western's Morristown Motor Inn is another choice, since you'll likely be heading this way on Sunday anyway.

Whatever your schedule, reserve some time for driving around one of the wealthiest areas in New Jersey—or anywhere else, for that matter—the hunt country of Somerset and Morris counties. They rank themselves among the top 20 counties in wealth in the country, and you won't doubt it if you travel down to Chester and through towns like Far Hills, Peapack, Gladstone, Mendham, Liberty Corners, and Basking Ridge. The very heart of the area is south of Route 24 and north of I-78, and the very best addresses are south of Mendham, Jacqueline Onassis's Far Hills country place among them.

Don't stick to the main roads. Try 525 or those wiggly lines on the map with no numbers to see the best estates of the horsey set. In the towns along the way you can explore the eclectic stores that occupy appropriately atmospheric Victorian houses. Antique shops are legion, especially in Mendham and in Oldwick, to the west.

A few backroads, some shopping stops, and Waterloo Village make for a Saturday well spent, leaving Sunday for all the history and natural scenery around Morristown.

Morristown was actually the nation's military capital for a while, the site of Washington's headquarters and the main encampment of the Continental Army during the winter of 1779–80, when the general was fighting to rally and rejuvenate his starving, freezing, and sometimes mutinous forces. Morristown National Historical Park has three parts, representing that crucial year.

The first, off Morris Avenue, is the museum, where you can see a color film about the area and exhibits of weapons and other pertinent artifacts. In front of the museum building is the Ford Mansion, the finest home in town in the 1770s, which was offered as headquarters to Washington and his wife by Mrs. Jacob Ford, a widow who obligingly moved with her four children into two rooms to make room for them. The house still has many original Ford furnishings.

Fort Nonsense, not far from the Morristown Green, got its name because no one could remember why soldiers had been obliged to work so hard to dig its trenches and embankments.

The actual Jockey Hollow encampment area is a few miles south of Morristown off 202. It contains typical log huts where the troops might have been quartered, as many as twelve to a shelter, plus the officers' huts, the parade ground where troops were drilled, and Wick Farm, a prosperous farm of the day used as headquarters for General Arthur St. Clair. It too retains some of its original furnishings. The area also includes a wildlife sanctuary with wooded hills, streams and flowers, and hiking trails.

There's more history to be tracked in Morristown. Speedwell Village was the home and factory of Stephen Vail, who manufactured the engine for the first steamship that crossed the Atlantic. It was also the home of Vail's son, Alfred, who perfected the telegraph with Samuel F. B. Morse, demonstrating it publicly for the first time right here. The house has period furniture and there are various exhibits of engines and the history of the telegraph.

Want more history? Acorn Hall and Schuyler-Hamilton House are, respectively, a Victorian and a Colonial mansion, each furnished appropriately, and the Macculloch Hall Historical Museum is an 1810 mansion with gardens and much Morristown memorabilia gathered by a family that lived here for 140 years.

But how much can a person absorb on one summer afternoon?

Maybe it's time for a different destination, the Frelinghuysen Arboretum, a 127-acre estate with rolling lawns and stately trees in a traditional English park design. On the grounds are flower gardens, a large peony collection, a lilac garden, areas set off to show various tree varieties, and a rose garden so lovely it has become a setting popular with local brides. There are also nature trails here and the unusual fern configurations of a swamp area. The arboretum couldn't be a nicer spot for a walk, and you may see some interesting things in the gardens, since this is one of the select all-American gardens that preview new varieties of flowers and vegetables. An added bonus on some Sunday afternoons are free concerts on the lawn.

At the end of the day you may want to check for just one more historic setting—a place to enjoy a good dinner before you head for home.

New Jersey Area Code: 201

DRIVING DIRECTIONS To Waterloo Village, take I-80 to Route 206 (exit 25), drive north 2½ miles to Waterloo Road, then left another 2 miles to Waterloo Village. Watch for signs. Follow 206 south to Chester and Bernardsville, 202 or 287 to Morristown.
Total distance: 50 miles.

ACCOMMODATIONS *Publick House,* 11 Main Street, Chester, 879-6878; $–$$ with breakfast • *Old Mill Inn,* Route 202, Bernardsville, 766-1150; $$ • *Best Western Morristown Inn,* 270 South Street, Morristown, 540-1700; $$–$$$.

DINING *Black Forest Inn,* Route 206, Stanhope, 347-3344, German and French dishes in a turn-of-the-century stone house; $$–$$$ • *Silver Springs Farm,* Drakestown Road, Flanders (south of Stanhope), 584-6660, French haute cuisine—reserve ahead; $$$ • *Van's Huong Viet,* Route 24, Chester Mall, Chester, 879-5232, Jersey's only Viet restaurant, and a good one; $$$ • *Black Horse Inn,* Route 24, Mendham, 543-7300, a Victorian inn with appetizer buffet table; $$–$$$ • *Governor Morris Inn,* 2 Whippany Road, Morristown, 539-7300, comfortable, reliable, typical Colonial; $$–$$$ • *The Tarragon Tree,* 225 Main Street, Chatham, 635-7333 (French and really fine); $$$$.

SIGHTSEEING *Waterloo Village,* Waterloo Road off Route 206, Stanhope, 347-0900. Hours: Tuesday to Sunday, 10 A.M. to 6 P.M.

Adults $4, senior citizens $3, children age 6–12 $2. Concerts vary in price, roughly $7 to $10 for seating in tent, $4 for lawn; phone for current schedule and prices • *Morristown National Historical Park,* Morris Avenue, Morristown, 539-2016. Hours: daily, 9 A.M. to 5 P.M. Admission paid at Historical Museum for all sites, adults 50¢, under 16 and over 62 free • *Speedwell Village,* 333 Speedwell Avenue, Morristown, 540-0211. Hours: April to October, Thursday to Saturday, 10 A.M. to 4 P.M.; Sunday 2 to 5 P.M. Adults 75¢, senior citizens, children age 12–18 50¢ • *Schuyler-Hamilton House,* 5 Olyphant Place, Morristown, 267-4039. Hours: Tuesday, Sunday, 2 to 5 P.M. Free • *Acorn Hall,* 68 Morris Avenue, Morristown. Hours: March to December, Thursday, 11 A.M. to 3 P.M., Sunday 1:30 to 4 P.M. All ages 50¢ • *Macculloch Hall Historical Museum,* 45 Macculloch Avenue, Morristown, 538-2404. Hours: April to November, Sunday, 2 to 4:30 P.M. Adults $1, senior citizens, children over 12 50¢, under 12 not admitted • *Frelinghuysen Arboretum,* Whippany Road (entrance from East Hanover Avenue), Morristown, 285-6166. Hours: mid-March to early December, Monday to Friday, 9 A.M. to 5 P.M.; weekends till 6 P.M. Free.

Stone-House Hunting in Ulster County

It may seem an unlikely place to look for the past. First there are the fast-food signs, then the funky shops filled with students from the local college. But drive on to the end of Main Street in New Paltz, New York, take a right turn onto Huguenot Street (just before the bridge)—and the clock turns back 300 years.

A national historic landmark that celebrated its tercentennial in 1978, Huguenot Street is the oldest street in America with its original homes intact. And the sturdy, steep-roofed stone houses on the block, their old-world architecture unique to New Paltz and its Ulster County environs, still evoke the feel of a rural European village just as they did for the homesick French Huguenot families who built them so long ago.

The houses are an unusual start to a weekend of beautiful back roads Ulster County scenery and a visit to one of America's unique hotels, Mohonk Mountain House.

The settlers of New Paltz were a small band of Huguenot families from Flanders villages. Fleeing from the religious persecution of Louis XIV, they first moved to the Rheinland Pfalz, or Palatinate, in

Germany. Eventually they emigrated to America and the Dutch settlements of Kingston (then known as Wiltwyck) and Hurley in the Hudson River Valley. In 1677 a dozen of these families banded together to buy from the Indians their own tract of land beside the Wallkill River. They named it New Paltz for the Rheinland Pfalz.

Happy to have found a safe haven at last, the Huguenots moved onto their land in the spring of 1678, and there they put down firm roots. Although their homes were enlarged as new generations grew and prospered, five of the first six houses on the street remained virtually unchanged for 250 years and were occupied by descendants of the original builders.

Even today many names of those original settlers—Deyo, Bevier, Elting, DuBois, and Hasbrouck—remain prominent in New Paltz life. Kenneth Hasbrouck, who claims to be related to 11 of the original 12 families, is now president and guiding light of the Huguenot Historical Society. It was under his leadership that in the 1950s efforts to buy and restore the earliest homes began. Each house museum is supported by a family association of descendants.

A tour of the homes begins at Deyo Hall, half a block off Huguenot Street. Here, displays give visitors some insight into the history of the area. An excellent introduction is the Jean Hasbrouck Memorial House, whose steep, shingled roof, great chimney and jambless fireplace have earned it a citation as the most outstanding example of medieval Flemish stone architecture in America. The gigantic internal chimney is one of the only originals of its kind in existence. Many of the furnishings, including the tavern table, Hudson Valley rush-bottom chairs, Dutch *kaas* (chests), and a cradle, belonged to the Hasbrouck family prior to 1700.

In the Abraham Hasbrouck House, unusual family heirlooms include an English four-panel chest that commemorated a 1609 marriage. There's also a rare seventeenth-century Dutch writing table with mother-of-pearl inlay and a cozy Dutch bed hidden behind paneled doors. The pride of this house is the mammoth medieval fireplace in the central "room of seven doors." As in most of the homes, you can still see much of the original woodwork, huge beams, and wide floorboards.

The two Hasbrouck houses, along with the equally interesting Hugo Freer and Bevier-Elting houses, represent living styles from the town's earliest days. The LeFevre House, built in 1799 with three stone walls and a front of brick, marks a transition to the Federal Period on the street. Deyo House, dating from 1692, was remodeled in the 1890s into an elegant Edwardian residence.

Huguenot Street's annual Heritage Day, usually the first Saturday in August, adds demonstrations of weaving, blacksmithing, and other arts and crafts of the past to the regular house tours.

Also on the street are two churches. A careful reconstruction of the 1717 French Church has been placed next to the original Huguenot Burying Ground. The 1839 red brick Dutch Reformed Church is a sign of the growing influence of Dutch neighbors on the Huguenots.

After you've seen Huguenot Street, then head four miles south on Route 32 to Locust Lawn, the other Huguenot Society property in the area. Built by Josiah Hasbrouck in 1814, this Federal-style house reflects the owner's travels to Washington and Virginia, and its furnishings are a textbook of period decoration, from Queen Anne to early Victorian. Also nearby is the Terwilliger Home, where the Hasbroucks lived until Locust Lawn was completed. Many consider this appealing home their favorite of all the stone houses.

Just west of Locust Lawn, 20 acres of woodland, thicket, and pond have been set aside as a wildlife sanctuary. Nature trails through the area may be reached from the entrance on Jenkinstown Road.

There's more spectacular nature awaiting, however, six miles west of New Paltz at Mohonk Mountain House. This absolutely huge old-fashioned Victorian fantasy of towers and turrets is wrapped around one end of a natural marvel, a mountain lake atop the Shawangunk Mountains. The dark blue, 60-foot-deep, spring-fed lake lies in a small fault running across the main line of the mountain, surrounded by cliffs—a truly spectacular sight.

It was the natural beauty of this place 1,200 feet high that captivated the twin Smiley brothers, Alfred and Albert, in 1869. Albert bought up 300 acres and a rundown tavern for $28,000, mortgaging his future in the process, while Alfred stayed at his teaching job to bring in some much needed cash. Paying guests were needed to add more income, so in 1870 a 10-room hotel was opened—with drinking, smoking, dancing, and cards outlawed by its Quaker owner.

More than 100 years later, Mohonk still belongs to the Smiley family. It has grown to 305 rooms; the grounds now total 7,500 acres (5,000 of them in protected undeveloped land known as the Mohonk Trust); and there are award-winning gardens, a cliff-top lookout tower to make the most of the view, artificial lakes, 30 miles of bridle trails, an 18-hole golf course and putting green, miles of gorgeous hiking trails, and tennis. There is still no bar and no smoking in the dining room, though drinks are allowed now at dinner or in your room. People come regardless of restrictions, for this remains a magnificent natural retreat.

You can happily spend a weekend or more at Mohonk, or you can come as a day guest, paying admission to enjoy hiking in the woods, strolling the gardens, or taking out one of the horses for hire at the stable. If you have a meal in the dining room, there is no admission charge.

Some Sunday, continue driving to the end of the Mohonk Road and you'll reach High Falls, a tiny town with one of the Hudson Valley's finest restaurants, the Dupuy Canal House, a historic stone structure that was once a lively tavern back in 1797. The old Delaware and Hudson Canal passed through here; in an old church's tiny and charming museum you can see replicas of the canal boats, panoramas of the canal and the adjoining towpath and fascinating miniature dioramas of early life in High Falls.

This is choice antiquing territory. The Canal Antiques Center is 10 shops in one and the Tow Path House across the street is another dealers' cooperative housing several stores.

It's also choice backroads country, the kind of area to just get lost on the side roads admiring the quaint stone houses and farms and the unspoiled Ulster County scenery.

One pleasant drive west on Route 213 brings you to Stone Ridge and five more antique shops, including The Thumb Print, housed in a picturesque old barn. Continue north on Route 209 to Hurley, site of the first Huguenot settlements in the county, and you'll see stone houses still occupied here, transformed into attractive homes for today.

If you have more time continue to Kingston, New York's first capital, with historical sites and museums and its own store of stone houses. Or head up Route 28 and 375 to Woodstock, the artists' colony that is chock-a-block with intriguing shops.

If time is up you can still fit in one last stop on the way home, at the Hudson Valley Wine Company in Highland. A 1½-hour winery tour, followed by a tasting that includes bread, fruit, and cheese, is a totally pleasant way to wind up the weekend.

Ulster County Area Code: 914

DRIVING DIRECTIONS George Washington Bridge to Palisades Parkway to exit 9N, New York Thruway to exit 18, New Paltz. Turn left onto Route 299, which becomes Main Street, then right onto Huguenot Street just before the river.
Total distance: 85 miles.

ACCOMMODATIONS *Mohonk Mountain House,* Mohonk Road, New Paltz, 233-2244 (inquire about many special weekends for nature lovers, photographers, tennis players, music fans—even fans of mystery novels); $$–$$$$ AP • *Brodhead House* Route 213, High Falls, 687-7700 (Victorian home owned by DuPuy Canal House across the street); $, no private baths • *The Anzor Motel,* Route 299, New Paltz, 883-7373; $ • *Three Penny Inn* (motel), Route 299, New Paltz, 255-1500; $ • *Williams Lake Hotel,* Rosendale, 658-3101 (pleasant resort, advance reservations in summer by the week only, but a possibility for last-minute accommodations); $$$$ AP.

DINING *DuPuy Canal House,* Route 213, High Falls, 687-7700; $$$–$$$$ • *Lake Mohonk House* (see above); $$ • *The Locust Tree Inn,* 215 Huguenot Street, New Paltz, 255-7888; an old stone house convenient for lunch $ or dinner $$ • *Top of the Falls,* Route 213, High Falls, 687-7565; for Sunday brunch $, dinner $$, jazz on Friday, Saturday nights.

SIGHTSEEING *Huguenot Street,* New Paltz, 255-1660. Hours: Wednesday to Saturday, 10 A.M. to 4 P.M.; Sunday 1 to 4 P.M. Each house $1, children 50¢. Guided tours at 10 A.M. and 3 P.M., complete tour $3, short tour $2 • *Delaware and Hudson Canal Museum,* Mohonk Road, High Falls, 687-9311. Hours: Wednesday to Sunday, 11 A.M. to 5 P.M. through October 30. Donation • *Ulster County Fair* is held annually in August at New Paltz fairgrounds. For information, contact Ulster County Public Information Office, P. O. Box 1800, Kingston, NY 12401, 331-9300.

Weekending with the Boston Symphony

Is there anybody out there who doesn't know about Tanglewood?

The summer home of the Boston Symphony has been one of the most popular destinations in the northeast ever since the concerts began here back in 1936. The 6,000 seats in the open-air shed are often sold out, and as many as 10,000 more people may be found on the lawn, spreading wicker baskets and wine bottles on blankets and settling back to enjoy a symphony concert under the stars.

Some people like the lawn even better on Sunday afternoon, when you can really appreciate strolling the 210 acres of William Aspinwall Tappan's former estate, viewing the formal gardens and the re-creation of the red house where Nathaniel Hawthorne worked, no doubt inspired by the beauty around him. The view of lake and mountains from the main house (now the administration building) is magnificent.

The question arose whether Tanglewood even needed mentioning here, especially since the Berkshires come up again for other reasons in fall and winter. However, since the fare of music as well as dance and theater is so rich here in the summer, plans for a weekend seem in order, if only to inspire those who haven't gotten around to making the trip.

For first-timers, then, a word about accommodations. You must make reservations several months ahead for the choicest of the inns, and even the motels may require you to stay a minimum of three nights. As for tickets, lawn seats are always available, but write ahead to Tanglewood or watch for the very first ad that appears in the Sunday *New York Times* to order tickets if you want to be sure of reserved seating for the concert of your choice.

As for accommodations, the list is long and there are many terrific choices, everything from an Italian villa to simple country inns, with dozens of motels in between.

A personal favorite is the Flying Cloud Inn in New Marlboro, about half an hour from Tanglewood, a former farmhouse way out in the country surrounded by a couple of peaceful acres of land. The rooms are simple, the furnishings are antique, the help-yourself bar works on the honor system, and the food, heavy on natural ingredients, is fine. There's also a tennis court and a rowboat on the spring-fed pond.

Other Berkshire lodgings that come highly recommended are the Williamsville Inn, a Victorian house in West Stockbridge with a swimming pool, a tennis court, a 10-acre garden and a dining room widely considered the best around; and the simple Colonial Egremont Inn, which also provides you with a pool and a fine dining room. The granddaddy of the inns is the wonderful Red Lion in Stockbridge, almost a prototype New England inn right on an historic main street; and for those with the wherewithal to pay the tab, Wheatleigh lets you live like the contessa who once owned this villa, with polished oak floors and chandeliers and period antiques. There's a pool once again, and you can walk to Tanglewood, an advantage you'll appreciate even more when you see the line of traffic.

All of the above are good choices for dinner. Some equally good suggestions are the Gateways in Lenox, for very elegant continental dining; The Old Mill in Egremont (which is just that), atmospheric, excellent and reasonable; and two offbeat places in West Stockbridge, Miss Ruby's Cafe, which may serve you anything from Tex-Mex to French depending on the mood of the chef, and The Orient Express, a Vietnamese restaurant in West Stockbridge. The locals swear by it.

Now that you have the basics, here's a quick rundown on some of the attractions you have to choose among, in addition to planning a night and/or afternoon at the symphony. Jacob's Pillow Dance Festival, the oldest such event in America, takes place in a rustic 100-acre setting in a barn named for its founder, Ted Shawn. You'll see the whole gamut of dance performed over the summer here. A recent season included the Joffrey II dancers; companies from India, Spain, and Brazil; modern dance; the Boston ballet; a week of premieres by the resident ballet; and an American sampler from classic to folk.

The Berkshire Theater Festival in Stockbridge, originally housed in a building designed in 1886 by Stanford White, was only the second summer theater in the nation when it began performances in 1928. Now there's top grade summer stock here in the Mainstage and two barn theaters, The Barn and The Unicorn, where there are special events and Sunday afternoon readings of new plays, and a children's theater in the courtyard.

If drama is a special interest, don't overlook the excellent Williamstown Theater Festival, which has done some experimental productions that attracted much critical acclaim.

The bard is the thing at Shakespeare & Company, played in a natural amphitheater on the grounds of The Mount, Edith Wharton's former estate high above Laurel Lake. There are normally two plays alternating, and you can picnic on the lovely grounds. The house itself is open for daytime tours.

Another pleasant place to hear music is at the South Mountain Concerts, chamber music performed in a barnlike shed that has attracted fine chamber groups and soloists for some 60 years. The grounds are the former estate of Elizabeth Sprague Coolidge, and once again, are idyllic, though the straight-back pews could benefit from cushions.

You won't have a lot of time left to worry about sightseeing, especially if you have sunshine during the day and a pool or a pond at your disposal. A couple of possibilities for lake swimming are Pontcosuc Lake in Pittsfield, York Lake in New Marlboro, or Beartown State Forest near Great Barrington.

Save a little time for a drive around and a walk through both Lenox and Stockbridge, the former a town that was the summer mountain retreat for millionaires in its heyday, the latter a picture-book New England town with a Norman Rockwell museum honoring the man who immortalized the town in his paintings.

If the clouds roll in, consider Saturday and Sunday matinees at the various theaters in the area, or go shopping in West Stockbridge, or antiquing in South Egremont or Sheffield, or visit the marvelous Clark

Art Institute in Williamstown. If you need further suggestions, check the attractions mentioned in the fall and winter Berkshire itineraries on pages 124 and 189.

You'll probably make plans to come back, because if a Berkshires weekend proves anything, it's that you really can't get too much of a good thing.

Berkshires Area Code: 413

DRIVING DIRECTIONS   Saw Mill River Parkway north to the Taconic Parkway to the New York Thruway Berkshire spur (Route 90) east to exit 2, then follow Route 102 to US 20 into Lenox. Tanglewood is on West Street, Route 183 in Lenox.

Total distance: 153 miles.

BY PUBLIC TRANSPORTATION   Amtrak serves Pittsfield, Greyhound services much of the Berkshire area. You might be able to stay close enough to walk to Tanglewood, but it is difficult to get around to other places without a car.

ACCOMMODATIONS   *The Flying Cloud Inn,* Route 57, New Marlboro, 229-2113; $$$$ ● *Williamsville Inn,* Route 41, West Stockbridge, 274-6580; $$ ● *Egremont Inn,* Old Sheffield Road, South Egremont, 528-2111; $$ MAP ● *Red Lion Inn,* Main Street, Stockbridge, 298-5545; $–$$ ● *Wheatleigh,* West Hawthorne Road, Lenox, 637-0610; $$$$ AP.

DINING   All of the above plus: *The Gateways Inn,* 71 Walker Street, Lenox, 637-2532; $$$; prix fixe entrées, $16.50 ● *Miss Ruby's Cafe,* Main Street, West Stockbridge, 232-8582; $–$$ ● *The Orient Express,* off Main Street, West Stockbridge, 232-4204; $ ● *The Old Mill,* Route 23, South Egremont; $–$$ ● For lighter fare, try *Ganest,* 90 Church Street, Lenox; $ ● *The Stockpot,* around the corner from the Red Lion, Stockbridge; $.

SIGHTSEEING   Check all for current dates, ticket prices, and starting times ● *Tanglewood,* West Street (Route 183), Lenox, 637-1940. Concerts: July to August, Friday, 9 P.M. (preludes at 7); Saturday, 8:30 P.M.; Sunday, 2:30 P.M. Reserved seats from $5.50–$17.50, lawn seats $4; open rehearsals on Saturdays at 10:30 A.M., $3.50 ● *Jacob's Pillow Dance Festival,* off Route 20 on George Carter Road, Becket, 243-0745. Performances Tuesday, Wednesday,

Friday, Saturday evenings; Thursday and Saturday afternoons. Admission $6–$8. Call for performance schedules • *Shakespeare & Company,* The Mount, Route 7, Lenox, 637-1197. Hours: Wednesday to Sunday, July to Labor Day, 8 P.M. Admission $6. House open Friday through Sunday, 10 A.M. to 2 P.M. Admission $2.50 • *South Mountain Concerts,* Route 7, one mile south of Pittsfield, 443-6517. Hours: June to August, Saturday, 3 P.M.; inquire for dates. $6. • *Berkshire Theater Festival,* Main Street, Stockbridge, 298-5576. Hours: Wednesday to Friday, 8:30 P.M., Saturday, 5 P.M., 9 P.M., Sunday 3 P.M., 7:30 P.M. Admission $5.95–$9.95 • *Williamstown Summer Theatre,* Park and Main (intersection of Routes 7 and 2), Williamstown, 458-8146. Hours: late June to August, Tuesday to Friday, 8:30 P.M.; Saturday 5 P.M., 9 P.M. Admission $3.25–$9.25 • *Searles Castle,* Main Street, Great Barrington, 528-0025. Tours: daily, 10 A.M. to 4 P.M. Adults $3, children age 12–16 $1.75. Chamber concerts Wednesday, Friday, and Saturday evenings, Sunday afternoons; inquire for current schedule and prices.

FOR FURTHER INFORMATION   Contact Berkshire Hills Conference, 205 West Street, Pittsfield, MA 01201, 443-9186.

Rhode Island's Unsung Shoreline

It was Sunday noon on a mid-July weekend, and all was right with the world at Weekapaug Beach—hot sun, ocean breeze, cloudless sky, and beach blankets spaced in a discreet checkerboard to allow everyone a patch of privacy to enjoy it all.

It is a scene repeated many times along 25 miles of sandy shoreline edging the area officially labeled Washington County, but affectionately known to everyone in Rhode Island only as "South County." The five state parks here spaced between Westerly and Point Judith draw their full share of sun worshippers, but the town beaches in between (by New York standards, at least) have plenty of room for all. And so does this relatively unheralded vacation area.

South County doesn't ape the chicness of the Hamptons or the quaintness of Cape Cod. It's a down-to-earth, wide-open area with a couple of nice inns, a scattering of adequate motels, a smattering of small towns, lots of nature preserves and fishing grounds, and just enough shops to fill the bill on a rainy day. There's little traffic, less hassle—and few better places for a truly relaxing weekend.

Westerly, population 14,497, is the hub of the western end of the county, and within the bounds of Westerly township are a variety of accommodations that should suit almost anyone. One of the best choices is Shelter Harbor Inn, about four miles out of town, an informal restored country farmhouse and barn that offers seclusion, a pleasant sundeck, a tennis court, big full breakfast included in the rates, and guest passes to that delightful residents-only beach at Weekapaug.

Weekapaug Inn is quite another matter—a handsome, weathered, shingled summer place that has been run by the same family for three generations and had some of its guests for almost as long. Here you'll find rockers on the porch, beautiful grounds with a water view, bowling on the lawn, tennis, sailing, golf privileges, and a private beach. It's expensive and with the atmosphere of a private club.

West of Weekapaug are two beaches that are poles apart. Misquamicut is a state beach, crowded with roller rink, water slide, seafood stands, tavern, discos, and all the other amusements of a slightly tacky beach area. Nevertheless, on one end is the nicest direct beachfront accommodation on the shore, the Pleasant View House.

Farther on, on a spit with Little Narragansett Bay on one side and the ocean on the other, is Watch Hill, an enclave of big Victorian homes and old wealth. But you can't exactly categorize Watch Hill. The shops here include expensive antiques and names like Lily Pulitzer and William Coppola that you'll also find in Palm Beach, but there are also souvenir places, a wonderful old used bookstore called the Book and Tackle Shop, and a very plain restaurant that is a local institution called the Olympia Tea Room.

The street runs directly across from the harbor, so one of the major events of the day here is watching the sun go down over the masts of the sailboats. Park benches are thoughtfully provided.

The oldest carousel in the country is at the end of the block, with horses hung on chains, and it fills the street at night with music to serenade strollers out for a homemade ice cream cone or fresh buttered popcorn.

Mansions notwithstanding, there's nothing forbidding about Watch Hill—in fact, it is pleasant and almost wholesome. But it is difficult to stay here. There's the huge old wooden Ocean House, the last remaining grand hotel, but it has seen better days. Narragansett House has the best spot in town for cocktails and sunset-watching on its deck, but the rooms are downright spartan. Which leaves Hartley's Guest House, a prototype guesthouse full of plants and magazines and old-fashioned furniture, and with one exception, bathrooms down the hall. It's neatly positioned on the block between Main Street and the ocean beach (it's free, reached by a craggy hidden path; the bay beach charges $3 admission), and the water view from the front porch is unbeatable. Unless you are just not the guesthouse type, it's the best bet in a town that most definitely *is* a best bet.

Proceeding east, the choice narrows to motels from Charlestown on. (Check to see that beach passes are provided; all the beaches charge to get in.) Narragansett seems to have lost its flavor when its famous old casino was downed by a 1938 hurricane and has become a bland modern town, but the Chamber of Commerce here has an interesting program of bed-and-breakfast lodging at moderate rates in some of the town's nicest private homes. At this end of things there are still plenty of beaches, and you're near the picturesque fishing village of Galilee and the Block Island Ferry and closer to Newport, if you want to drive over the bridge.

If the weather is with you, a place to stay and a few restaurant recommendations are all you'll need on the Rhode Island shore. But if the clouds roll in or you're beginning to burn, all is far from lost. Visit some of the lovely conservation areas along the shore, and take advantage of nature walks and field trips for visitors scheduled at Kimball Wildlife Refuge and the Ninigret Conservation Area. And remember that this is fisherman's paradise—write ahead and the state tourist office will send you a free guide telling where to cast for what.

Or go to Westerly and its library—not for a book but to admire the wood paneling, fireplaces, stained glass, marble mosaic floors, and leaded-glass hanging lamps in this surprisingly lovely building. Look out back for another surprise. Wilcox Park is one of the loveliest to be found anywhere in a city this size. The park is used for free summer concerts, so check in the library for a schedule.

Also in Westerly, though open only on Sunday afternoons, is the 1732 Babcock Smith House, one of Rhode Island's architectural landmarks, restored and elegantly furnished by the local historical society.

For antiquing head for Wakefield (though it is the only place on the shore where you will encounter traffic), and while you are there have a meal at the Larchwood Inn, a gracious antique-filled home in town. (You can stay here, too, if you want to be a bit inland.) Two shops to watch for are Dove and Distaff on Main Street in Wakefield, with really fine early furniture, and The Trestle off Route 108 in neighboring Peace Dale, with a bit of everything. For more shops, ask for the free printed guide to antique stores on the South Shore; most stores have them.

Some other pleasant shopping stops are Windswept Farm (also a restaurant) on Route 1 outside Westerly for antiques and gifts;

Charlestown's Artists Guild and Gallery; and also in Charlestown, the Fantastic Umbrella Factory, a crazy mish-mash of pottery, china, posters, clothes, gifts, and what-have-you in ramshackle, old farm buildings with a few goats and chickens still wandering in the barnyard. For lunch or dinner, there's a good restaurant in the complex called Heart's Desire.

Some other dining possibilities: Shelter Harbor is a good choice (the place to sample Rhode Island johnnycakes) as is the Olympia Tea Room, which serves fresh seafood and homemade bread as well as tea. George's in Galilee is the special spot for seafood, and if the food at the Wayfarer in Westerly isn't unusual, the after-dinner fare is—Bogart, the Marx Brothers, and other classic films. Another pleasant evening diversion is the Theater-by-the-Sea in Matunick, which specializes in summer stock musicals.

By all means, stop at some of the roadside stands near the beach (especially those near Weekapaug) where lobster goes for about $5, a dozen clam cakes cost $3, and you take your meal and your chowder outside to the picnic tables in the back. The food, like the area, doesn't come in fancy wrappings, but it can't be beat.

Rhode Island Area Code: 401

DRIVING DIRECTIONS I-95 to Route 2 (exit 92), Westerly exit. Follow into Route 78 (Westerly bypass) to US 1 and bear north for Shelter Harbor Inn, Charlestown or Narragansett (watch for town signs to guide you); 1A south leads to Watch Hill, Misquamicut, and Weekapaug.
Total distance: 145 miles.

ACCOMMODATIONS *Shelter Harbor Inn,* Route 1, Westerly, 322-8883; $–$$ including full breakfast • *Weekapaug Inn,* Weekapaug, 322-0301; $$$$ AP • *Pleasant View House,* 65 Atlantic Avenue, Misquamicut, 348-8107; $$$ MAP • *Hartley's Guest House,* Larkin Road, Watch Hill, 348-8253; $ • *Larchwood Inn,* 176 Main Street, Wakefield, 783-5454; $$.

DINING *Shelter Harbor Inn* (see above); $$ • *Larchwood Inn* (see above); $ • *Heart's Desire* (at Fantastic Umbrella Factory), Route 1, Charlestown, 364-3935; complete dinner $11.95 • *The Wayfarer,* 2 Canal Street, Westerly, 596-4512; $ (movies extra) • *Georges,* near the fishing dock, Galilee, 783-2306; $–$$ • *Olympia Tea Room,* Watch Hill, 348-8211; $–$$ • *Narragansett Inn,* Watch Hill, 348-8912; $$.

A Taste of Victoriana at Nyack-on-Hudson

There was a lively argument the other day on a street corner in Nyack, New York. A young man, gesturing upward toward the round towers of an ornate Victorian home, kept insisting that this was the house to buy. His wife continued to shake her head and point across the street to an old house with a wraparound porch perched above the Hudson.

Neither house was for sale that day, but Nyack is a town that inspires first-time visitors to wishful househunting. An antiques and handicrafts shopping center, Nyack is also an old-fashioned village filled with delightful gingerbread Victorian homes. It is a town that proudly declares itself one of the last remnants of "Small Town, USA."

The town's scenic location on the west bank of the Hudson once made it a busy river landing and later allowed it to decline gracefully into a peaceful resort community. Grover Cleveland spent summers here, Ben Hecht and Carson McCullers found the atmosphere conducive to writing, and Helen Hayes bought a gracious white house on North Broadway where she still lives today. Nyack's best-known native son, artist Edward Hopper, memorialized his town's homes in his paintings.

In recent years, however, Nyack had come on hard times, and its charm seemed threatened by the specter of housing developments and shopping centers. Instead, the combination of low rents and artistic atmosphere inspired the town's renaissance as a shopping and strolling mecca. On a pleasant weekend, the sidewalks are filled with visitors.

A good plan would be to arrive Saturday morning, take in a few shops on Broadway in the center of town, then buy a picnic lunch (there's a deli on Broadway) and go two miles north to Hook Mountain State Park. Picnic tables are right at the river's edge; the view is hard to beat. Thus refreshed, you'll be ready to explore the town at length.

Nyack's homes remain its pride. Most are not mansions but well-kept examples of comfortable Victoriana in its turn-of-the-century heyday, displaying the gables and porches, balconies and bay windows, cupolas, and whimsical carving that give this style its special appeal.

To appreciate the houses, you must get out and walk, preferably accompanied by the Village Guide and Walking Tour, a booklet available in most shops for about 25 cents. It will give you a fast lesson in spotting Victorian architecture, and then point out the most interesting houses on five different loops along the treelined village streets and the waterfront. If you're on your own, an easy route to follow is south on Broadway to Washington Avenue, then one block left to Piermont at the water's edge.

All roads eventually lead to Broadway and the shops. On one block alone (South Broadway between Hudson and Cedar Hill Avenues), there are at least two dozen stores offering everything from baskets to beads, furniture to works of art. Stroll the side closest to the river and you can prowl among places like The Art Couple (moderately priced framed prints), Christophers (lots of handsome oak furniture and a greenhouse), or Horsefeathers (a potpourri of Mexican pottery, Icelandic sweaters, Chinese food, and American antiques).

At the end of the block, the Vintage Car Store will gladly sell you a souped-up Ferrari for about $22,000. If you've left your checkbook at home, you're still welcome to browse.

There are more stores on Main Street, including Gallery 110, which is five shops in one. If you continue on Route 9W into Upper Nyack you'll find another cache of shops, including four that call themselves the Upper Nyack Antique Center.

When hunger pangs strike, there are lots of pleasant possibilities. For lunch Strawberry Place is an ice cream parlor with an interesting sandwich menu, Herbal Gardens has crepes and vegetarian dishes, and Old Fashion is a chop house with seafood and hot sandwiches in a tavern atmosphere. At dinner time the Bully Boy, an English pub not far away in Congers, is very popular locally.

Make it an early dinner, and you can then drive across the Tappan Zee Bridge for music under the stars at Lyndhurst. Concerts are held every Saturday night from July through mid-August on the 67-acre grounds of this Gothic Revival mansion overlooking the Hudson River. It is located on Route 9, a half-mile south of the bridge, and you can picnic there, too.

Spend the night at the Tarrytown Hilton or the even newer and nicer Marriott, and you may choose to spend Sunday sunning at the pool or hitting a few tennis balls. The new Marriott, with an indoor pool, is another good bet.

Or you are perfectly situated to explore Sleepy Hollow Country, the three restorations that provide a look at life in early Hudson River days. Starting with the farthest point, Van Cortlandt Manor at Croton-on-Hudson is a Revolutionary War estate where Benjamin Franklin was once a guest. Beautifully situated overlooking the river, the gracious 1680 stone house with railed porch, double stairway, and pitched roof is surrounded by eighteenth-century gardens, peach, pear and apple trees, and a brick-paved Long Walk lined with lush flowerbeds. Costumed hostesses take you through the house, pointing out the prize furnishings and telling of life during the home's heyday.

Philipsburg Manor in North Tarrytown was also the preserve of a prominent family, one that once owned about a third of what is now Westchester County. The trilevel home bears witness to New York's Dutch-English origins. One of its most appealing rooms is the big beamed kitchen, where the hostesses show you how food was prepared in Colonial times. At the gristmill and barn on the grounds, you'll learn about some of the daily activities on an early Colonial farm.

The last of the restorations, Sunnyside in Tarrytown, was the home of Washington Irving, who immortalized the area with his stories of Rip Van Winkle and Ichabod Crane, the legends of Sleepy Hollow. Irving once described his Victorian home as "a little old-fashioned stone mansion, all made up of gable ends, and as full of angles and corners as an old cocked hat." The house stands on the east bank of the Hudson surrounded by orchards, gardens, and wooded paths planned by Irving himself. Much of his original furniture and personal possessions also remain, including his massive desk in the library.

You may also want to return to Lyndhurst for a house tour, stepping back into the gilded age when Jay Gould lived here very much like a king. The house is maintained by the National Trust for Historic Preservation.

If all that househopping has built up an appetite, have a last dinner at the Tappan Hill restaurant, a scenic spot high on a hill at Benedict and Highland avenues, only about four blocks off Route 9 near the center of Tarrytown.

Nyack Area Code: 914

DRIVING DIRECTIONS   Take the George Washington Bridge to New Jersey, then the Palisades Interstate Parkway to exit 4. Continue north on 9W until you come to Broadway, then bear right into the center of Nyack. The parkway also leads back to the Garden State Parkway and the connection to the Tappan Zee Bridge, which leads directly across the river into Tarrytown.

Total distance: about 25 miles.

BY PUBLIC TRANSPORTATION   For Nyack only: Take the IND *A* train to the George Washington Bridge Bus Terminal at 175th and Broadway in Manhattan, then board one of the Red & Tan buses that leave for Nyack every hour weekdays and weekends.

ACCOMMODATIONS *Tappan Zee Town House,* Route 9W, Nyack, 358-8400; $$ • *Tarrytown Hilton Inn,* Route 9, Tarrytown, 631-5700; $$$ • *Marriott,* 670 White Plains Road (Route 119), Tarrytown, 631-2200; $$.

DINING *Old Fashion,* 83 South Broadway, Nyack, 358-8114; $–$$ • *Angel Cafe,* foot of Burd Street on River, Nyack, 353-1843 (seafood); $–$$ • *Bully Boy Chop House,* 117 Route 303, Congers, 268-6555; $$–$$$ • *Tappan Hill,* Highland Avenue, Tarrytown, 631-3030; $$–$$$.

SIGHTSEEING *Sleepy Hollow Restorations,* three properties all along Route 9, Tarrytown, New York 10591, 591-7900. Hours: daily, 10 A.M. to 5 P.M. Each house, adults $4, children $2.50, combination tickets for all three houses, $10 and $6.50 • *Lyndhurst,* Route 9, Tarrytown, 631-7766. Hours: May to October, Tuesday to Sunday, 10 A.M. to 5 P.M.; rest of year until 3:15 P.M. Adults $3, children and senior citizens $2.

FOR FURTHER INFORMATION Free map and shopping guide is available by mail from the Art and Antique Dealers Association of the Nyacks, P. O. Box 223, Nyack, NY 10960.

Long Island Beaches for Beginners.
Part 1: The Fabled Hamptons

Yes, that was definitely Cheryl Tiegs at the next table in the restaurant. And yes, that was unmistakably Dina Merrill and Cliff Robertson coming down the aisle of the John Drew Theater. And it could well have been Lee Radziwill window-shopping on Job's Lane.

Celebrities are commonplace in the Hamptons. Socialites spend their summers in Southampton, artists and writers and publishing executives in East Hampton—and prominent faces from the worlds of arts and entertainment are easy to spot in either town or in any of the villages in between. But their presence is possibly the least of the reasons for planning a weekend on Long Island's eastern end.

The main attraction remains the thing that brought the beautiful people here in the first place—the beach. There are miles and miles of it, broad stretches of soft sand lined with sheltering dunes, some of it still amazingly unpopulated. You'll search hard to find better beaches anywhere, and if you are an ocean lover and a sun worshipper, you may never notice or care who else is around sharing nature's bounty with you.

There are other reasons for making the trip, of course. Lots of people enjoy the browsing possibilities in an area filled with chic shops and art galleries. Others are attracted by resort towns where a Colonial heritage remains dominant in spite of the influx of summer visitors and where picturesque windmills still stand. There are many fine restaurants to choose from. And let's face it—it's fun to peek at the mansions behind the hedges.

All in all, the popularity of this area is well deserved, and though you'll encounter annoying traffic not only driving out from the city but clogging the streets of the shopping centers after you arrive, this remains a prime summer destination.

The Hamptons officially begin with Westhampton, which is considerably closer to the city than the rest, but that proximity seems its only advantage. It is by far the most built up of the towns, with houses and condominiums lining the beach road.

Adjoining Westhampton Beach, however, is Quogue, a quiet village that is almost all gracious private homes, one of them an inn worth noting. The Inn at Quogue was taken over a few years back by one of the owners of New York's Summerhouse Restaurant and done over into an informal, breezy place with airy dotted Swiss curtains, old-fashioned furniture, and a breakfast room overlooking a garden of wildflowers. It is easy to feel at home here—and it is less than a mile to the very private town beach. Mark this one down as a sleeper.

Southampton was discovered long ago—even earlier than you might have guessed. The marker at Conscience Point off North Sea Road bears a plaque reading, NEAR THIS SPOT IN JUNE 1640 LANDED THE COLONISTS FROM LYNN, MASS., WHO FOUNDED SOUTHAMPTON, THE FIRST ENGLISH SETTLEMENT IN THE STATE OF NEW YORK.

Visit the Old Halsey House here and you'll be entering the oldest frame house in the state. The Southampton Historical Museum offers relics even older, all the way back to Indian days—not to mention a whaling captain's living room, a Colonial bedroom, a one-room schoolhouse, a country store, a carpenter's shop, and exhibits of early farm equipment. The restored Silversmith Shop on Main first opened about 1750.

Many tourists overlook all the history, preferring instead to head for Job's Lane to look at the men's velvet slippers and plaid pants in the windows of Shep Miller's or the flowery print dresses at Lily Pulitzer's, or the fashions both staid and strictly kicky in boutiques along the way. The antique shops on Job's Lane don't deal in junktique—if you don't believe it, just check the price tags.

While you're on Job's Lane, don't get so carried away with window shopping that you miss the Parrish Art Museum. The changing exhibits are well worth a look.

Southampton has long been a favorite wateringhole for society, and its mansions are legendary. Best roads for seeing them are parallel to the ocean on Meadow Lane (also the site of the handsome town beach) and Gin Lane, and on intersecting streets such as Halsey Neck, Cooper's Neck, and First Neck Lanes. Wait until you see the size of these shingled "cottages"—and the cars in the driveway. In addition to the sports cars that seem universal, many people own classic cars that they keep almost shiny enough to qualify for the antique auto museum in town. (The museum, incidentally, trots out its cars for a run every Fourth of July, giving Southampton one of the more unusual Independence Day parades.)

If you want to stay in Southampton and share that inviting public beach, the Village Latch Inn on Hill Street puts you within walking distance. Otherwise, it's motel time outside of town.

Driving farther east on Route 27 you'll pass through appealing small villages such as Water Mill (named for its windmill) and Bridgehampton, each with many shops for later exploring, and into East Hampton, where you could well be driving into another era. The approach as you turn left onto Main Street is pure Colonial, handsome white houses facing a green and a narrow pond that was a cattle wateringhole for early settlers and is a gathering spot for ducks today. The first stretch of Main Street is labeled Woods Lane, probably because it once ran through a forest.

East Hampton is another settlement founded more than three centuries ago, and in this case many descendants of the original families remain. Most of the older homes have been declared historic landmarks, and this town would make interesting strolling even if it were landlocked.

Almost every old home has a story to tell. On the west side of the pond, the second house from the *V* where Woods Lane turns into Main Street is The Studio, the home of noted watercolorist Thomas Moran. Two doors down at 217 is the home that was summer White House for President John Tyler. Across the green is the South End Burying Ground, and on James Lane, a short street bordering the eastern edge of the cemetery, are some of the oldest homes in town. Among them are Winthrop Gardiners' saltbox, Mill Cottage, and Home Sweet Home, a 1750 home named for its owner John Howard Payne, who wrote the song of the same title. It is open to visitors. Mulford Farmhouse next door, built in the 1650s, is the oldest of all the homes and was a working farm until the late 1940s.

Back on Main Street is Guild Hall, art museum and home of the John Drew summer theater and cultural center of East Hampton. Across the way is the town library and next door, Clinton Academy, the first chartered secondary school in New York state. It is currently home to the East Hampton Historical Society, which holds exhibits and lectures there regularly. Next is Towne House, a tiny 1730 structure that has been both school house and town hall and is currently being restored.

Hook Mill at the end of town is very much a landmark, and tours of the wind-powered grinding mill, which is still in working order, are a favorite with children. Hook Mill Burying Ground is even older than the South End cemetery, and it is not unusual to see people taking rubbings of the stones, which date back to 1650.

The East Hampton Chamber of Commerce, in a parking lot behind Main Street near the corner of Newtown Lane (paths go back from both) has free walking guides to the village and lots of other printed information. Shops in town begin on Main and continue down Newtown. Some are interesting, but as a whole are not in a league with Southampton's.

The beach in East Hampton is located at the end of Ocean Avenue, a right turn south at a blinker as you approach town. Lily Pond Lane, which runs west off Ocean Avenue, is this town's mansion row.

For your own weekend home there are some very appealing inns back on Main Street. The Maidstone Arms, across from the green, is sunny and simple with a Victorian feel and lots of wicker. 1770 House lives up to its name with Colonial decor, wide-planked floors, antiques, and canopy beds. Across the street, the Hunting Inn, which dates back to 1751, is also Colonial, though the accommodations are secondary to the restaurant downstairs, an outpost of New York's classy The Palm.

Farther east is Amagansett, which is really a Hampton in all but name. More boutiques and shopping complexes seem to spring up here every year, changing the face of what used to be a small charming town with Colonial flavor diluted only by the modernistic beachhouses near the shore. They haven't overrun the place yet; there are still enough saltbox homes, Colonial shutters, and geranium boxes to make the town wonderfully appealing, even if the famous once-authentic farmer's market has succumbed to commercialism.

All the new shops do make for interesting browsing, and Balasses House, an old standby on Main Street, has beautiful English country antiques. If you need other diversions there is a little marine museum on Bluff Road, as well as an historical museum known as Miss Amelia's cottage, with excellent period furniture, particularly clocks and other pieces made by the Dominy family, well-known Colonial craftsmen of East Hampton.

Amagansett has several town beaches. One of them, Coast Guard Beach, is popular singles territory, sometimes called "Asparagus Beach" for all the bodies standing around.

One of the most appealing places to stay in the whole area is in Amagansett. Just off Main, the Mill Garth is a 100-year-old main house with another half dozen or so studios and apartments winding around a complex of lawns and gardens, all antique-filled and offering charm as well as privacy. It is only half a mile to the beach, but if you're feeling lazy, they will lend you a bike or provide parking passes.

Hamptons weekends can't be run by schedules. Both East Hampton and Southampton can easily take half a day just for sightseeing, but if the weather is right the beach and the ocean may be the only sights you care to see.

Not only is Amagansett pleasant to visit, but Water Mill and Bridgehampton also have many interesting specialty shops worth a stop, particularly for the folk art, Appalachian art, and quilts in Bridgehampton. All of Route 27, in fact, offers galleries and shops that will tempt you to pull off the road for a bit.

If you want tennis, golf, or fishing, all are available; just ask at your lodging for the most convenient spots. And you can take a trip to Montauk, or Sag Harbor, or Shelter Island.

There's enough to keep you busy here for many a day—and many a weekend. Why do you think all those people spend the summer here?

Hamptons Area Code: 516

DRIVING DIRECTIONS   Long Island Expressway to exit 70, right for three miles to Sunrise Highway (Route 27) eastbound. Follow 27 to Southampton; it continues to be the only main route to the end of the island.

Total distance to Southampton: 100 miles.

BY PUBLIC TRANSPORTATION   Long Island Railroad has regular service to the Hamptons. Hampton Jitney provides autobus service from Manhattan; call (212) 537-3008 for information. It is perfectly possible to settle into any one town and get around without a car; there is also intertown service via Hampton Jitney, which can be hailed anywhere along Montauk Highway.

ACCOMMODATIONS   Many places have three-day minimums in summer • *The Inn at Quogue,* Quogue, 288-1300; $$$–$$$$ • *The Village Latch Inn,* 101 Hill, Southampton, 283-2160; $$–$$$ with breakfast • *The Maidstone Arms,* 207 Main Street, East Hampton, 324-5006; $$–$$$ • *1770 House,* 143 Main Street, East Hampton, 324-1770; $$$–$$$$ with continental breakfast • *Hunting Inn,* 94 Main Street, East Hampton, 324-0410; $$–$$$ • *East Hampton House,* Montauk Highway, East Hampton, 324-4300; a particularly nice motel with many kitchenettes; advance reservations for seven days minimum, but it's worth a call for last minute weekend accommodations; $$–$$$$ • *The Mill Garth,* Windmill Lane, Amagansett, 267-3757; $$–$$$$.

DINING   *The Inn at Quogue* (see above), fresh caught seafood, fresh grown vegetables; $$ • *John Duck, Jr.,* North Main Street, Southampton, 283-0311, no atmosphere, just delicious homestyle roast duckling and lots of it; $$–$$$ • *Herb McCarthy's,* more because it's a town landmark than for the food; $$–$$$ • *Carol's,* 419 North Highway (Route 27), Southampton, 283-5001, currently chic, with good food; $$–$$$ • *The Palm* (see Hunting Inn above), steaks and lobster— the best of everything with outrageous prices to match; $$$–$$$$ • *Georgettes,* Three Mile Harbor Road, East Hampton, 324-9776, nouvelle cuisine; $$–$$$ • *Leif Hope's Laundry,* 31 Race Lane, East Hampton, 324-3199, brick walls, skylights, mixed menu, popular; $$–$$$ • *Gordon's,* Main Street, Amagansett, 324-9793, a longtime local favorite; $$–$$$ • *Gosman's Dock,* Montauk, a tradition for lobster; no reservations and long waits but worth it; $$–$$$.

SIGHTSEEING   *Southampton Historical Museum,* 17 Meeting House Lane off Main Street. Hours: mid-June to September, 11 A.M. to 5 P.M.; Sunday 2 to 5 P.M. Adults $1, children 25¢ • *Parrish Art Museum,* 25 Job's Lane, Southampton, 283-2118. Hours: Tuesday to Saturday, 10 A.M. to 5 P.M.; Sunday 2 to 5 P.M. Free • *Halsey Homestead,* South Main Street, Southampton, 283-3527. Hours: mid-June to mid-September, 11 A.M. to 4:30 P.M.; Sunday 2 to 4:30 P.M. Adults 75¢, children 25¢ • *Long Island Automotive Museum,* Route 27, Southampton, 283-1880. Hours: daily, mid-June to Labor Day, 9 A.M. to 5 P.M.; early June and September, Saturday and Sunday. Adults $2, children $1 • *Olde Mill,* Route 27, Water Mill, 726-4594. Hours: mid-June to September, Monday, Wednesday, Saturday, 10 A.M. to 4 P.M.; Sunday, 1 to 4 P.M. Donation • *Home Sweet Home House and Windmill,* 14 James Lane, East Hampton, 324-0713. Hours: July to Labor Day, Monday to Saturday, 10 A.M. to 4 P.M.; Sunday 2 to 4 P.M. Adults $1, children 50¢ • *Historic Mulford House,* James Lane, East

Hampton, 324-6850. Hours: late June to mid-September, Thursday to Saturday, 11 A.M. to 4 P.M.; Sunday 2 to 4 P.M. Adults $1, children 50¢ • *Hook Mill,* 36 North Main Street, East Hampton, 324-0173. Hours: daily, late June to Labor Day, 10 A.M. to 5 P.M. Adults $1, children under age 12 50¢ • *Guild Hall,* 158 Main Street, East Hampton, 324-0806. Hours: June to October, Monday to Saturday, 10 A.M. to 5 P.M.; Sunday 2 to 5 P.M. Art exhibits free. Check for current summer theater schedule at John Drew Theater, 324-4050 • *Clinton Academy,* 151 Main Street, 324-6850. Hours: late June to September, Tuesday to Sunday, 1 to 6 P.M. Donation • *Miss Amelia's Cottage,* Main Street, Amagansett, 267-3020. Hours: Tuesday to Sunday, 1 to 4 P.M. • *East Hampton Town Marine Museum,* Bluff Road, Amagansett, 267-6544. Hours: July to Labor Day, Tuesday to Sunday, 10:30 A.M. to 5 P.M. Weekends, June through September, adults $1, children 50¢.

FOR FURTHER INFORMATION Contact the Southampton Chamber of Commerce, 79 Main Street, Southampton, NY 11968, 283-0402 • East Hampton Chamber of Commerce, 74 Park Place, East Hampton, NY 11937, 324-0362.

Long Island Beaches
Part 2: Unaffected Montauk

Boutiques and babies don't always mix. Small children and country inns aren't always comfortable with each other. And people who love wide open seascapes and shell searching often hate tourist-clogged sidewalks and busy town beaches.

That's why many people prefer to keep right on going when they get to the Hamptons. Instead of heading for the action, they want to get away from it on the easternmost end of Long Island.

The scene changes dramatically on Route 27 as soon as you pass the outer limits of Amagansett. No more shops. After a while, no more clumps of beachhouses. At Napeague there is a small inn and a couple of seaside motel-type mini-resorts (desirable places, by the way, but usually available only by the week during the peak season). And then there is nothing except beach grass and dunes and the unmistakable scent of the sea growing stronger all the time.

Bear right onto Old Montauk Highway and you'll see the sea, Hither Hills State Park, and a few exceptional places for beach lovers. Gurney's Inn is the oldest, best known, and most luxurious. Panoramic

View, terraced up a steep hillside, offers dramatic sea views, private beach and pool, simpler accommodations, and a much smaller tab. Wave Crest is another nearby spot for wave watching. All of these provide comfort and extraordinary private powdery beaches. Leave the small groups clustered in front of each hotel, and in either direction, there's open space for walking, jogging, or shelling as far as the eye can see and the feet can carry you.

Children are in the definite minority here—very young ones, at least. They're more likely to be found farther on in Montauk, where about a dozen unpretentious motels are grouped near the ocean, none of them offering much in the way of charm but all providing something equally hard to come by—direct access to the beach. There couldn't be a better place for young families. It's easy for one parent to take a little walk back to put the baby in for a nap while the other stays on the beach with the rest of the family. Many of these motels offer refrigerators and/or cooking facilities, helping to save on restaurant bills. And if there are children too old to want to sit around with parents in the evening but too young to drive, Montauk offers a special bonus. The beach (and the beach motels) are only a block off the Main Street of town, meaning that it's an easy walk to the local movie or mini-golf course or pinball parlor.

Don't look for Hamptons chic in Montauk. This is a fisherman's town, and though a few new shops have begun to open, until very recently the best place in town to find anything including clothes was White's Drug Store. There are eating places for breakfast and dinner in town, a pizza palace; and a handful of stores and one interesting art gallery, the Bittersweet Gallery, which stocks crafts and paintings (lots of nauticals) by Long Island artists.

So what do you do in Montauk when you're not on the beach? Get back to nature in other ways. Go hiking or biking on dirt roads beside ocean, sound, lake, and fresh ponds. Watch for birds—you're in the crossroads of a major migratory pattern. Go berrypicking for shadberries, blackberries, or blueberries—or, in September, for beach plums and wild grapes. Go horseback riding on the beach or sign up for lessons in surf sailing, scuba diving, or ballooning.

There are many ways to go out to sea in Montauk. You can sign on for the deep-sea fishing trips that go out of the harbor daily, or sign up for a 2½-hour sail on the *Delta Lady,* a 65-foot sailing schooner. You can take a day-long whale-watching expedition aboard the *Okeanos,* a working scientific research boat. Or you can take the ferry to Block Island, just a 1½-hour cruise away.

Whether you get on a boat or not, you'll surely want to watch them returning to the docks with the day's fresh catch of fish. One prize spot for viewing is Gosman's Dock, where fresh fish is available in the fish store as well as in the restaurant, one of the most popular places on all the island.

Gosman's lobsters are legendary; there is often at least an hour's wait for a table on weekend evenings. There are no reservations; you'll just have to wait your turn, keeping occupied with a drink from the bar and the activity of the boats around you. If you don't want to wait, there is a clam bar and a take-out where you can get "lobster in the rough" to eat at picnic tables nearby. If not as pleasant as the restaurant, it is, at least, cheaper. (The crowds at Gosman's, incidentally, have inspired the only shops in town that might qualify as touristy—all right at the dock.)

The other "don't-miss" attraction in Montauk is its lighthouse, which has stood on the very eastern tip of the island since 1795. Kids absolutely love clambering up the rocks here, and grown-ups with cameras go crazy looking for the best angle on the cliff-top view.

If you find yourself stuck indoors with kids in the rain, there are just enough diversions within driving distance to save the day. Two standbys are the whaling museum in Sag Harbor and East Hampton's windmill. If the children are old enough to appreciate a bit of history, you can also visit the museums in the various Hamptons towns.

Are the motels in Montauk tacky? Does the town lack class? Some Hamptons lovers might say so, but you couldn't prove it by the many people who swear by the place and can't wait to get back.

Montauk Area Code: 516

DRIVING DIRECTIONS   Follow directions to Southampton, continue east on Route 27 to Montauk.
Total distance: 120 miles.

BY PUBLIC TRANSPORTATION   Once again, Long Island Railroad and Hampton Jitney, limited local bus service. Montauk motels are right in the town.

ACCOMMODATIONS   Expect minimum-stay requirements in season ● *Gurney's Inn,* Old Montauk Highway, 668-2345; $$$$ MAP ● *Panoramic View,* Old Montauk Highway, 668-3000; with kitchenettes, terraces; $$–$$$ ● *Wave Crest,* Edgemere Road, 668-2872; several sections—one on old Montauk Highway is the most private and nicest, others are in town; all share pool and tennis court; $$–$$$ ● *Royal Atlantic Motel,* South Edgemere Street, 668-5103; pool, some kitchenettes; $$–$$$ • *Ocean Beach Motel,* Box 728, 668-5790, refrigerators in rooms; $$–$$$ • *The Ocean Surf,* South Emerson Avenue, 668-3332; $$–$$$ with some efficiencies • *The Imperial,* Montauk, 668-3400; pool, playground, barbecue grills, some efficiencies; $$–$$$ • Two places opposite The Inn at Napeague, worth noting in case of last-minute weekend availabilities: *Driftwood,* Route 27, 668-5744; some efficiencies, tennis on premises, golf privileges; $$$ • *Sea Crest,* Route 27, 267-3159; efficiencies, lighted tennis, pool; $$–$$$.

DINING   *The Inn at Napeague,* Route 27, 267-8103, owner/chef formerly at New York's Quo Vadis; $$ • *Gurney's Inn* (see above); $$–$$$ • *Gosman's Dock,* at the end of the docks, 668-5330; $$–$$$ • *Shagwong Restaurant,* Main Street, 669-3050, an old favorite, low on atmosphere, but good food; $$ • *Fish,* Main Street, 668-9300; $$ • *Allie's,* Main Street, for breakfast and snacks, Belgian waffles; $ • *Jody's Country Kitchen,* 688-9602, breakfast through dinner, good homemade food; $.

SIGHTSEEING AND ACTIVITIES   *Bicycle rentals:* Pfunds Hardware Store, Main Street, 668-2456 • *Delta Lady,* 688-2145, 65-foot sailing schooner from Tuma's Dock. Hours: daily, 10 A.M., 1 and 4 P.M. 2½-hour ride $15 • *Viking Fishing Fleet,* 668-5700; fishing trips from Montauk Harbor, half and whole days, night fishing; phone for current rates and hours • *Hidden Echos Ranch,* Route 27 opposite Ditch Plains Road, 668-5453; horseback riding. Hours: 9 A.M. to 6 P.M., night rides to beach; phone for current rates • *The Dive,* Montauk Plaza, 668-3330, scuba and skin-diving center; phone for details • *Up, Up & Away Balloon Co.,* Box 5, Montauk, instruction and rides; write for info • *Okeanos Whale Watching Cruises,* P.O. Box 361, Jamesport, 728-4522. Hours: daily from Montauk Marine Basin at 10 A.M.; returning approximately at 4 P.M. Adults $20; children under 13, $15. Reservations required two weeks in advance • *Montauk Point State Park,* end of Route 27, 668-2461, parking $1.50.

FOR FURTHER INFORMATION   Contact the Montauk Chamber of Commerce, Box cc, Montauk, NY 11954, 668-2428.

Shipping Out in New London

The ship is caught midstream, its decks aflame, the crew in peril. But never fear. To the rescue comes the U.S. Coast Guard, that relatively unheralded seagoing service whose mission since 1790 has been the saving of lives and property at sea.

On the first Saturday in August each year the Coast Guard has its day, showing off for the public the kind of colorful rescue exploits that often go unseen, and doing it in a blaze of fireworks, music, and watery daring.

The annual Coast Guard Day is a tritown celebration anchored in New London, home of the Coast Guard Academy, and shared by the neighboring nautical centers of Groton and Mystic. The actual events vary each year, but spectators on New London's City Pier usually can expect to see firsthand a dramatic Coast Guard air and sea rescue of the crew of a burning ship on the Thames River.

There are diving demonstrations and other kinds of displays, and boats to board across the river in Groton and 10 miles away in Mystic, but most of the hoopla remains in New London. Music here often begins on Friday night, with a dancing and dining moonlight ferry cruise. Bands play at various spots Saturday, and often the 65-piece Coast Guard Band is at hand near the pier on Saturday night as a prelude to the big fireworks display off a barge in the river. Check the New London Chamber of Commerce for an accurate schedule of this year's activity.

Coast Guard Day will offer many festive one-of-a-kind events, but it will give only the smallest sampling of the pleasures available in this salty section of the Connecticut shore. Together, New London, Groton, and Mystic cover the historic waterfront, comprising, respectively, a one-time whaling center, the nation's submarine capital, and the 17-acre living museum at Mystic Seaport, which is the largest maritime complex in the world. Also, all offer a scenic, sandy shoreline along Long Island Sound.

New London is a city fighting hard to reclaim some of its illustrious past as a wealthy whaling outpost. The New London Historic Walking Tour, posted prominently along the main street, a restored pedestrians-only mall known as Captain's Walk, begins with the city's pride, its beautifully restored nineteenth-century train station and includes the restored Nathan Hale schoolhouse. It moves on to the 1930s Custom House, whose front door was once part of the frigate *Constitution,* and then to the four imposing, columned whaling merchants' mansions now known as Whale Oil Row. One of the houses is the Tale of the Whale Museum, housing relics of the whaling era, including a fully equipped whaleboat. The compact tour covers other historic homes, including the Shaw Mansion, now the headquarters and museum of the local historical society.

As you proceed south from Whale Oil Row, Hempstead Street has several fine old homes, including one of Connecticut's oldest, Hempstead House, a 1637 homestead, where the family of the original owners remained until 1937. The only house remaining that escaped burning by British troops in New London in 1781, it is open to the public for a look into the past every afternoon.

Head back to town via Starr Street, where the old homes have been restored to form a charming contemporary neighborhood. Back near the waterfront, Bank Street is another area being refurbished store by store, adding atmosphere and lots of nightlife to the city with lively cafés like Pier I and Anna Christie.

Drive out toward Ocean Beach Park to Pequot Avenue and you'll find Monte Cristo Cottage at number 325, the boyhood home of *Anna Christie*'s author, playwright Eugene O'Neill. The Victorian home is being restored, and tours are by appointment. For information, call the Eugene O'Neill Theater Center in Waterford. Also, check to see whether the center's annual summer series of readings by promising new playwrights is in session.

New Yorkers may find a familiar look to New London's Ocean Beach, done by the designer of Jones Beach. There's a mile-long boardwalk, rides, a pool, miniature golf, and a wide beach on the sound.

A few miles west of New London in Waterford on a breezy promontory is the luxurious summer estate of Edward and Mary Harkness, 27 buildings on 235 acres including spacious lawns, formal Italian gardens, and 200-year-old trees. Now known as Harkness Park, about half the area is open to summer visitors, including the gardens, the mansion, a bird painting exhibit, and a beach for strolling (no swimming allowed).

Back on the other side of I-95 in New London on Mohegan Avenue is the Coast Guard Academy, a cluster of handsome, traditional red brick buildings on 100 acres high above the Thames. It has inviting grounds, a well-endowed museum, and a multimedia center at river's edge, where you can learn about the service's glory days from the era of George Washington to the present. There's a bonus when the *Eagle* is in port. Each summer the 295-foot square rigger, which led the Bicentennial parade of tall ships, is a magnificent floating classroom for cadets.

Across from the Academy on Mohegan Avenue is the campus of Connecticut College and the Lyman Allyn Museum, named in memory of a famous sea captain. It contains art, antiques, and a wonderful collection of dollhouses, dolls, and toys.

Also on the campus is the Connecticut Arboretum, a particularly fine nature preserve, which offers 415 acres with hiking trails.

Across the Thames at Groton, the U.S. Navy Submarine Base, the largest in the world, provides still another perspective on America's maritime traditions. The submarine has a longer history in the New London area than most visitors realize. The first submarine, *"The Turtle,"* invented by David Bushnell of nearby Saybrook, was launched in 1776. Although an attempt to sink a British flagship failed, the seven-and-half foot vessel paved the way for today's underwater fleet.

The Submarine Memorial on Thames Street in Groton centers around the U.S.S. *Croaker,* a veteran World War II sub open to visitors. You can inspect the torpedo and control rooms, learn about diving, surfacing, and maneuvering, and tour the crew's less-than-spacious quarters.

From the deck of the *Croaker,* you can see today's nuclear submarines being built at the Electric Boat yards nearby.

Groton has its own share of nautical history. Up the hill from the *Croaker* is Fort Griswold State Park, where colonial troops were massacred by Benedict Arnold's British forces in 1781. An obelisk standing 127-feet high marks the spot, and the fort still offers the same commanding view of the river that made it ideal as a Civil War lookout for British ships.

Monument House nearby holds the D.A.R. Collection of both Revolutionary and Civil War memorabilia. The Ebenezer Avery House is furnished with household accoutrements from Colonial times. It was moved from its original site on Thames Street, but it is the very same building in which the wounded from the battle were brought to be treated.

Groton is not a city that wears its history well, but the Groton Bank Historical Association publishes an interesting pamphlet, which sells for one dollar and can be found in local stores. It tells the long story of the town, and it indicates excellent examples of the two-and-a-half centuries of architecture from the Colonial era through whaling days, places easy to miss on your own. It begins with the oldest home in town, the Joseph Latham House on Meridian Street, and guides you on to Thames and Broad streets.

All of this sightseeing is hardly going to leave enough time to do justice to Mystic Seaport, one of America's prime maritime attractions. There are the majestic sailing vessels to board; a whole nineteenth-century village with working shops to explore; buildings filled with rare boats, ship's models, figureheads, scrimshaw, and art; the chance to watch boats being built; and continuing demonstrations of arts such as sail setting, ropework, oystering, or fireplace cooking. It might be well to save Mystic for a weekend of its own or tack an extra day onto your present tour.

Note that each of these sea-centered communities offers ample opportunity to actually get out on the water. In New London, ferries ply back and forth to Fishers Island, Block Island, and Orient Point. The *Mystic Belle,* a pint-sized replica of a Mississippi paddle-wheeler, tours the Thames Harbor from Groton. Visitors to Mystic Seaport can have a half-hour day cruise on the jaunty little coal-powered steamboat *Sabino* or a 90-minute river cruise at night, often with music.

And should all that nautical atmosphere move you to want to go farther out to sea, you can ship out on the *Mystic Whaler,* a 100-foot replica of the old two-masted nineteenth-century schooners that sails out of Mystic regularly for one-, two- or five-day windjammer cruises.

New London Area Code: 203

DRIVING INSTRUCTIONS I-95 to exit 83, New London, exit 85 for Groton.
   Total distance: about 125 miles.

BY PUBLIC TRANSPORTATION Amtrak has trains to New London from Grand Central, but it's hard to get beyond the center of town without a car.

ACCOMMODATIONS Motels only: *Holiday Inn,* North Frontage Road, New London, 442-0631; $ • *Lamplighter,* I-95, exit 81, Waterford, 442-7227; $ • *Holiday Inn,* Bridge Street, Groton, 445-8141; $ • *On the Thames Motel-Boatel* (on the river in the middle of town), 193 Thames Street, Groton, 445-8111; $.

DINING *Ye Old Tavern,* 345 Bank Street, New London, 442-0353, saloon atmosphere; $$ (closed Sundays) • *Anthony's Steam Carriage,* in restored Union Station, New London, 443-8316; $–$$ • *Ship's Wheel,* Captain's Walk, New London, 442-9433; $–$$ • *The Butterfly,* 223 Thames, Groton, 445-7238; $ (a sleeper, plain but with riverside deck, inexpensive dinner specials; also sourdough and oatmeal pancakes and waffles, lots of omelets for breakfast, crepes for lunch) $2.75–$3.95.

SIGHTSEEING   *Coast Guard Day,* write or call Chamber of Commerce of Southeastern Connecticut, 105 Huntington Street, New London, CT 06320, 443-8332 ● *Tale of the Whale Museum,* 3 Whale Oil Row, New London, 442-8191. Hours: daily except Monday, 1 to 5 P.M. Adults 50¢, children under age 16 35¢ ● *Shaw Mansion,* 11 Blinman Street, New London, 443-1209. Hours: Tuesday to Saturday, 1 to 4 P.M. Adults $1, children 50¢ ● *Nathan Hale Schoolhouse,* Captain's Walk next to City Hall, New London, 447-3106. Hours: Memorial Day to Labor Day, Monday to Friday, 10 A.M. to 3 P.M. Free ● *Hempstead House,* 11 Hempstead Street, New London, 443-7949. Hours: Tuesday to Saturday, 1 to 5 P.M.; Sunday 2 to 5 P.M. Free ● *Ocean Beach Park,* Ocean Avenue, New London, 447-3031. Hours: daily, 9 A.M. to 1 A.M. Adults 50¢, children 20¢. Parking $1, Sunday $2 ● *U.S. Coast Guard Academy,* Mohegan Avenue, New London, 444-8270. Hours: daily, 9 A.M. to sunset. Free ● *Harkness Memorial State Park,* Route 213, Waterford, 443-5724. Hours: mansion open daily, Memorial Day to Labor Day, 10 A.M. to 5 P.M.; grounds open all year. Admission $1 ● *Connecticut Arboretum,* Connecticut College Campus, New London, 447-7700. Hours: daily during daylight. Free ● *Lyman Allyn Museum,* 625 Williams Street (near college), New London, 443-2545. Hours: Tuesday to Saturday, 1 to 5 P.M.; Sunday, 2 to 5 P.M. Free ● *U.S.S. CROAKER,* 359 Thames Street, Groton, 448-1616. Hours: daily, 9 A.M. to 5 P.M.; offseason, 9 A.M. to 3 P.M. Adults $2, children $1 ● *Fort Griswold State Park,* Monument and Park avenues, Groton, 445-1729. Hours: daily, Memorial Day to Columbus Day, 9 A.M. to 5 P.M. Free ● *Ebenezer Avery House,* Fort Griswold, Groton, 446-9257. Hours: June to August, Friday to Sunday, 2 to 4 P.M. Free ● *Mystic Seaport,* Route 27, Mystic, 536-2631. Hours: daily, 9 A.M. to 5 P.M. Adults $7.50, children age 6–12 $3.75.

Gingerbread by the Sea in Cape May

With more than 600 prize gingerbread Victorian houses within 2.2 square miles, how do you ever decide which ones deserve special status? In historic Cape May, New Jersey, they didn't even try. They simply declared the whole town a national landmark.

Hop aboard the sightseeing trolley or join the weekly Sunday morning walking tour of the nation's oldest seashore resort and you'll soon know why. While erosion has diminished Cape May's once lavish beaches, fire has leveled the legendary nineteenth-century hotels that hosted presidents and royalty, and the usual quota of innocuous resort motels and eateries have sprung up around the beach, nothing has touched the treelined residential streets of old Cape May. They remain a serene world apart, a gracious enclave of pastel paint and lacy curlicues, mansard roofs and fish-scale shingles, ornate railings and columned porches, with widows' walks, cupolas, towers, and turrets looking out to sea.

Because of its unique heritage, the largest collection of Victorian homes in America, Cape May is a seaside retreat like no other—and possibly at its most appealing during the tail end of summer, after Labor Day. The water remains warm, there is more room for strolling on the beach promenade, and you have a better chance of getting reservations in the guesthouses in the historic district where you will sample the best of Victorian living.

If you get in early enough, try to make the 9 P.M. Friday-night film showing at the Welcome Center opposite the bandstand. Called "Victorian Capers," it is an excellent introduction to Cape May's fascinating and unusual history. The film shows again on Saturday night, but it's most helpful before you see the town.

You'll learn that the unusual concentration of homes of the 1880s results from a fire that all but destroyed the city in 1878. Before that date Cape May was the prime vacation spot on the east coast. It had attracted Colonial luminaries from Philadelphia as early as the 1770s, and in the years following local guesthouse and hotel registers included the names of seven U.S. presidents, including Andrew Jackson and Abraham Lincoln, as well as Henry Clay, Horace Greeley, actress Lily Langtrey, and composer John Philip Sousa. Huge old wooden hotels like the Mansion House, the Mount Vernon, and the United States had been vulnerable to fires all along, but the blaze of 1878 was so devastating that 30 acres of the town were laid bare by the flames.

Ironically, it was that disaster that prompted so many wealthy people, most from the Philadelphia area, to come in and build on the suddenly available tracts of land. They were further encouraged by the railroad, which offered a year's free transportation for anyone who would help recoup their tourist trade.

The homes that went up were smaller than Cape May's original structures but were even showier, products of an era when having money meant flaunting it in the form of elaborate exterior home decoration. The fancier the better seems to have been the Victorians' motto.

Trolley tours of the town run daytime and early evening daily, but you'll get a much better look at the architecture on the Sunday morning walking tour that leaves at 10 A.M. from the information booth at Washington and Ocean, the end of the stone-paved, gaslamp-lit pedestrian shopping mall. It takes you down streets like Ocean and Beach, Gurney and Stockton, Columbia and Howard, with an enthusiastic local resident to fill you in on who was who in the homes and hotels along the way. You'll learn how the Chalfonte Hotel on Howard Street, the only remaining survivor of the 1878 fire, once qualified for a local liquor license by counting "accommodations" such as linen closets and bathrooms as rooms; about the wife of a sea captain living near Howard and Ocean who confessed in her diary that she was afraid when her husband went to sea, leaving her to deal with the Indians and pirates who roamed the Cape; and about the socialite from Baltimore who came to the Columbia Hotel in the summer of 1917 to plan her coming-out party. Her name was Wallis Warfield, later known as the Duchess of Windsor.

Most of the homes are private residences, but you can get a feel for their interiors by visiting some of the guesthouses in the historic district. The acknowledged showplace in town is the Mainstay Inn, also known as the Victorian Mansion, once an elegant gambling club, still with its original 14-foot ceilings, tall mirrors, ornate plaster moldings, elaborate chandeliers, and cupola with an ocean view. The current young owners, Tom and Sue Carroll, have kept many of the original furnishings, and they offer tours and tea in the parlor (on the veranda, weather permitting) on Saturdays and Sundays at four.

Catty-corner from the Mainstay at the corner of Gurney is The Abbey, an 1869 Gothic villa that once belonged to coal baron John B. McCreary. It is furnished with tall carved walnut headboards, marble-topped dressers, and ornate lighting fixtures from its original era, and the first floor also can be toured at teatime on weekends. The second floor bedrooms have private baths; if you stay on the third floor you share the Tower Bath, big as a bedroom, with claw-foot tub, pedestal sink, brass fixtures, Oriental rug, and stained glass.

These two homes are the pick of the guesthouse accommodations, and two or three months ahead is none too soon for reservations. Some other pleasant inns are Victorian Rose, the Queen Victoria, The Brass Bed, and the Washington Inn. No rooms at the inns? You'll have to settle for a motel and teatime tours.

Cape May's beaches are a lot slimmer than they used to be, but there is still enough room for sunning and the promenade is perfect for walking or jogging with an ocean view. A 30-minute bike ride from town takes you to Cape May Point, where the Atlantic meets Delaware Bay and where you can sift through the sand for pieces of polished quartz known as Cape May diamonds. These have more sentimental than monetary value, but they are pretty and when polished can be set into jewelry souvenirs. Cape May Point State Park has a pleasant bird sanctuary and also one of the country's oldest lighthouses, dating back to 1744. The Point's Sunset Beach is the favored local spot for sunset watching.

Back in Cape May you can play tennis at the Cape May Tennis Club, next to the Physick Estate at 1048 Washington Street, and while you are in the neighborhood have a look at the elegant 1881 home being restored as a community center for concerts and films. The Cape May County Art League holds changing exhibits in the carriagehouse on the estate.

On Washington Mall you'll find three blocks of shops as well as sidewalk cafés, ice cream parlors, and a bookstore where you can pick up the Sunday papers. Just off the mall is the Pink House, an antique shop that is the ultimate in Victorian frills. It's the house you see most of the time when you see a photo of Cape May.

You'll hardly need any further diversions if the weather is right, but for cloudy days or a very worthwhile detour on the way home, don't overlook Wheaton Village, about an hour away in Millville, New Jersey. This relatively unknown attraction is a re-created Victorian Village on the site of a former glass factory. The 1888 factory has been restored and gives demonstrations of early glass-blowing techniques daily at 11 A.M., 1:30 P.M., and 3:30 P.M. The crafts arcade demonstrates nineteenth-century arts such as weaving, woodcarving, printing, and pottery making; and an old barn provides an agricultural history of South Jersey, with lots of waterfowl and farm animals to delight the kids. Young visitors also love the ¾-mile train trip around the lake in an old-fashioned train.

But the main attraction here is the Museum of Glass, one of the best collections of its kind anywhere, in an attractive building around a court that makes excellent use of its tall windows to highlight the glass displays. You'll view the first handblown bottles, used for drinks, strong and otherwise; goblets, pitchers, ornamental glass, medicine bottles, perfume and ink bottles, early lamps, pressed glass, cut glass, lead crystal, works of art by Tiffany, Art Nouveau glass, Art Deco glass—just about every kind of glassware ever made by hand or machine. You can buy glassware in the Village store and paperweights in a shop that has a most comprehensive collection of this art ranging in price from $3 to $3,000.

Wheaton Village is a surprise in this quiet, nontouristy farm area, and it is a fascinating look at another kind of 1880s—a perfect counterpoint to a weekend in Victorian Cape May.

Cape May Area Code: 609

DRIVING DIRECTIONS Take the Garden State Parkway to its last exit.

Total distance: 160 miles.

BY PUBLIC TRANSPORTATION Bus service via Transport of New Jersey from the New York Port Authority; for schedules and rates, phone (800) 772-2222.

ACCOMMODATIONS *Mainstay Inn,* 635 Columbia Avenue, 884-8690; $–$$ MAP • *The Abbey,* Columbia and Gurney streets, 884-4506; $–$$ with continental breakfast; tours and tea, Saturday, Sunday, 5 P.M. $2 • *The Brass Bed,* 719 Columbia Avenue, 884-8075; $–$$ • *Victorian Rose,* 715 Columbia Avenue, 884-2497; $–$$ • *Washington Inn,* Washington and Jefferson, 884-5697; $$ MAP • *Queen Victoria,* 102 Ocean Street, 884-8702; $–$$ with breakfast • *Chalfonte Hotel,* 301 Howard Street, 884-8934; last of the pre-1878 biggies, especially worth noting for spring work weekends when guests stay free in return for helping keep the place up; $–$$.

DINING *The Mad Batter,* 19 Jackson Street, 884-5970, nouvelle cuisine in a gingerbread house; $$, brunch $ • *Chalfonte Hotel* (see above), southern specialties; $$ • *The Lobster House,* Fisherman's Wharf, 884-8296, nautical decor and menu; $$–$$$ • *Watson's Merion Inn,* 106 Decatur Street, 884-8363, a local standby; $$–$$$.

SIGHTSEEING *Trolley Tours* from Rotary Bandstand in rear of Washington Street Mall. Hours: daily, every 45 minutes from 10 A.M. to 1 P.M. and 5 to 8 P.M. Adults $2.50, children $1.50 • *"Victorian Capers,"* the Cape May film at Welcome Center, Lafayette and Decatur streets. Hours: Friday, Saturday, 9 P.M. Admission $1 • *Walking Tours* from Mall Info Booth. Hours: Wednesday, Sunday, 10 A.M. Adults $3, children $1 • *Mainstay Inn* (see above), tea and tours. Hours: May to September, Saturday, Sunday, Tuesday, Thursday, 4 P.M. Adults $2, children under 12 $1 • *Physick Estate,* 1048 Washington Avenue, 884-5404. Tours: Tuesday to Sunday in summer season, 11 A.M. to 3:30 P.M. Adults $3, children $2 • *Wheaton Village,* Route 552, Millville (from Cape May take Route 47 north and west and watch for signs), 825-6800. Hours: daily, 10 A.M. to 5 P.M. Adults $3.50, students $2, children under 5 free; family of 2 adults and 2 children $7.50.

FOR FURTHER INFORMATION Contact the Cape May Chamber of Commerce, P.O. Box 365, Cape May Courthouse, Cape May, NJ 08210, 465-7181.

The Pick of the Past in Massachusetts

Brimfield. The founding fathers must have had a premonition when they named the place, because brim it does—on every field as well as sidewalk and front porch and any other place where there is room to set up a booth.

Brimfield, Massachusetts, a tiny town near the southern border of the state, is the flea-market capital of the world, the place where some 2,000 vendors congregate three times a year for a sale that must be seen to be believed. Trinkets, trunks, beer bottles, brass beds, Victorian sofas, vintage postcards—you'll be hard pressed to name any item that won't be for sale somewhere in Brimfield during these weekend gatherings held in May, July, and September each year.

The early September date usually brings the best weather for browsing and makes for a perfect end-of-summer weekend, for when you've made the rounds and gathered all the tea caddies and copper pots and other treasures that you can afford, you'll find yourself right next door to the sights of Sturbridge and perfectly positioned for a backroads meander home through some quaint and undiscovered Connecticut towns.

The gathering of the flea market clans began more than 20 years ago, brainchild of an entrepreneurial dealer named Gordon Reid, who hosted the first affairs at his farm called Antique Acres. Reid's daughters, Jill and Judith, run things now on the same spot, with some friendly competition from brother Gordon, Junior, who has his own place, Auction Acres, just down the road. Between them, the Reids corner the cream of the dealers who come to town, but they aren't quite the whole show. May's Antique Market usually has more than 300 sellers dealing exclusively in antiques and collectibles, and there is almost no end in sight to the variety of vendors who show up to take advantage of the crowds. Try to come early, when you can pick and choose with the least amount of elbowing. Whole busloads of shoppers tend to show up as the day goes on.

Sturbridge is only a five-minute drive east of Brimfield on Route 20. The best-known attraction here is Old Sturbridge Village, a 200-acre re-creation of a rural New England village of the early nineteenth century, and one of the outstanding developments of its kind. It's a wonderful place no matter what your age, beautifully landscaped and with more than 45 old buildings moved from their original sites to form a realistic town where costumed "residents" go about the everyday activities of an earlier time.

You'll see the farmer hoe his crops or plow the fields, watch spinners weave wool carded at the waterpowered carding mill, find the cobbler's daughter sewing shoe uppers at home, or a woman binding books in the printing office. You just might also be on hand when the farmer appears at the blacksmith shop with a broken hoe to be mended, or find a farm wife picking vegetables to cook over an open hearth for the noon meal, or encounter the members of the Ladies' Benevolent Society gathering for their regular meeting.

Every day there are fireplace cooking demonstrations and 15 different early nineteenth-century crafts in the making, fife and drum music at 12:45 and 3:15, and a musket-firing demonstration at 4 P.M. You can hop aboard the horse-drawn wagon anytime of day or tour the parsonage, with guided tours by the minister's family on any half hour in the mornings.

Sturbridge Village can take an hour or a whole day, depending on how much time you have to give it. Snacks and refreshment and whole meals are available on the premises and there are picnic tables if you want to bring your own fare.

There's a real village of Sturbridge to be explored as well, an authentic New England town with its original green and many historic buildings intact. If you can handle more shopping, here's a town full of shops, including Sturbridge Yankee Workshop, which makes faithful reproductions of Early American furniture designs, and The Seraph, which makes its reproduction designs to your order. There's Basket-ville and Quilters Quarters on Route 20, a secondhand bookstore and more antique stores on the green, and west on Route 20 you can watch for signs to Arnold Road and Hyland Orchards to pick up some of the new apple crop right off the trees.

If you do Brimfield on Saturday morning, the real Sturbridge in the afternoon, and Sturbridge Village on Sunday, your visit will be more than complete. But if you can tear yourself away with time left for exploring on the drive home, there are some detours along the Connecticut back roads that are delightful alternatives to turnpike driving. One of these is Woodstock, not the famous one but a country cousin slightly east on Route 169, a little town of stone walls and historic houses that dates back to 1686.

There is no Main Street as such here, just clusters of homes and occasional shops. About midway through the town on the crest of a long ridge is Woodstock Hill, where huge old trees shade handsome country houses spanning a couple of centuries in architecture. One that stands out is Roseland Cottage, a bright pink Gothic-style house built in 1864 for a wealthy gentleman named Bowen, a New York newspaper publisher, who installed the best of everything right down to a private bowling alley. The house and gardens and barns are open to visitors, owned and operated by the Society for the Preservation of New England Antiquities. Woodstock Academy is almost directly across the common and about a mile south on 169 is Quasset School, a little red-brick schoolhouse (open to the public in the summer months only). The Woodstock Fair each Labor Day weekend is a real old-fashioned country fair, worth keeping in mind for another time.

Woodstock offers its own small group of shops, including Sawmill Brook Workshop and Gallery with a resident woodworker, metal worker, and potter, and Woodstock Pottery, which specializes in reproductions of New England redware, slipware, and stoneware. Windy Acres has dried and silk flowers as well as fresh blooms, and the Christmas Barn and Shop has 12 rooms of gifts, candles, tree decorations, and fabric, and a very special little spot called The Little Mouse House filled with miniatures. A mile off 169 on Woodstock Road in East Woodstock there's another furniture showroom where handcrafted pieces in pine and oak are available.

Keep heading south on 169 for Brooklyn, another of those out-of-the-way discoveries off the tourist paths. Brooklyn's New England Center of Contemporary Arts is a charming rustic gallery with monthly new exhibits of work by recognized living artists. There is usually an artist in residence to talk about his or her work.

It's a gentle way back to the present, and if you connect with Route 205 below Brooklyn and then Route 14, you'll soon be back on Route 52, the Connecticut Turnpike, and speeding back to reality with all your new-found treasures from the past.

Brimfield-Sturbridge Area Code: 617

DRIVING DIRECTIONS   New England Thruway or Hutchinson River Parkway and Merritt Parkway to I-91 north; at Hartford cut off to I-86 and continue to Sturbridge, exit 3. Brimfield is about 7 miles west of Sturbridge on Route 20.

Total distance: about 160 miles.

ACCOMMODATIONS   *The Publick House,* Main Street (Route 131), Sturbridge, 347-3313; a charming 1771 inn; $$–$$$ ● If you like smaller inns, ask for the *Colonel Ebenezer Crafts Inn,* a restored 1786 home under Publick House management; $$$ ● *Treadway Sturbridge Motor Inn,* I-86 (service road), 347-3391; $–$$ ● *Sheraton Sturbridge Inn,* Route 20, 347-7393; indoor pool, tennis; $$ ● *Wildwood Inn,* 121 Church Street, Ware, 967-7798; antique-filled Victorian home, just five rooms, serving homemade breads and muffins for breakfast—20 minutes from Sturbridge and a bargain!; $ with continental breakfast.

DINING *Publick House* (see above); $$ ● *Salem Cross Inn,* West Brookfield (north of Sturbridge), 867-2345; restored 1705 inn, Yankee fare; $ ● *Bald Hill,* Route 169, South Woodstock, 974-2240; setting of plants and flowers; $–$$, Sunday brunch, $$.

SIGHTSEEING *Brimfield Flea Market,* Route 20, Brimfield; outdoor fair dates for 1982: May 7, 8; July 9, 10; September 10, 11; for later dates, phone Antique Acres, 245-3436. Admission $1 ● *Old Sturbridge Village,* Route 20, 347-3362. Hours: daily April to October, 9:30 A.M. to 4:30 P.M.; shorter hours off-season. Adults $7, children age 6–15 $3, under 6 free ● *Roseland Cottage,* Route 169, Woodstock, 928-4074. Hours: June to mid-October, Tuesday to Sunday, noon to 5 P.M. Adults $2; children under 12 $1.

Fall

Antiquing in Old Connecticut

Any experienced actress knows that a well-staged revival can be big box office. So, though June Havoc says that they called her the "Madwoman of the Crossing" when she began in 1978, she had high hopes when she set about to bring Cannon Crossing back to life.

This tiny crossroads village, bounded by the red and white Cannondale railroad station on one side and the Norwalk river on the other, was a serious victim of neglect at the time—paint peeling, roofs sagging, walls on the verge of tumbling down. Today it is as spiffy as a stage set and sometimes close to SRO on busy weekends, when visitors come to browse for antiques, watercolors, candles, fabrics, and other finds housed in the nostalgic nineteenth-century buildings.

A shopping expedition alone doesn't quite justify a whole weekend, of course, not even in such an unusual setting. But by good luck Cannon Crossing is located within easy reach of Ridgefield, a beautiful Connecticut town with a long history, a wide Main Street canopied by stately elms, three highly regarded restaurants, and a top country inn. And to cap things on Sunday, you can journey farther up Route 7 to Kent, another country charmer with a tiny jewel of a museum where tools become works of art.

Route 7, the road north of Norwalk that leads to the Crossing, used to be known as Antique Row for its abundance of shops. Shopping centers have taken their toll on the small dealers, but if you drive past some of the more mundane establishments, you'll still find a few choice stores in the Wilton area. Blackmar Antiques, for example, housed in a dark red 1700s farmhouse, puts the emphasis on American country accessories. A recent visit uncovered a bentwood high chair, Victorian wire planters, and an ornate wire birdcage, along with old advertising tins for collectors, ranging from under $10 for the smallest to $30 or more for oversized double-handled tobacco tins.

Just about everything is for sale at the Wayside Exchange, a high-quality consignment shop packed full of wooden and upholstered furniture, stacks of dishes and silver, trunks, books, copper pots, and endless miscellany. A stop here might net you a handpainted child's chest and matching mirror for less than $50, a tall grandfather's clock for $900, or a silvery dinner bell for $15.

Vallin Gallery is well known for its exquisite Oriental antiques.

Chests, tables, lamps, vases, porcelains, and scrolls may be found, all of high quality and priced accordingly.

Neighboring Toby House specializes in early porcelains, particularly English Wedgwood and lusterware. Figurines and paintings of dogs are another specialty. Small Limoges pieces can be had for under $25; Wedgwood starts at around $75.

When you spot the sign for Cannon Crossing, turn east and you'll soon have a whole cache of shops to explore, a mix of antiques and crafts. The formerly rundown general store is now Greenwillow Antiques, with trunks, cradles, and chairs lined up across the wide front porch. A watercolorist and multitalented candlemaker and tinsmith occupy part of the building, and there are also fabrics and quilts supplied by the tinsmith's wife.

Some other high spots are The Dovetail, featuring handmade reproductions of eighteenth-century furniture, Suzy and Carol Antiques with Victorian pieces, The Silver Shuttle for handloomed fabrics, and a tiny potter's shed nestled on the river's edge.

Behind all this is a barnlike structure with outbuildings containing a fireplace shop, more antiques, and McArthur's Smokehouse, where you can stock up on smoked hams and bacon, savory cheeses, and unusual jams and relishes.

Miss Havoc, incidentally, lives in the restored millhouse at the river's edge.

Take a break at the Old Schoolhouse Café and Riverside Garden, where the blackboards now bear menus instead of multiplication problems, and then it's on to Ridgefield. Serious collectors, however, will want to make one last stop before the turnoff on Route 35, at Tontine's Emporium, where there is room after room of choice eighteenth-century furniture, glassware, orientalia, jades and ivories, African sculpture, and an enormous collection of blue and white onion-pattern porcelain. Chairs are in the hundreds, Chippendale tallboys in the thousands, but there are a few less expensive items—glass hurricane lamps and the smallest of antique duck decoys.

There are more shops, too, on Route 33, an alternate country road connection to Ridgefield that takes you past many lovely Colonial homes. Ask for a complete listing of area antique shops if you want to do further shopping; it is available in most of the stores. You might take scenic Route 33 anyway, just to see the sights the next time you return to Route 7.

Either way will bring you onto Ridgefield's broad Main Street lined with mansions that were once the summer retreats of wealthy residents of New York. The principal bit of history on the street is Keeler Tavern, which was in operation from 1772 to 1907 and has been meticulously restored with authentic furnishings and accessories. Costumed hostesses will show you the sights, including the cannonball that remains imbedded in the shingles outside as a memento of a British attack during the Revolutionary War.

Down the street in a 1783 white house, The Aldrich Museum, is a surprise in this tradition-oriented town. Its three floors are filled with the latest in modern art, and there is an abstract sculpture garden in back.

Ridgefield's three highly regarded eating places, all Colonial and favoring continental fare, are The Inn and The Elms in town, and Stonehenge, a 1799 house off Route 7, where fresh trout from the collecting pool behind the waterfall is a house specialty.

The inn in town is the West Lane, and it is an elegant Victorian beauty, with mahogany paneling, designer fabrics, and working fireplaces in four of the 14 rooms. There are also half a dozen simple rooms in a separate building at Stonehenge.

If you are at West Lane, they'll let you sleep late and serve you breakfast until 11. Then it's Route 7 time again and the drive north to Kent, another pretty Colonial town, and its special treasure, the Sloane Stanley Museum. Artist Eric Sloane's outstanding collection of early American tools is housed here in a rustic barnlike building donated to the state by the Stanley Tool Works as a gift marking that company's 125th anniversary.

Sloane sees handcrafted tools as the nation's first works of art, and you'll likely agree when you see his artistic displays of wooden bowls, buckets and barrels; tiny hinges and huge plows; tools carefully crafted to follow the shape of the grain of the wood they are made from; and others, such as hoes, rakes, and handles, with shapes by nature that could not be improved upon. Some of the most interesting displays show how the tools were used. Many of the wooden pieces, elegantly carved and high polished, are unmistakably pieces of art.

Outside there is a small cabin reflecting the austere conditions of frontier life, and just below the museum is the ruins of an iron furnace. Partial restoration of the Kent Furnace is planned for the future.

You can see a totally different kind of craftsman at work, giving new twists to an old art, at Bull's Bridge Glass Works. Stephen Fellerman is usually present to demonstrate his award-winning glass-blowing techniques, creating art glass in flowing shapes and glowing colors. Iridescent lusterware is one of his specialties. Bull's Bridge, incidentally, is the name of the covered bridge just west of Route 7 across the Housatonic River.

Another pleasant distraction is a visit to Kent Falls State Park, also right on Route 7. An easy footpath leads to the top of the 200-foot falls, with the sights and sounds of the cascading water beside you all the way.

For Sunday dinner, Kent's best offering is the Fife and Drum, where you'll not only enjoy excellent food but entertainment by owner-pianist Dolph Trayman, a top musician.

Then it's back home to find the right places for all your newly acquired treasures, permanent souvenirs of the weekend.

Connecticut Area Code: 203

DRIVING DIRECTIONS   Hutchinson River Parkway to the Merritt Parkway, exit 40, Route 7 north. Cannondale and Cannon Crossing are a right turn clearly marked; Routes 33 or 35 lead to Ridgefield.
Total distance: 60 miles.

ACCOMMODATIONS   *West Lane Inn,* 22 West Lane, Ridgefield, 438-7323; $$$ with continental breakfast • *Stonehenge,* Route 7, Ridgefield, 438-6511; $$ with continental breakfast.

DINING   *Stonehenge* (see above); $$$, prix fixe dinner $23.50 • *The Inn* at Ridgefield, 20 West Lane, Ridgefield, 438-8282; $$$, prix fixe dinner $23.75 • *The Elms,* 500 Main Street, Ridgefield, 438-2541; $$–$$$ • *Fife and Drum,* Route 7, Kent, 927-3509; $$.

SIGHTSEEING   *Cannon Crossing,* Cannondale, off Route 7 north of Norwalk. Hours: shops open Tuesday through Sunday, 11 A.M. to 5 P.M. • *Keeler Tavern,* 132 Main Street, Ridgefield, 438-5485. Hours: Wednesday, Saturday, Sunday, 2 to 5 P.M. Adults $1, children 50¢ • *Aldrich Museum of Contemporary Art,* 258 Main Street, Ridgefield, 438-4519. Hours: Saturday, Sunday, Wednesday, 1 P.M. to 5 P.M. Adults $1, children 50¢.

Shakers and Scenery in the Berkshires

The trilevel round stone dairy barn is not only the most striking building at Hancock Shaker Village but also an apt symbol for the extraordinary people who once lived on this site.

The barn's shape is as ingenious as it is beautiful. Hay wagons could enter at the top, traverse the interior on a sturdy balcony, and dump the hay into the center to a middle level where as many as 54 head of cattle, radiating around the central manger in stanchions, could easily be fed by a single farmhand.

The Shakers had a way of finding the most functional way of doing things. The simple classic lines of their chairs and chests made more than a century ago were a precursor of modern design. They were the first to think of packaging garden seeds or herbal remedies, and such handy devices as the circular saw, the flat broom, and the common clothespin were their inventions. They made work easier for themselves as well as for an eager public who bought these products and thus helped support the community that thrived here for more than 100 years.

The order had all but vanished, done in perhaps by its own rule of celibacy, when the last surviving buildings were acquired in 1960 by a group resolved to create a memorial to the sect by restoring their unique village. It is a fascinating place to visit, conjuring a vivid picture of the life-style of a unique people.

Since the village is also near the heart of the Massachusetts Berkshires, it is an ideal autumn destination, allowing you to enjoy the year-round attractions of the area while the mountains are aflame with autumn color.

Of the 20 buildings that remain of the original 100 structures on 1,250 acres, 16 have been restored. The visitors' center outside the historical village sells tickets and will provide you with a pamphlet to lead you through the various buildings, where guides are posted to answer questions. Exhibits at the center and through the buildings will tell you about the community from its founding in 1790 to the opening of the restoration in 1960. You'll learn that the Shakers were actually an outgrowth of the Quakers, but took a different path, believing that Christ had already returned in the person of their founder Mother Ann Lee. Mother Ann decreed that religion was to be the dominant force in every area of their lives, requiring separation from the world, communal property, regular confession of sin, and celibacy. Though the sexes were separated, they were considered equal, a very advanced notion in the 1700s. In England they acquired the name Shaking Quakers for the ritual dances that were part of their worship, literally shaking off sin, and were eventually simply dubbed Shakers.

Mother Ann fled from England, where her ways were frowned upon, and came to America to preach her special gospel. Hancock was the third of the 18 communities the sect eventually established throughout the northeast and midwest. At the town's height in the 1830s there were six "families" in residence with a total membership of about 300.

At the restoration you'll visit the Garden House and Herb Garden, which is planted with materials that constituted some of the major crops of the Hancock herb and extract industry. One of the most important buildings is the Brick Dwelling that housed 100 and contained the communal dining room and meeting room used for weekday worship. The basement level contains the Great Cook Room and the appropriately named Good Room, where homemade baked goodies are still made and sold to visitors. Also in the building are typical sleeping quarters, a pharmacy, a nurse shop, the children's room, and the schoolroom.

In the Brethren's and Sisters' shops you'll see the chair, broom carpentry, cobbling, and clockmaking industries run by the men; and the dairy, medical department, and weaving rooms that were the women's province. The famous Shaker chairs are displayed in the Brethren's Shop, and reproductions are sold in the Ministry Shop.

A few other sights are the most recently completed structures, the Hired Men's Shop and the Printing Office, and the Wash House, Tan House, Laundry, Machine Shop, and Meeting House, all contributing to a realistic picture of what life was like for this devout band who left the world to build a successful self-sufficient community for themselves.

It takes at least half a day to really appreciate Hancock Shaker Village, and with lunch, you'll have just a couple of daylight hours left. Considering the season, you might choose to spend them enjoying the scenery from one of the two prime viewing points, Mount Greylock, the area's highest peak, to the northeast in North Adams, or the next highest point, Mount Everett, to the south in Mount Washington. Mount Washington, a sky-high village with just 100 residents, also gives you a view of Bash Bish Falls, which makes a spectacular 50-foot plunge.

All the inns and restaurants that serve music lovers in the summer are available in fall as well, so you'll have many pleasant choices for dinner and lodgings.

On Sunday you can see some of the sights that are often missed in the busy summer season in Lenox and Stockbridge, which were magnets for both the wealthy and the literary greats of the mid-1800s. Drive around Lenox to see the fine homes in the town that was referred to as the "inland Newport." Longfellow, Melville, Hawthorne, Henry Adams, and Edith Wharton were among the literati who were attracted by the area's beauty, along with several prominent artists.

Tanglewood's grounds with their magnificent gardens are open for strolling year round and here you'll see a re-creation of the little house where Hawthorne wrote many of his novels.

The traditional New England main street of Stockbridge was immortalized by one of the area artists, Norman Rockwell, whose paintings can be seen in the Old Corner House on Main Street, a restored eighteenth-century home that is now a museum dedicated to Rockwell.

There are other interesting sights on the historic street. The oldest house, the 1739 Mission House, was the home of John Sergeant, who was a missionary sent to convert the Indians. It is filled with fine Early American furnishings and has an authentic Colonial herb garden out back. The Merwin House, also known as Tranquility, was built around 1825 and is Victorian in its decor. There are two old churches on the street and the Village Cemetery is the resting place of Indian chiefs as well as early Colonial settlers.

The Children's Chimes, erected in 1878 on the site of the original Mission Church, were built by David Dudley Field as a memorial to his grandchildren; they serenade the town every evening at sunset from apple-blossom time until frost.

If you aren't staying there, do stop for a drink or a meal at the Red Lion. It's the most delightful Colonial inn, full of eighteenth-century furniture and Colonial pewter, with charm in every corner. If it is still warm enough, the courtyard is a particularly nice place for refreshments. On Main Street and in other courtyards just off it, you'll also find a few interesting shops and galleries for exploring.

Another spectacular home just west of Stockbridge is Chesterwood, where sculptor Daniel Chester French created the casts for his famous "Seated Lincoln" for the Lincoln Memorial in Washington. You can still see the casts in the studio along with other bronzes and working models. The home itself, set beside the Housatonic River overlooking Monument Mountain, is certainly a setting that might lead to inspiration. French referred to his home simply as "heaven." Chesterwood has been beautifully maintained by the National Trust for Historic Preservation.

If you still have time to spare, West Stockbridge will hope to provide another kind of inspiration—the spending of cash for the jewelry, folk art, pottery, health foods, dried herbs, and what have you in the shops comprising a town that calls itself "New England's Yankee Market."

If you prefer to concentrate on antiques, drive south on Route 7 to Sheffield, a gracious town with a covered bridge and a main street lined with stately homes—at least a dozen of them transformed into antique shops. There's no problem finding most of the stores, since they are right on Main Street, but one complex worth seeking out is Twin Fires Antiques on Route 41—12 shops in two large barns with lots of special pieces of antique English stripped pine furniture.

By the time you've done the shops, the autumn color should be fading into the twilight, telling you it's time to get back to the highway and home.

Berkshires Area Code: 413

DRIVING DIRECTIONS   Saw Mill Parkway north to the Taconic State Parkway to the New York Thruway (Berkshire Spur, Route 90) east to Route 22; north on Route 22 to 295, east on 295 to Route 41, north on 41. The village is at the junction of routes 20 and 41, five miles west of downtown Pittsfield. To get to Lee and Lenox, take exit 2 off 90 and proceed north on Route 7.
Total distance: about 163 miles.

ACCOMMODATIONS AND DINING   See "Weekending with the Boston Symphony," page 84.

SIGHTSEEING   *Hancock Shaker Village,* Route 20 at 41, Pittsfield, 443-0188. Hours: daily, June to October, 9:30 A.M. to 5 P.M. Adults $3, children age 6–12 $1 ● *Missions House,* Main and Sergeant streets, Stockbridge, 298-3383. Hours: May to mid-October, Tuesday to Saturday, 10 A.M. to 5 P.M.; Sunday, 11 A.M. to 4 P.M. Adults $1.40, children age 15–18 50¢, under 15 30¢ ● *Merwin House,* 39 Main Street, Stockbridge, (617) 227-3958. Hours: June to September, Tuesday, Thursday, Saturday, Sunday 1 to 5 P.M.; weekends only May to October. Adults $1 ● *Old Corner House,* Main Street, Stockbridge, 298-3822. Hours: daily except Tuesday, 10 A.M. to 5 P.M. Adults $1, children age 5–12 25¢ ● *Chesterwood,* Route 183, 2 miles west of Stockbridge, 298-3579. Hours: daily, May to October, 10 A.M. to 5 P.M. Adults $2, senior citizens, children age 6–18 $1.

FOR FURTHER INFORMATION   Contact Berkshire Hills Conference, 205 West Street, Pittsfield, MA 01201, 443-8186.

 # Going Back to Old Kingston

The hostess seemed to know all of the old home's secrets—the Revolutionary War documents that were hidden under the hearth, the unusual beaded siding that had been rediscovered and lovingly restored to its original 1760s hue.

Her store of lore is not so surprising, however, since the house in question is her own. She's one of the owners of historic private homes in Kingston, New York. Homes open to the public one day only each year, during the city's annual Fall Festival held on the second Saturday of October.

If the oldest homes in Kingston could talk, they could tell of three centuries of drama in New York's first state capital and one of its earliest settlements. Settled in 1652 by the Dutch, who were forced to build a stockade in 1658 to keep out hostile Indians and who were subject to a continuing tug of war between the Dutch and English, Kingston was burned and its people massacred by the Esopus Indians in 1663. The city was burned again by the British during the Revolutionary War. Only one of the original 103 stone houses survived—the Tappan House, later to be Governor George Clinton's house. The festival date in October commemorates that British attack.

Kingston's later history was less violent. The city was rebuilt, and prospered in the 1800s with the completion of the Delaware and Hudson Canal, which transported Pennsylvania coal to Kingston for shipment. The city also became a nineteenth-century center of commerce for blue stone, brick, and cement, and a hub of shipbuilding.

The homes built over this period form their own 300-year mini-history of architecture, from seventeenth-century Dutch stone houses through Federal, Greek Revival, and Hudson Valley Cottage styles; Italianate, Victorian, Romanesque, and art deco.

Among the most charming are the remaining early Dutch stone structures. Some of these are always included on the festival walking tour. The Henry Sleight House, virtually unchanged in appearance since the late eighteenth century and now the home of the local DAR chapter, is a regular. Others frequently chosen for the tour are the Van Buren House, built in the early 1700s by a cousin of Martin Van Buren, and the eighteenth-century Van Keuren House.

Other houses that may be visited are the Kersted Home, one of the earliest frame houses in Kingston (and the bearer of that beaded siding); the two-story Federal-style home of Dr. Matthew Jansen; and the handsome, two-story Greek Revival house now owned by Herbert Cutler, who has added an exquisite hidden formal garden behind the house.

Not all homeowners are present to chat with visitors, since the tours are ably led by knowledgeable guides versed in the histories of the homes they show. The walking tours leave from the Old Dutch Church, whose tall gray spire is Kingston's most prominent landmark. The tours begin with the church itself, the handsome interior, the church museum, and the burying ground dating from the mid-seventeenth century.

Also part of the tour is the 1676 Senate House and adjoining museum. Kingston, incidentally, is where New York State's constitution was adopted and where its first governor was sworn into office.

All tour sites are either in or adjacent to the Kingston historic district known as the Stockade because of the protective walls that once surrounded it. To see more of the interesting homes in the district, pick up an inexpensive, self-guided walking tour map at the church or a local bookstore. You'll also want to check out the traditional Merchants' Market Place, a sidewalk sale under the shelter of the striking pillared canopies of the main shopping area along Wall and North Front Streets, just down the street from the church. Many local groups also choose this day for book, bake, plant, and harvest sales.

A few other areas of interest in Kingston are Fair Street, a block of pleasant Victorian houses south of the Stockade area; Ponckhockie, a quaint nineteenth-century residential section near former mine operations in the hills; and West Chestnut Street in Rondout, where the town's nineteenth-century mansions are located. This riverfront area was settled by Dutch fur traders in 1615 before the Pilgrims came.

For a quick and inexpensive lunch, the ladies of the Old Dutch Church offer homemade sandwiches and desserts. Or you may want to try the sandwich boards, pastries, and other German-American specialties at Schnellers on John Street, which bills itself as "The Wurst Place in Town." To keep to the spirit of the day, there's the Hoffman House, a restored sixteenth-century stone house in the historic Stockade district, offering a traditional American menu.

There are plenty of motels near Kingston, but considering the time of year, you may prefer to venture farther afield to take advantage of the glorious autumn scenery on the back roads and in the nearby Ulster County Catskills. One excellent choice, if you're lucky (it offers three rooms only), is the Victorian Brodhead House in High Falls. It's owned by the people who run the DuPuy Canal House across the street, an eighteenth-century restored stone tavern that is a national landmark as well as a four-star restaurant. It's worth the splurge.

Travel west about 30 miles northwest of Kingston on Route 28, turn north on 42 to Shandaken, and you'll find the most spectacular location of all, the Auberges Des Quatre Saisons. Your simple lodge room or chalet-type motel accommodations come with a breathtaking mountain view, and the rates include breakfast and dinner prepared by a genuine (and genuinely talented) French chef.

Farther west on 28, the chairlift at Belleayre Ski Area offers sky-high panoramas of autumn colors. Heading back on Route 28, detour on 28A for the scenery at the Ashokan reservoir, then follow Route 375 into Woodstock for pleasant browsing in the picturesque artists' colony that's chock-a-block with shops and galleries. Pick up Route 212 out of Woodstock to Saugerties and take in the annual chrysanthemum festival in full bloom in Seamon Park.

For a fitting historic end to the weekend, stop off on the way home in New Paltz, whose Huguenot Street is the oldest street in America with its original homes still intact. There are a half dozen stone houses here, some dating back to the 1600s, all filled with fine furnishings and heirlooms of descendants of the original owners.

And if you want to take home some fresh-picked apples as a souvenir of the weekend, Stone Ridge Orchards on Route 213 in Stone Ridge northwest of New Paltz and Stanley Orchards on Route 32 in Modena to the south are two places where you can pick your own.

Kingston Area Code: 914

DRIVING DIRECTIONS New York State Thruway north to exit 19 for Kingston. To reach the Stockade Area, take second right off traffic circle (Washington Avenue), proceed to third light and turn left for public parking.

Total distance: about 95 miles.

ACCOMMODATIONS *Sky Top Motel,* Route 28, Kingston, 331-2900; mountaintop view in better rooms; $ • *Howard Johnson's Motor Lodge,* Route 28, 565-4100; indoor pool; $$ • *Auberge des Quatre Saisons,* Route 42, Shandaken, 688-2223; doubles in chalet with private bath, shared bath in lodge; $$–$$$ MAP • *Brodhead House,* Route 213, High Falls, 687-7700; shared bath; $.

DINING *Schnellers Restaurant,* 61-63 John Street, Kingston, 331-9800; entrées and sandwich boards; $ • *Hoffman House,* 94 North Front Street, Kingston, 338-2626; $–$$ • *DuPuy Canal House,* Route 213, High Falls, 687-7700, best restaurant in the area; prix fixe five-course dinner, $30; $$$–$$$$ • *Cafe St. Jacques,* Motel du Moulin, Route 28, Shandaken, 688-2231; prix fixe dinner $15; $$.

SIGHTSEEING *Kingston Fall Festival.* Reception center, schedules and maps, guided tours available at Old Dutch Church, corner of Wall and Main streets, in the Stockade area right on the main street of town. Hours: second Saturday in October, 10 A.M. to 5 P.M. Admission to homes: around $4. For exact prices for this year and updated information, contact Kingston Fall Festival, 124 Green Street, Kingston 12401, 338-1164 or 246-7097 • *Huguenot Street,* New Paltz. Hours:

Wednesday to Saturday 10 A.M. to 4 P.M.; Sunday 1 to 4 P.M. Each house $1, children age 6–14 50¢; guided tours offered 10 A.M. and 3 P.M. Complete tour $3; short tour $2.

FOR FURTHER INFORMATION Contact Ulster County Public Information Office, Box 1800, Kingston, NY 12401, 331-9300.

Foliage Watch on the Connecticut River

A cloud of smoke, a cheerful toot of the whistle, and we were off—chugging our way to a rendezvous with the Connecticut River. Outside the windows of the old steam train, the countryside passed in review, dressed in its best fall colors. Marshes and meadows rolled by, an old freight station here, a tiny lace factory there, until at last we spied the sparkling water and two festive riverboats waiting at the dock to provide the second half of one of the region's most unusual foliage tours.

The Valley Railroad has been operating in Essex, Connecticut, since 1970, offering 10-mile excursions into the past aboard the same kind of steam train that grandpa might have ridden when he was a boy. More than 140,000 people took the ride last year—a nostalgia trip for some, a new adventure for others.

The century-old railroad, abandoned in 1968, is one of more than 90 steam trains flourishing again across the country by giving samples of what travel was like in the not-too-distant past. But this line is unique for its connection with the Connecticut River.

The river completes its 110-mile journey to the sea just a few miles downstream from Essex. Seven nearby towns that call themselves the Gateway Group have taken pains to see that the pristine beauty of the steep riverbanks remain unspoiled. For train passengers who board the double-decker riverboats, the stately river still offers only vistas of untouched woodland, with an occasional diversion—a hilltop mansion, the stone turrets of Gillette Castle, or the gingerbread facade of the Goodspeed Opera House—to whip photographers into action. With the coming of autumn foliage, it is a spectacular scene.

After the hour-long cruise, the train returns passengers to the depot, where they can have photos taken in costumes that match the train's vintage, dine in a 1915 grill car, or browse through a shop of memorabilia to warm the hearts of railroad buffs. There are many, according to Valley Railroad officials. Some phone ahead to check whether Engine No. 40 or No. 97 is on duty that day. No. 40, it seems, has a particularly mellow whistle.

On board, conductors oblige railroad fans with a history of the cars in service that day, which may include an open gondola and plush-seated Pullman cars, as well as the standard wicker-seated coaches. In the trainyard there are cabooses, work cars, locomotive cranes, and a unique double-ended snowplow.

When you've had your fill of railroad lore, head for Essex and a second look at the river from one of its most charming landings. The history of Essex, a picture-book town of picket fences and white clapboard Colonial and Federal homes, is inextricably tied to its river. The first wharf at the site of the present Steamboat Dock was in existence in 1656. Essex also thrived as an early shipbuilding center.

The 1878 three-story clapboard Dockhouse with its graceful cupola became a landmark on the river. The Connecticut River Foundation has restored the exterior and a portion of the interior to its warehouse days. It also houses a small but interesting River Museum that tells the story of the waterway with tools, models, and a fascinating model of *The Turtle,* the first submarine, designed in 1776.

There are several river excursion trips offered from the dock; ask about them at the museum.

Pick up a walking tour of Essex at the museum and you can while away a delightful hour seeing the fine houses lining the winding lanes in town. Watch for the Pratt House on West Avenue above the Congregational Church. It was recently restored by the New England Society for Antiquities, and the Essex Garden Club has planted a lovely Colonial herb garden around the home.

There's also shopping galore on Main Street for antiques, nautical and otherwise, and all the handcrafts, gifts, and geegaws you'd expect in a town full of strollers. In keeping with the town, however, everything is tasteful.

By car, River Road offers a scenic drive with glimpses of the water and many fine homes.

There is just one inn in Essex, the famous Griswold, which has been open for business on Main Street since 1776. Spring is not too early to reserve a room for fall foliage season, but it's always worth a call in case of last-minute cancellations. The Gris is a must, at least for a meal and a visit. The Tap Room, with its busy antique popcorn machine, was once an early Essex schoolhouse; the Steamboat Room simulates the dining salon of an old riverboat, complete with motion from a gently rocking mural at the end of the room; and the Covered Bridge Dining Room, constructed from an abandoned New Hampshire bridge, contains an important collection of Currier & Ives steamboat prints.

No room at the inn? There are two others to try in neighboring Ivoryton, including the Copper Beech, which many consider the best dining place in the area, although I find it a bit formal for its rural setting.

Another local attraction requiring reservations many weeks in advance is the Goodspeed Opera House. Musicals of the 1920s and 1930s and new shows aiming for Broadway are served up here in a restored Victorian theater that has been aptly described as a "jewel box." *Annie* and *Man of La Mancha* both debuted at the Goodspeed. The theater is right on the banks of the river, and the Gelston House next door is a scenic spot for before- or after-theater dining and drinks.

Come Sunday, one of the pleasantest afternoon diversions along the river is a picnic at Gillette Castle State Park, where you'll munch your sandwiches with a spectacular clifftop view. A tour of the castle is a unique experience. It was built by actor William Gillette, a somewhat eccentric gentleman who gained fame and fortune for his portrayal of Sherlock Holmes on stage. The structure cost over a million dollars, quite a pretty penny when it was built in the early 1900s, and was meant to emulate the Rhine Valley castles Gillette had admired in Europe—with turrets, balconies, and the rest.

The interior of the castle is a curiosity. Each of the 24 rooms bears witness to Gillette's eccentricity. No two of the 47 doors are alike, and all are fitted with wooden locks operated by hidden springs. A system of mirrors enabled Gillette to observe visitors without being seen, and a secret panel in the study permitted him to escape if he didn't like what he saw.

Gillette also apparently had an aversion to metal. He insisted that no nails or other metal objects be exposed, and even his light switches are made of wood. The interior walls are also made of handhewn and carved oak. There is so much wood that Gillette had fire hoses and a sprinkler system installed, safety features that were many years ahead of their time.

After the Castle, there are pleasant sights in either direction. A short drive northwest on Route 9 is Middletown, with the art gallery and pleasant campus of Wesleyan College and dining at Town Farms Inn on the river's edge. To the east are Old Saybrook, where you can sample fresh seafood at little outdoor cafés on the harbor and Old Lyme, a gracious Colonial town with two fine inns and some worthwhile sightseeing. The Florence Griswold House here is a late Georgian mansion that housed one of America's first art colonies; the Lyme Art Association galleries next door show contemporary artists' works.

Or you can end your weekend with a visit to Old Lyme's one-of-a-kind attraction, the Nut Museum, with exhibits that include the world's tallest nutcracker plus nut art, music and lore, all housed in a Victorian mansion.

Essex Area Code: 203

DRIVING DIRECTIONS   I-95, New England Thruway, to exit 69, Route 9 north three miles to Essex (exit 3).
  Total distance: about 100 miles.

BY PUBLIC TRANSPORTATION   Amtrak service to Old Saybrook, Valley Railroad Connection to Essex. Check current schedules.

ACCOMMODATIONS   *Griswold Inn,* Main Street, Essex, 767-0991; $ with breakfast • *Copper Beech Inn,* Main Street, Ivoryton, 767-0330; $$ • *Ivoryton Inn,* Main Street, Ivoryton, 767-0422; $.

DINING   *Griswold Inn* (see above); dinner entrées $$, Sunday hunt breakfast $ • *Copper Beech Inn* (see above); dinner entrées $$–$$$ • *The Gull,* Essex Harbor, 767-0916; $$ • *Old Lyme Inn,* 85 Lyme Street, Old Lyme, 434-2600; $$ • *Bee and Thistle,* 100 Lyme Street, Old Lyme, 434-1667; $$ • *Town Farms Inn,* River Road, Middletown, 347-7438; $$ • *Restaurant de Village,* 59 Main Street, Chester, 526-5058, a French bistro; $$–$$$ • *Gelston House,* Goodspeed Landing, East Haddam, 873-9300, a Victorian mansion next to Opera House; $$.

SIGHTSEEING   *Valley Railroad,* Essex, 767-0103. Hours: Saturday, Sunday, 11:45 A.M. and 1 P.M., 2:15 P.M. to connect with one-hour cruise, 3:30 P.M. train without cruise. Ride and cruise $6.75, children age 4–11 $4, under 4 free. Train only $3.75, children $2 • *Goodspeed Opera House,* 873-8668. Tickets $9–$17.50 • *Gillette Castle,* Gillette Castle State Park, East Haddam, 536-2336. Hours: to mid-October, 11 A.M. to 5 P.M. Adults 50¢, children under 12 free. No fee for visiting park.

Family Fare around Fallsington

"Perhaps the most remarkable thing about Fallsington Village is that it exists at all," says a local guide.

It is indeed improbable in busy and built-up lower Bucks County to find an untouched oasis of two dozen homes mirroring 300 years of the history of this area, founded in the 1600s by William Penn, whose own historic residence is only five miles away on the Delaware River.

Penn's home has been restored, and you can see it anytime, but only once a year on Historic Fallsington Day, the second Saturday in October, can you tour the historic stone houses that remain private residences in Fallsington. Since this is also a festive day with lots of activities on the village green, you might mark the calendar and make it the occasion for a family trip to Bucks County, just in time to see the foliage at its peak.

The core of Fallsington grew up around an early Quaker meeting-house where Penn himself used to come to worship. That structure no longer stands, but three successive ones do, clustered around Meeting-house Square. When you get to town go to the Information Center in Gillingham Store, the site of an old town store and post office located on lower Morrisville Road, just off the square. Get a brochure for your own walking tour or join one of the guided tours of the town.

It will take you past mellowed stone residences dating back to Colonial days, including the Burges-Lippincott House, which sparked the entire town restoration effort when it was threatened with demolition in the early 1950s. Luckily, its beautiful doorway, delicate carved fireplace, and unique wall-bannister have been saved and the home is now filled with period furniture and open to the public.

The Stage Coach Tavern, a stage stop in the late 1700s, has also been restored and furnished, and some of the other structures including the Schoolmaster's House and the 1728 Gambrel Roof House built as a meetinghouse are in the process of restoration.

On this day only you will be invited into places you can only walk past the rest of the year: Pleasants House, a 1788 home at 14 Meetinghouse Square; Manor House, which dates back to 1690, and some of the three Federal Houses that stand on Yardley Avenue. Owners of several of these houses participate in Historic Fallsington

Day to raise funds to continue the town's ongoing preservation efforts.

The last house on the walking tour is the oldest of all, built of logs around 1685. The two huge sycamores, known as "bride and groom" trees, were probably planted by the original settlers; and the house itself is back to its original state, the Victorian "improvements" added in the 1800s having been removed during its restoration.

While the house touring continues, all kinds of festivities are going on outdoors—jugglers, singers, displays of spinning and other old crafts; a chicken potpie luncheon and other homemade foods for sale at various locations around the town; and artists demonstrating and selling their work. Stop in at the Information Center Gift Shop for fall flower arrangements, door swags, and unusual Christmas decorations, and visit the resident Pumpkin Peddler for your Halloween needs.

There should be just enough time at the end of the day for a visit to Pennsbury Manor, William Penn's country home, a self-supporting plantation that has been restored complete with gardens and orchard and outbuildings such as the bake-, brew-, ice- and smokehouses that demonstrate some of the activities of an earlier day. The furnishings in the house represent a period 75 to 100 years before the American Revolution and are the largest collection from this time in Pennsylvania. It's all a look at gracious living, circa 1680. The house is located on Route 13 near Tullytown, off Bristol Pike.

Lodgings are in short supply in this area. You can try motels by heading south toward Philadelphia, or drive half an hour to New Hope for more variety. If you have children under 12 along, stay in the vicinity so that you can start Sunday with a visit to Sesame Place, the family play park in Langhorne that is one part innovative playground, one part do-it-yourself science exhibit, and one part computer game gallery. It has the largest collection of educational computer games in the country, and kids aren't the only ones who have a good time here.

Take a drive on Route 413 to Newtown to see another of the oldest communities in the county. The old section here is an historic district, and you can pick up a self-guided walking tour at the Court Inn, Court Street and Centre Avenue.

Then follow General Washington's footsteps to River Road (Route 32) and Washington Crossing State Park, where you'll learn about the frigid river crossing on that fateful Christmas night in 1776 that turned the tide of the Revolutionary War. Start at the visitors' center for a sense of the history of the event. Inside, along with displays, is a painting that is an exact replica of the famous "Washington Crossing the Delaware." (You can see the original in New York at the Metropolitan Museum.)

North of the building is a statue of George Washington and a reflection pool surrounded with flags of the thirteen original states and the Betsy Ross flag.

Next, on to McConkey Ferry Inn, where Washington and his staff held their final meeting before the crossing, the Durham Boat House, where you'll see reproductions of eighteenth-century cargo boats, and the Bowman's Hill and Tower, the site of the observation point used by the Continental Army, where a memorial tower with a similar view was built in 1930. It's 121 steps up for the view.

There's more to see and do in the park. The restored and operating Thompson Grist Mill and its barn are interesting examples of eighteenth-century life. And what could be nicer than an autumn ramble through a 100-acre wildflower preserve.

If your energy holds out, continue north to New Hope and take a ride on the old mule-drawn canal barge or a chugging tour into the flaming countryside aboard an old-time steam train. Once again, it's fun that has no age limit.

And if you want more scenery, just hit the back roads of Bucks County, where the stone houses, barns, and covered bridges against colors of autumn just beg for a camera—or a canvas. See page 15 for further details.

Bucks County Area Code: 215

DRIVING DIRECTIONS   New Jersey Turnpike to Exit 6, Pennsylvania Turnpike westbound to Exit 29, Route 13, take 13 north, following historical markers, five miles to Fallsington.

Total distance: 80 miles.

ACCOMMODATIONS   *Holiday Inn Northeast,* 3499 Street Road, Bensalem, 638-1500; $$, under 18 free in room with parents • *George Washington Motor Lodge,* US 1 at Pennsylvania Turnpike, Trevose, 357-9100; $ (sometimes gives free tickets to Sesame Place). For New Hope accommodations see page 19.

DINING   See New Hope page 19.

SIGHTSEEING   *Historic Fallsington,* 4 Yardley Avenue, Fallsington, PA 19057, 295-6567. Write or call for details of annual open house. Tours: mid-March to mid-November, Wednesday to Sunday, 1 to 5 P.M. Adults $2, students $1, under 12 50¢; self-guided tour map, $1. • *Historic Fallsington Day,* 2nd Saturday in October, 10 A.M. to 4:30 P.M., guided tours, adults $4 • *Pennsbury Manor,* 5 miles from

Fallsington on the Delaware River, Morrisville, 946-0400. Take Route 13 south to Bordentown Fry Road, then go 5 miles northeast to Manor. Hours: May to October, Tuesday to Saturday, 9 A.M. to 5 P.M.; rest of year, 10 A.M. to 4:30 P.M.; Sunday, 1 to 5 P.M. all year. Adults $1.50, children under 12 free • *Sesame Place,* Oxford Valley Mall off US 1 Bypass, Langhorne, 752-7070. Hours: daily, April to Labor Day, 10 A.M. to 7 P.M.; September, October, to 6 P.M.; rest of year indoors only, 10 A.M. to 10 P.M.; $5.95 all ages • *Washington Crossing State Park,* Route 32, 7 miles from New Hope, 493-4076. Hours: May to October, 9 A.M. to 5 P.M.; November to April, 10 A.M. to 4:30 P.M.; Sunday all year, noon to 5 P.M. Adults $1, over 65 and under 12 free. • *Mule-drawn barge rides,* New Street at southern end of New Hope, 862-2842. Hours: daily, mid-April to October, 11:30 A.M. and 1, 2, 3, 4:30 P.M. Adults $3.75, children age 2–11 $1.75 • *New Hope Steam Railway,* Bridge Street (Route 179) near the center of New Hope, 345-0292. Hours: May and October, Saturday, Sunday, 1, 2:30, 4 P.M.; June to September weekends 12:50, 2, 3:15, 4:30 P.M. Adults $4, children $2 • For more on Bucks County see "Mercer Mile" spring trip, page 15.

FOR FURTHER INFORMATION (New Hope) Contact New Hope Chamber of Commerce, South Main and Mechanic streets, New Hope, PA 18938, 862-5880 • For free pamphlet, "Highways of History," Bucks County Historical Tourist Commission, One Oxford Valley, Suite 410, Langhorne, PA, 752-2203.

Tailgating and Other Diversions in New Haven

It's a matter of pride in New Haven, Connecticut, that football was born here. The first Yale intramural game was played on the village green some 200 years ago, and football has been a welcome fall tradition ever since.

The origins of tailgate picnics are more obscure, but a visit to the Yale Bowl parking lot on a football weekend clearly demonstrates that this diversion, too, has become a local tradition—and one that is observed with style. Hibachis and outdoor grills send out tempting aromas, cocktail shakers clink merrily, folding tables are set with cloths and cutlery, and even the informal picnickers seem to have particularly attractive hampers—or box lunches labeled *Trattoria* or *Brasserie*.

It's a happy custom on a fine fall day—the picnic, the game, the Yale marching band clad in blue blazers putting a bit of wit into its casual halftime show—and if you want to join the fun, you'll find yourself in a town that has a lot to offer both before and after the game.

New Haven has a long history, the largest collection of British art to be found outside of Britain, Yale's magnificent Gothic campus for strolling, top museums, some of the best regional theater in the country, and last—but certainly not least—pizza that is unsurpassed. It will take some juggling to fit it all in. One plan might be to do the campus Saturday morning, take in a bit of New Haven history after the game, and reserve Sunday for museums and some autumn leaves in the city's scenic parks.

Begin by visiting the Information Center on the Green, where you can pick up a walking tour map, then head for the Green across the way. One of the nine squares laid out in 1638 in America's first planned city, the Green offers three particularly fine churches, one Gothic, one Federal, and one Georgian in design. The Center Congregational (1813) is considered a masterpiece of American Georgian architecture.

The main entrance to Yale is just off the green through the William Lyon Phelps Gate on College Street. Free one-hour tours of the campus are offered from the Information Center inside the gate from 9 A.M. to 4 P.M. on weekends, but you can spend an equally pleasant if less informed hour just roaming through the ivied courtyards and past the Gothic facades of the college. Though Yale is now a university of 11,000 students that spreads over many blocks, the heart of the school still remains the old campus bounded by Chapel, High, Elm, and College Streets. Nathan Hale, Noah Webster, and William Howard Taft all studied in Connecticut Hall, the oldest intact building on campus.

The Green and Yale recall New Haven's Colonial and cultural history, but the city also has an important industrial history. Among its prides are New Haven clocks, Winchester rifles, and Gilbert toys, which include that all-time favorite, the erector set. Eli Whitney manufactured his cotton gin here and in 1812 led the way to mass production by turning out rifles with interchangeable parts. New Havenite Charles Goodyear invented vulcanized rubber in this town.

After the game, visit the New Haven Colony History Society, where you can see samples of some of these early products, Whitney's cotton gin among them, as well as displays of decorative arts, tableware of New Haven from 1640 to 1840, and antique dolls and toys. Nearby at High and Grove streets, an impressive Egyptian gateway leads to the

Grove Street Cemetery, a parklike retreat where Whitney and Good-year are buried, along with Samuel F. B. Morse and Noah Webster.

New Haven has many excellent restaurants patronized by the many visitors to Yale and by theatergoers in town, but at dinner hour many make a beeline straight for Wooster Street, the heart of the Italian district. Some of the restaurants here are highly regarded, too, but it is the pizza that makes Wooster Street legendary. It is authentic Italian tomato pie—you have to order mozzarella on top if you want it—and it is delicious. There is a longstanding war between devotees of Pepe's (medium-thick crust) and Sally's (super-thin), but there are enough fans to do justice to both. Come very early, or be prepared for long lines.

Early dinner isn't a bad idea anyway, since you will probably want to get to the theater in the evening. Those who follow theater will need no introduction to Long Wharf, the regional company named for its home in a former food terminal near the water. *The Shadow Box* and *The Changing Room* are just two of numerous productions that got their start in New Haven and moved on to Broadway. Long Wharf is a pleasant theatergoing experience, a small and intimate theater-in-the-round with invariably creative staging. Write or call in advance for tickets, and if the main theater is sold out, don't hesitate to take the smaller production next door at Stage II. It, too, is dependably high quality. Yale Repertory Theater is another place where you will usually find well-performed experimental theater in New Haven.

One other possibility for evening entertainment is next door in Milford, where jai alai is played daily through November. The game is fast and the betting furious. If you've never seen it played, here's your chance.

Since museums don't open until afternoon on Sunday, you might sleep late, enjoy brunch, or take a drive to one of New Haven's parks. The city's flat terrain is interrupted by two towering red rock cliffs that are centerpoints for two lovely parks, each with views of harbor and Long Island Sound. East Rock Park also is the site of the city's arboretum, Pardee Rose Gardens, a bird sanctuary, and hiking trails at their best in the colors of autumn. West Rock Park contains a 40-acre zoo.

Your first museum stop should be Yale's (and New Haven's) newest attraction, the Yale Center of British Art. This modern structure holds the extensive Paul Mellon collection covering British life and culture from Elizabethan times to the present, with numerous paintings by Turner, Constable, and other noted British painters. There are often concerts and lectures scheduled here on weekends; check the desk for the current offerings.

Across Chapel Street, the Yale University Art Gallery, the nation's oldest college art museum, has a varied collection of American and European art of all periods, American decorative art spanning three centuries, African sculpture, Pre-Columbian, Near and Far Eastern art. There is also a sculpture garden.

Another unique attraction is the Yale Collection of Musical Instruments, 850 antique and historical instruments dating from sixteenth to nineteenth centuries. The Peabody Museum of Natural History is also an excellent one of its kind, and the Beinecke Library has many rare displays, including a Gutenberg Bible, original Audubon bird prints, and medieval manuscripts.

There is a lot to see—you'll have to pick and choose. And then you'll have the pleasant prospect of picking one of those many fine restaurants in the city to finish off the day.

New Haven Area Code: 203

DRIVING DIRECTIONS   Take I-95 or the Hutchinson, Merritt, and Wilbur Cross parkways to downtown New Haven exits.
Total distance: 75 miles.

BY PUBLIC TRANSPORTATION   Conrail services New Haven, as does Amtrak. Some bus transportation available in town.

ACCOMMODATIONS   *Sheraton Park Plaza Hotel,* 155 Temple Street, 772-1700; $$–$$$ ● *Colony Inn,* 1157 Chapel Street, 776-1234; $$ ● *Holiday Inn at Yale,* 30 Whalley Avenue, 777-6221; $$ ● *Howard Johnsons-Long Wharf,* 400 Sargent Drive, 562-1111; $$ ● *New Haven Motor Inn,* 100 Pond Lily Avenue, 387-6651; $.

DINING   *Fitzwillys,* 338 Elm, 624-9438, for sandwiches, quiches, salads—very popular, open till 2 A.M.; $ ● *Leon's,* New Haven, 321 Washington Avenue, 789-9049, one of best Italian restaurants in town; $–$$ ● *La Rotisserie Normande,* 1157 Chapel Street, 776-1234, good French food; prix fixe dinner $14.95; $$ ● *Bourbon Street,* 883 Whalley Avenue, Westville Center, 389-6200, New Orleans fare—try for Sunday brunch; $, dinner $$ ● *Delmonaco's,* 232 Wooster Street, 865-1109, for southern Italian food; $$–$$$ ● *Valente's Cafe Reale,* 100 Wooster Street, 624-5289, for northern Italian food; $$–$$$ ● *Sally's Pizza,* 237 Wooster Street, 624-5271; $ ● *Pepe's,* 157 Wooster Street, 865-5762; $ ● *Sherman's Taverne,* 1032 Chapel Street, 777-2524, on the green, atmospheric; $$–$$$.

SIGHTSEEING *Yale Football,* contact Yale Department of Athletics, Box 402A, Yale Station, New Haven 06520, 436-0100, for current schedule and ticket prices ● *New Haven Colony Historical Society,* 114 Whitney Avenue, 562-4183. Hours: Tuesday to Friday, 10 A.M. to 5 P.M.; Saturday, Sunday, 2 to 5 P.M. Free ● *Yale University,* guided one-hour walking tours from Phelps Gateway off College Street at New Haven Green. Call 436-8330 for current schedule. Free ● *Yale Center for British Art,* 1080 Chapel Street, 432-4594. Hours: Tuesday to Saturday, 10 A.M. to 5 P.M.; Sunday 2 to 5 P.M. Free ● *Yale University Art Gallery,* 1111 Chapel Street, 436-0574. Hours: Tuesday to Saturday, 10 A.M. to 5 P.M.; Sunday, 2 to 5 P.M. Free. ● *Peabody Museum of Natural History,* 170 Whitney Avenue, 436-0850. Hours: Monday to Saturday, 9 A.M. to 5 P.M.; Sunday 1 to 5 P.M. Free Monday, Wednesday, Friday; other days adults $1, children 50¢ ● *East Rock Park,* East Rock Road. Hours: daily, during daylight. Free ● *West Rock Park,* Wintergreen Avenue. Hours: zoo open weekdays, 9:30 A.M. to 4:15 P.M.; Saturday, 10 A.M. to 4 P.M.; Sunday, noon to 4 P.M. Free ● *Long Wharf Theatre,* 222 Sargent Drive, 787-4282. Write or phone for current schedule and ticket prices ● *Yale Repertory Theater,* Chapel and York streets, 436-1600. Contact for current schedule and ticket prices ● *Milford Jai Alai,* 311 Old Gate Lane (I-95, exit 40), (800) 243-9660. Hours: Monday to Friday, 7:30 P.M.; Saturday, noon, 7 P.M. General admission $1.75, reserved seats $2–$6.

FOR FURTHER INFORMATION Contact New Haven Convention and Visitors Bureau, P. O. Box 1857, New Haven, CT 06058, 777-4205; and Visitors Center, 155 Church, New Haven, CT, 767-8367, open daily, 10 A.M. to 4 P.M.

A Vision of the Past in Deerfield

Many consider The Street in Old Deerfield, Massachusetts, the loveliest in all New England—and you'll find it at its very best in autumn.

More than 50 fine Colonial and Federal homes line this mile-long avenue, each one carefully restored to its original condition. In the 11 houses open to the public, visitors can see more than 100 rooms filled with china, glassware, silver, pewter, fabrics, and furniture that are a testament to the good taste of our early settlers.

The difference between Deerfield and other restorations is that this town remains alive and well today. People still live in its historic homes. Even the museum-houses have apartments in the rear for the faculty of Deerfield Academy, the noted boys' school that has stood on The Street since 1797. From the moment you arrive, you will sense the town's continuity with the past.

Seeing this peaceful, elm-shaded village today, it is hard to believe it was once a frontier outpost whose fate was uncertain from day to day. Twice Deerfield was almost destroyed by Indian attacks, in the Bloody Brook Massacre of 1675 and the Deerfield Massacre of 1704. Fifty settlers died in the latter battle, and another 111 were taken prisoner and marched off on a brutal mid-winter trek to Canada.

But instead of fleeing, the survivors set out to rebuild their town and rework their farms. The town revived and thrived as a center of the wheat industry and an important cattle market. Its more primitive houses were replaced by gracious clapboard homes in the Connecticut Valley tradition. Though rustic compared to homes of this period in Boston or Philadelphia, their very simplicity makes them seem all the more beautiful today.

Deerfield's hardbitten farmers used the new wealth to bring in the finest furnishings they could buy, particularly the work of the excellent craftsmen and cabinetmakers of their own valley.

By a combination of luck, vision, energy—and money—this era of good taste has been preserved. When the center of farming moved away from New England in the mid-nineteenth century, Deerfield, by then the home of three schools, survived as a center of education. In the next 100 years many local residents began efforts at restoration, but the town's real renaissance was fostered by Mr. and Mrs. Henry Flynt, who came to Deerfield in the 1930s because their son was enrolled at the academy. The Flynts' first move was to buy and restore the white-columned Deerfield Inn in the center of town. They next acquired one of the old houses for themselves, and from then on one house led to another. In 1952 Mr. Flynt and his wife founded Historic Deerfield, Inc.

Though Deerfield is only a village, you can't rush through it in an hour or two. Allow at least a full day—or better yet, a weekend.

Start by just strolling The Street, savoring the town's setting among wooded hills and observing the exteriors of the saltbox houses, with their steep-pitched gambrel roofs, weathered clapboard sidings, and distinctively carved doorways. Note the academy buildings, the old Brick Church, and the delightful post office, a replica of a 1696 meetinghouse. Then head for the Hall Tavern Information Center, where color photos will help you make the difficult choice of which houses to visit during a limited stay. Each house tour takes from 30 to 45 minutes.

You can begin with the Tavern itself, once a hostelry for travelers. One of its seven rooms is an unusual ballroom with gaily stenciled walls.

A must on any tour is Ashley House (circa 1730), the home of Deerfield's Tory minister during the American Revolution. Many may have quarreled with Reverend Jonathan Ashley's politics, but no one could fault his taste. The north parlor, with blue walls setting off red shell-crowned cupboards, a gold satin settee, and rich Oriental rugs has been called one of the most beautiful rooms in America.

Each of the other houses has its own special attractions and a knowledgeable guide to point them out. Many of the guides are longtime Deerfield residents who have family stories to add to the town's history.

The Sheldon-Hawks House (1743), home of the town's historian, contains fine paneling, a display of sewing equipment, and a memorable bedroom with brilliant flame-stitch bed hangings and red moreen curtains and chairs. The Wells-Thorn House (1717/1751) combines an austere, Colonial exterior with urbane, Federal-period furniture. The Dwight-Barnard House (1750) has an elegant parlor and a doctor's office behind its weathered exterior.

The Asa Stebbins House (1799), the town's first brick edifice, was built by the wealthiest landowner and decorated with French wallpapers and freehand wall drawings. Like many of Deerfield's homes, this one has an excellent collection of early export china.

Mr. Stebbins also built the town's other brick house for his son, Asa, junior, in 1824. Now called Wright House, it is distinguished for its Chippendale Room, its handsome dining room, and a bedroom hung with crewelwork.

Frary House (1720/1768), a home with a double history, is another highly recommended stop. Its location on the town common made it a refuge for the Frary family in pioneer days and a profitable tavern for the Barnards later on. The house contains a ballroom, many examples of country furniture, and a variety of cooking, spinning, and weaving equipment. There is also a "touch it" room where children and adults may handle some of the tools that are off limits elsewhere.

For a change of pace, step into some of the specialized buildings such as the Wilson Printing House, restored to its original site and used as a printing office and bookbindery, or the Parker and Russell Silver Shop, a farmhouse containing a smith's workshop, a clock collection, and an outstanding display of American and English silver. Both date from around 1815.

Helen Geier Flynt Fabric Hall is a Victorian barn that houses Mrs. Flynt's remarkable collection of American, English, and European needlework, textiles, quilts, bed hangings, and costumes.

Last stop, and a delightful place to stay, is Deerfield Inn, where you can end the day with tea before a roaring fire or stronger refreshments in the tavern room. The Inn serves excellent meals in an elegant, candlelit dining room.

With luck you'll be able to get a room at the inn. If not, there are other good inns in the college towns nearby, and wherever you stay, you're in good position on Sunday for a tour of the Pioneer Valley, home of the well-known Five Colleges, haven for craftsmen and antique dealers and a bucolic area with more than its share of autumn scenery.

A college tour is a good plan for seeing the sights, and you'll be getting a good cross section of college architecture while you're at it—Amherst with its halls of ivy and picture-book green; the modern University of Massachusetts, a virtual city that actually has a building tall enough for a top-floor restaurant with a view; rustic Hampshire College; and the mix of old and new along the quadrangles of Smith in Northampton and Mount Holyoke in South Hadley. Smith has an excellent and varied art museum with French Impressionists, Renaissance sculpture, eighteenth-century English paintings, and—you name it. Amherst's Mead Art Gallery is smaller but does have one curiosity, the Rotherwas Room, dating from 1611 and given to the college by an alumnus who had brought it to America from a British castle. Walnut carved paneling, an ornate mantel, and stained glass windows give the room an authentic baronial flavor.

There's interesting shopping in this area, particularly around Northampton, though you can't be sure who will be open on Sunday. American Indian products are the specialty at a gallery called White Star at 46 Green Street, just off the Smith campus. Lillian Stone and Family Jewels are two antique shops on the same block, and most dealers will hand you a map for 18 other antique shops in Northampton and nearby Hadley.

The best-known crafts center in the region is Leverett Craftsmen and Artists in Leverett Center, just northeast of Amherst. It's a cooperative venture of some 100 craftsmen, and their fall and pre-Christmas shows are particularly good ones. There are often artists in residence as well in this converted factory building.

For foliage vistas, try Mount Tom on US 5 in Holyoke, where an observation tower is open daily until 8 P.M. On Mount Sugarloaf off Route 116 in Sunderland near Amherst, another state park with an observation tower offers a sweeping view of the river valley and the flaming hillsides on either side.

Heading home, you may want to make a detour into Springfield, where four free museums for art, fine arts, and natural history are clustered together in a quadrangle downtown. Of more interest to any sports fans along may be the Naismith Memorial Basketball Hall of Fame at Springfield College, which has a replica of the original basketball court dating back to 1891, displays on the sport, and free movies.

From Springfield it's an easy drive back onto Route 91 and straight back to the city.

Deerfield Area Code: 413

DRIVING DIRECTIONS Take I-95 or Hutchinson River Parkway and Merritt Parkway to I-91 north; follow I-91 to exit 24 and follow Route 5 into Deerfield center.
Total distance: 187 miles.

ACCOMMODATIONS *Deerfield Inn,* Deerfield, 774-5587; $$ • *Lord Jeffrey Inn,* Amherst, 253-2576; $ • *The Autumn Inn,* 259 Elm Street (Route 9), Northampton, 584-7660; $ • *Yankee Pedlar Inn,* Route 5, Holyoke, 532-9494; $ • *Northampton Hilton Inn,* Routes 91 and 5, Northampton, 586-1211, the only one of the lot that isn't an inn but is a very pleasant lodging of its type; $–$$.

DINING *Deerfield Inn* (see above); $$ • *Lord Jeffrey Inn* (see above); $–$$ • *The Inn at Huntington,* Worthington Road, Huntington, 667-8888, out of the way, but chef is a Culinary Institute alumnus and Sunday 2 P.M. dinners are followed by a Beaux Arts concert series; $$–$$$ • *Beardsleys,* 140 Main, Northampton, 586-2699, a French cafe; $$.

SIGHTSEEING *Historic Deerfield,* P. O. Box 321, Deerfield, MA 10342, 773-5401. Hours: Monday to Saturday, 9:30 A.M. to 4:30 P.M.; Sunday, 1 to 4:30 P.M. Admission $1 to $2.50 per building; combination ticket valid for a week is $10 • *Mead Art Gallery,* Amherst College, 542-2335. Hours: Monday to Friday, 10 A.M. to 4:30 P.M.; Saturday, Sunday, 1 to 5 P.M. Free • *Smith College Museum of Art,* Elm Street, Northampton, 584-2700. Hours: Tuesday to Saturday, 11 A.M. to 4:30 P.M.; Sunday 2:30 to 4:30 P.M. Free • *Naismith Memorial National*

Basketball Hall of Fame, Alden Street, Springfield College campus, 781-6500. Hours: daily, 10 A.M. to 5 P.M. Adults $2, senior citizens $1.50, students $1.25, children age 6–14 75¢.

A Capital Trip to Albany

How about a ride on the A train, 1940s edition, with wicker seats and ceiling fans—and without graffiti? Or a stroll down Fifth Avenue, peeking into the windows at Delmonico's, where the diners are dressed in their 1890s best?

These and much, much more—replicas of a tenement sweatshop, the old port of New York, an old Chinatown store, an antique trading post from the Stock Exchange, the "Sesame Street" TV set, and a 1925 city bus, just for starters—are among the features of the "The New York Metropolis," the most comprehensive exhibit on the city ever assembled.

But if you want to see it, there's a catch. You'll have to travel 150 miles from Manhattan to the New York State Museum, part of the Empire State Plaza in Albany.

New York's capital rarely used to attract anyone who wasn't forced to make the trip for official state business, but that was before the completion of the plaza, late Governor Nelson Rockefeller's legacy to the city of Albany. Not everyone agreed with Rockefeller's grandiose plan to clear 98 acres of downtown land and dislocate 3,000 people in order to build glass and marble monuments costing a billion dollars of taxpayers' money. But 16 years later, when it was all finished in 1978, there was little doubt that Albany had acquired not only a striking government complex but a first-rate cultural center, one that has sparked a renaissance in the city.

The futuristic plaza, built around a landscaped mall of pools and fountains, gardens, and grandiose sculpture, has a huge collection of modern art on display and the largest state museum in the nation. It is definitely worth a visit, particularly in fall when the leafy countryside surrounding Albany is putting on its annual autumn spectacular. Apple picking, hiking, and a look at the fascinating history of the Shaker sect can also be part of the weekend scenario.

Your first stop in Albany should be the plaza itself, perhaps for a bird's-eye view from the forty-second floor observation deck of its tallest building, known simply as The Tower. Across the mall four smaller Agency Towers house many state departments. At one end of the mall are the lower scale structures of the Legislative Office Building and the Justice Building; at the other end is the handsome Cultural Education Center, which contains the State Museum. The many-tiered steps to the center form a seating area that can accommodate 2,500 people for the free music and entertainment that frequently takes place on the Mall.

Next to the Tower is a restaurant, and next to that the most unusual of all the edifices, the Performing Arts Center, universally known as The Egg. The name's origin will be obvious when you see the shape of this flying saucer on stilts.

Having gotten your perspective, you'll be descending underground to the half-mile concourse that connects all the mall buildings. Free guided tours of the plaza are offered hourly from the visitor services headquarters at the north end of the concourse, the same place to make arrangements for a tour of the state capitol. Along the tour you'll be seeing some of the monumental pieces of sculpture standing amid the buildings, most notably a series of painted steel structures by David Smith and large pieces by Noguchi and Calder.

The entire concourse is a gallery of modern art, some of it highly experimental. The collection indoors and out totals almost 100 pieces. To make sure you don't miss anything, ask at the visitor services desk for a map to help you find works by Frankenthaler, Motherwell, Oldenburg, Kelly, Gottlieb, Nevelson, and many other noted artists.

You'll probably want to return and linger in the State Museum, which has amazing resources for an institution in a city the size of Albany. In addition to the many unique features of the New York metropolis exhibit, there are some interesting special effects in the section called "Adirondack Wilderness," particularly a small dark room where you can hear the awesome sound of a giant tree falling in the forest. Well-made films enhance all of the museum's displays.

When you've had your fill of the plaza, you might take a walk to the west (behind the agency buildings) to Hamilton Street and Robinson Square, a series of galleries, shops, and restaurants in restored nineteenth-century brownstones. The entire area behind the plaza known as Center Square, once a slum, is being restored house by house into a totally charming neighborhood well worth the time for a stroll to appreciate the fine Victorian architecture. The area is bounded by Washington and Madison avenues, Lark and South Swan streets.

After lunch on Hamilton or in one of the plaza restaurants, it's time for a second free tour, this time a look at the ornate state capitol building with its "million-dollar staircase," adorned with carvings, and the beautifully restored Senate and Assembly chambers.

There are several other prize historic homes and churches to visit in Albany. Choice among the houses are Cherry Hill, whose furnishings reflect the changing life-styles of five generations of the Van Rensselaer family, who lived here from 1787 to 1963, and the Schuyler Mansion, home of a prominent early family and a center of activities during the Revolutionary War. George Washington, Benjamin Franklin, and Alexander Hamilton visited this house; Hamilton, in fact, married Elizabeth Schuyler at the mansion. One other important home is the Ten Broeck Mansion, home of a delegate to the Continental Congress and filled with many fine Colonial artifacts.

Among the more notable churches are First Church, whose pulpit, carved in Holland in 1656, is the oldest in America; St. Peters, a Gothic Revival structure containing a silver communion service donated by Queen Anne; the first Episcopal Cathedral in America, with stalls built by monks in 1623 and some of the finest European wood carving in America; and Congregation Beth Emeth, one of the first four reform Jewish congregations in America, with a great folded roof reminiscent of the tent Moses prepared as a desert tabernacle.

As the state capital Albany is used to visitors and there are numerous places to stay and to dine in the area. If you want to make this a country weekend, you might want to choose one of two inns out a ways from the city, your choice depending perhaps on the direction you plan to take on Sunday. The Greenville Arms, a comfortable Victorian homestead with attractive grounds, is about 28 miles southwest of the city in a peaceful tiny town on the edge of the Catskills. In the other direction, handier to the Shaker Museum, is The Inn at the Shaker Mill Farm, which is indeed an old mill and is furnished in the spare look of the Shakers. It is a little spartan for some tastes, but the setting is superb.

As for evening entertainment, if you are in the city you should find something of interest going on in one of the two arenas of The Egg, which has an ongoing schedule of drama, dance, and music.

Come Sunday, you'll have to pick and choose your destinations. One strong recommendation is to bring along your hiking shoes and make your first stop the John Boyd Thacher State Park, about 18 miles west of the city on Route 157. The clifftop view here is one of the best around; on a clear day you can see the peaks of the Adirondacks, the Massachusetts Taconics, and Vermont's Green Mountains plus the Hudson-Mohawk Valley and the profusions of trees covering the slopes—oaks, elms, red maples, birches, lindens, and white pines, producing a rich palette of fall color.

The hiking shoes are for the ½-mile Indian Ladder trail paralleling the Helderberg Escarpment, a cliff of limestone and shale that geologists have declared to be one of the richest fossil-bearing formations in the world. The trail takes about 45 minutes.

If you continue from the park to Route 146 in Altamont, you can pick your own peck of apples at Indian Ladder Farms. If the season is right you may find raspberries ripe for picking as well, and there's always fresh pressed cider for sale as well as fresh grown vegetables.

From here you can choose your direction. If you continue west on Route 20 for perhaps 20 miles you'll come to another natural wonder, Howe Caverns. An 80-minute tour here of the underground caves and subterranean waterways includes an underground boat ride. If you are going to the caverns bring a jacket; temperatures in the caves are in the chilly fifties.

Another alternative is to drive south. If you have children along you may want to stop at the Catskill Game Farm on Route 32. Otherwise on to Route 23A, the spectacular road to Hunter Mountain, with cliffs and waterfalls along the way and more magnificent foliage vistas. If you take this route make a detour to Elka Park for Sunday dinner at the Redcoat's Return, a rustic farmhouse whose booklined dining room is highly recommended in the area.

Or you might choose to make your way back about 20 miles southeast of Albany for a visit to the Shaker Museum on Route 66 in Old Chatham, a complex of eight buildings in a calm and beautiful farm setting showing the enterprise and ingenious simple designs of this industrious sect, who invented such practical aids as the circular saw, the flat broom, and the clothespin. You will see a cabinetmaker's shop; a small chair factory; a smith's shop; galleries of textiles and the looms that produced them; craft shops used by tinsmiths, cobblers, broom-makers; and the Shaker seed and medicine industries; an herb house adjacent to the herb garden; and nine period rooms and a Shaker schoolroom, all incredibly neat, spare, and functional, with the clean-lined furniture that has inspired so many latter-day craftsmen. If the Shakers interest you make a note that the third Saturday in September is the annual Crafts Day at the museum, when special demonstrations are scheduled. Also note that the museum store sells reproductions of Shaker furniture and of their handsome oval storage boxes.

If time remains take a drive through the appealing old towns and the pastoral countryside of the various Chathams and New Lebanon, then drive home via Route 22, where there are some splendid choices for dinner. Two are in Hillsdale, the French L'Hostellerie Bressane and the German Swiss Hutte. The third, farther down in Patterson, is a real curiosity. It's an offbeat Mexican restaurant called the Texas Taco where you'll share eating quarters with the most amazing collection of odd memorabilia and animals, including parrots and a monkey. Some people find it so appealing they make a special point of driving home via this route just to stop in again.

Albany Area Code: 518

DRIVING DIRECTIONS New York State Thruway (Route 87) to exit 23. Follow signs to I-787 into Albany, watching for signs reading South Mall. Elevated traffic loop leads into and under the Empire State Plaza. Parking is available in underground garages, free after 5 P.M. and on weekends.

Total distance: 150 miles.

BY PUBLIC TRANSPORTATION Amtrak to Albany is the most scenic route you can take, paralleling the Hudson River almost all the way.

ACCOMMODATIONS *Albany Hilton,* Ten Eyck Plaza, State Street, 462-6611; $$$ • *Americana Inn of Albany,* 660 Albany-Shaker Road, 869-9271, indoor pool; $$$ • *Quality Inn,* 1 Watervliet Avenue, 438-8431; $$ • *Albany Best Value Inn,* 44 Wolf Road, Colonie, 459-5670; $ • *Tom Sawyer,* 1444 Western Avenue, 438-3594; $ • *Best Western Inn Town,* 300 Broadway, 434-4111, convenient if you have no car; $$ • *Greenville Arms,* Greenville, 966-5219; $$–$$$, MAP • *The Inn at the Shaker Mill Farm,* Canaan, 794-9345; $$$–$$$$ MAP (less on weekdays).

DINING *Piccolo's at the Plaza,* Empire State Plaza, 465-2361, elegant; $–$$$ • *Bleeker Restaurant,* 32 Dove Street, 463-9382, international with a Middle Eastern flavor; $–$$ • *Ogden's Restaurant,* Howard Street at Lodge Street, 463-6605, interesting menu, in restored office building; $–$$ • *Chez Rene,* Route 9, Glenmont, 463-5130, French cuisine in a Colonial home; $ • *L'Auberge,* 351 Broadway, 465-1111, French fare in restored steamship ticket office; $$ • *Jack's Oyster House,* 42 State Street, 465-8854, noisy, old favorite downtown eatery with famous cheesecake; $$ • *Market Place,* 6 Grand Street, 463-4478, light fare in a former banana warehouse, especially good for lunch; $ • *Yorkstone Pub,* 79 North Pearl, 462-9033, hamburgers, soups, sandwiches; $ • *Joe's Restaurant,* 851 Madison, 489-4062, deli with takeout counter if you want a picnic lunch; $ • *Redcoat's Return,* Dale Lane, Elka Park, 589-6379; $–$$ • *L'Hostellerie Bressane,* off Route 22, Hillsdale, 325-3412; $–$$$ • *Swiss Hutte,* Route 22, Hillsdale, 325-3333; $–$$$ • *Texas Taco,* Route 22, Patterson, 878-9665; $.

SIGHTSEEING *Empire State Plaza,* information 474-2418. Tours: daily, hour-long regularly, from Visitor Services headquarters at north end of the underground concourse, 9 A.M. to 4 P.M. Free. Observation deck, daily, 9 A.M. to 5 P.M. Free • *New York State Museum,* Empire State Plaza, 474-5877. Hours: daily, 10 A.M. to 5 P.M. Free • *State Capitol Building,* Empire State Plaza, 474-2418. Tours: on the hour, daily, 9 A.M. to 4 P.M. Free • *Cherry Hill,* 523½ Pearl Street, 434-4791. Hours: Tuesday to Saturday, 10 A.M. to 4 P.M.; Sunday, 1 to 4 P.M. Adults $1, students 50¢, children age 6–16 25¢ • *Schuyler Mansion,* 27 Clinton Street, 474-3953. Hours: Wednesday to Sunday, 9 A.M. to 5 P.M. Free • *Ten Broeck Mansion,* 9 Ten Broeck Place, 436-9826. Hours: Tuesday to Sunday, 2 to 4 P.M. Free • Churches usually open daytime hours; phone to check; all free: *First Church in Albany,* North Pearl near Clinton, 463-4449 • *St. Peter's Church,* 107 State Street, 434-3502 • *Cathedral of All Saints,* 62 South Swan Street, 465-1342 • *Congregation Beth Emeth,* 100 Academy Road, 436-9761 • *John Boyd Thacher State Park,* Route 157 off Route 85. Hours: 9 A.M. to 10 P.M. through Labor Day, closes earlier after Labor Day. Free • *Indian Ladder Farms,* Route 156 (two miles west of Voorheesville) Altamont, 765-2956. Hours: Monday to Saturday, 9 A.M. to 5 P.M.; Sunday 10 A.M. to 5 P.M. • *The Shaker Museum,* Route 66, Old Chatham, 794-9100. Hours: May 1 to October 31, daily, 10 A.M. to 5 P.M. Adults $3, senior citizens $2.50, students $2, children age 6–14 $1 • *Howe Caverns,* Route 7, Howes Cave. Hours: daily, 9 A.M. to 6 P.M. Adults $4, children age 10–14 $2, under 9 free • *Catskill Game Farm,* Route 32, Catskill, 678-9595. Hours: April 15 to October 31, daily, 9 A.M. to 6 P.M. Adults $4.50, children age 4–12 $2.25.

FOR FURTHER INFORMATION Contact Albany County Convention and Visitors Bureau, Inc., 80 State Street, Albany, NY 12207, 434-1217.

Hounds and Houses in Chester County

For more than 40 years, it has been a ritual. Promptly at 9 A.M. on the first Saturday in October, the huntsman's horn sounds in Chester County, Pennsylvania. It is the signal for the running of horses and hounds for one of the frequent fox hunts in this fabled horse country— and it is the traditional start of the once-a-year celebration known as Chester County Day.

For the rest of the year much of this lush hilly region located roughly midway between Philadelphia and Pennsylvania Dutch country is somewhat private about its charms, except for the three major sights on the fringe of the county, Longwood Gardens, the Brandywine River Museum, and Valley Forge. But for this one day only, the entire county blows its own horn for the benefit of the local hospital, showing off dozens of its finest residences as well as the covered bridges, old mills, Quaker meetinghouses, gardens, and other historic sites that are all the more appealing just because they aren't widely touted. The day is so special that 6,000 people have been known to attend.

The crowds don't get overwhelming, however, because so many houses are open, everything from Federal-era rowhouses and columned mansions on the brick-paved streets of West Chester, the county seat, to stone manors and restored barns and carriagehouses in the country. So many homeowners take part in the day that two separate day-long itineraries are offered in different areas. Some of the owners also help to make the day more memorable with touches like the aroma of fresh-baked bread from the kitchen and spectacular arrangements of flowers and fruit in the rooms.

One of the particular pleasures of the tour is occasionally meeting some of the hosts whose families have lived in this area for generations. Chester County has been strongly influenced by its Quaker origins. People here don't show off. Their homes and possessions were made to last, and many live quietly everyday with family furniture, antiques, and china that would do credit to a museum.

When the owners aren't present, helpful guides will point out some of the treasures.

Because the county covers such a large area, tours alternate locale and emphasis each year. Recent ones have centered on the ironmasters country to the north, the special greenish-tint serpentine stone houses that are unique to this district, and for the 1982 tricentennial year, the focus will be homes associated with William Penn, who settled the area 300 years ago. Slide-show previews of the homes included are offered on Friday night at Longwood Gardens and the West Chester court-house to help visitors make the difficult choice of which houses they want to see most. If you can't make these 7, 8, and 9 P.M. showings, early-bird shows are given on Saturday morning at the hospital in West Chester, where bus tours are available for those who prefer not to drive themselves. The slide shows are included in the price of the tour.

A good plan is to write well ahead for a copy of the *County Day* newspaper, which is usually published in August and outlines the year's current tours. The itineraries may influence where you decide to stay for the weekend, but two safe bets any year are West Chester and the Longwood area, both with plenty of accommodations.

The tour will keep you so busy on Saturday you probably won't want to take time for a long lunch. However, a stop at the Marketplace Deli or at the perfectly elegant French Corner takeout shop in West Chester center will equip you with a fine portable meal to be enjoyed along the way. Come dinnertime, you can choose from a whole roster of charming country inns.

If you can spare a few minutes on Saturday, do have a look at the small but exceptional Chester County Historical Society Museum in West Chester (closed on Sundays). It is filled with exquisite clocks, furniture, inlaid chests, embroidery, Tucker porcelain, and majolica pottery made by local craftsmen, the kinds of pieces that are often featured on the covers of magazines for antique collectors.

Sunday offers other delightful possibilities. You might want to head for Marshallton to see the annual Triatholon Race beginning at noon, sponsored by the Marshallton Inn. It's a unique and wacky event, competition via canoe, bicycle, and Olympic walk-step. Normally this is a quaint quiet village, but on this day the Inn and the nearby Oyster Bar restaurant set up food stands out-of-doors. The place is jumping all afternoon and into the evening, when a Dixieland band holds forth.

If you didn't really see much of the town on Saturday, a walking tour of West Chester is a quieter and quite interesting occupation. The town is a parade of architectural variety—green serpentine stone, brick townhouses, gingerbread porches, porticoed doorways, iron-lace fences, Greek columns. The courthouse, a bank, and a church are massive-columned Greek Revival structures designed by the architect of the nation's capitol, which once caused the little town to be dubbed the Athens of Pennsylvania. The firehouse and public library are Gothic buildings adorned with Tiffany windows. The residential life of the 1800s can be seen in restored houses on Portico Row, Pottery Row, Stone Row, and Wayne Square.

Another special pleasure in the area is the little Dilworthtown Country Store, located south of West Chester on Brinton Bridge Road just off Route 202. It has been at the same stand since 1758, and the original stone walls and low beams add atmosphere to a tantalizing stock of penny candy, country antiques, bolts of calico, hand-fired tools, hand-dipped candles, folk toys, baskets, quilts, and all manner of one-of-a-kind creations from neighborhood craftsmen. The Dilworthtown Inn right next door is one of the best in the area, a good bet for Saturday or Sunday dinner.

Take a drive up Birmingham Road, just past the inn, to see the magnificent gentlemen's farms, a Quaker meetinghouse, an octagonal schoolhouse and a historic old cemetery.

If the day is fine and you want to enjoy the out-of-doors, take a stroll around the Brandywine Battlefield State Park near Chadds Ford, where you can visit restorations of Washington's and Lafayette's headquarters. Or, a half-hour's drive will take you to the 2,200-acre national park at Valley Forge, resplendent in autumn colors. Longwood Gardens and the Brandywine River Museum with its Wyeths are other perennial attractions, different with each change of seasons.

Between Longwood and the Museum, Route 1 is lined with antique shops, and a busy flea market is in action every Sunday. While you are in Kennett Square, you can also make a stop at the Mushroom Museum and Shop at Phillips Place. The giant mushrooms for sale here in the town that calls itself the world's mushroom capital will make the ones in your local supermarket look like miniatures.

On the less traveled roads to the north you can visit a former elegant spa at Yellow Springs, now an arts and crafts center, or St. Peters Village, a restored Victorian settlement of stores and crafts shops near another state park along French Creek.

North or south, the backroads of Chester County don't get a lot of attention compared to those in nearby Bucks or Lancaster counties, yet they are full of unexpected discoveries—historic, scenic, and just plain fun. You'll find that whatever direction you choose to explore, it's almost impossible to make a wrong turn.

Chester County Area Code: 215

DRIVING DIRECTIONS   Take the New Jersey Turnpike south to exit 6, Pennsylvania Turnpike, then west to exit 24, Schuylkill Expressway (Route 76), then south to route 202 south to West Chester. Continue on 202 to Route 1 west to Longwood Gardens.
Total distance: 120 miles.

ACCOMMODATIONS   *West Chester Inn,* Route 202, West Chester, 692-1900, a motel, but a nice one; $–$$ ● *Chadds Ford Ramada Inn,* Routes 1 and 202, Chadds Ford, 358-1700; $–$$ ● *Brandywine Inn,* Route 202, near Delaware line, 459-0995, dining and a few inn-type rooms; $–$$ ● *Longwood Inn,* Route 1, Kennett Square, 444-3515; $.

DINING   All of the following are attractive old country inns; pick one that is convenient and phone for exact driving directions: *Brandywine Inn* (see above); $$ ● *Chadds Ford Inn,* Route 1, Chadds Ford, 388-7361; $$ ● *Mendenhall Inn,* Route 52, Mendenhall, 459-2140; $$ ● *Red Rose Inn,* Routes 1 and 796, Jennersville, 869-3003; $ ● *Historic Dilworthtown Inn,* Old Wilmington Pike and Brinton

Bridge Road, Dilworthtown, south of West Chester, 399-1390; $$–$$$
● *Warren Tavern,* Old Lancaster Avenue, Malvern, 296-3637; $$$
● *Marshallton Inn,* 1300 West Strasburg Road (Route 162), Mar-
shallton, 692-4367; $$ ● *La Cocotte,* 124 West Gay Street, West
Chester, 692-4367, French local favorite; $$ ● *Pace One,* Thornton-
Concord Road, Thornton, 459-9784, a restored barn; good for Sunday
brunch, $$, dinner $$$.

SIGHTSEEING *Chester County Day,* tours $10 (no children under
12); bus tours from Chester County Hospital beginning at 8:15 A.M.
(first two buses depart for the hunt), $15; tickets include slide show
previews. For information, tickets, copy of *County Day* advance
newspaper, write Chester County Day, P. O. Box 1, West Chester, PA
19380. For phone information and additional information on Chester
County accommodations and attractions, contact Chester County
Tourist Promotion Bureau, 33 West Market Street, West Chester, PA
19380, 431-6365 ● *Longwood Gardens,* US 1, Kennett Square,
388-6741. Hours: daily, 9 A.M. to 6 P.M.; conservatories 10 A.M. to 5
P.M. Adults $3, children age 6–14 $1 ● *Brandywine River Museum,* US
1, Chadds Ford, 388-7601. Hours: daily, 9:30 A.M. to 4:30 P.M. Adults
$1.75, children age 6–12 75¢ ● *Brandywine Battlefield Park,* US 1,
Chadds Ford, 459-3342. Hours: Tuesday to Saturday, 9 A.M. to 5 P.M.;
Sunday noon to 5 P.M. Free ● *Mushroom Place Museum,* US 1,
Kennett Square. Hours: daily, 10 A.M. to 6 P.M. Free ● *Valley Forge
National Historical Park,* near Pennsylvania Turnpike exit 24,
783-7700. Hours: daily, 8:30 A.M. to 5 P.M. Free. Guided bus tours,
adults $3, children age 6–16 $2.

Fairs, Festivals, and Big Apples in the Nutmeg State

There was music coming from a carousel on the midway, an oxen draw
scheduled at one, a corn husking contest at two, and a wild west show
about to begin.

But for one towheaded four-year-old named Billy, it was all an
anticlimax. The highlight of his day had been a new acquaintance
named Elsie. She was the first cow he had ever seen outside of a
storybook.

From July to October country fairs are in high gear all over the state
of Connecticut, a harvest ritual that gives farmers a showcase for their

crops and livestock, homemakers a place to exhibit their prize baking and canning, and everyone the opportunity for some old-fashioned fun.

For many a suburban or city parent, however, the best show of all is watching youngsters like Billy wide-eyed at their first sight of real, live farm animals.

A stamped self-addressed envelope will get you a full listing of current dates and times of fairs in the Nutmeg State from the Association of Connecticut Fairs.

Often the last fairs of the season offer a bonus since they are strategically located in scenic central and northwestern parts of the state that offer fine foliage as well as other special fall pleasures—hayrides, harvest festivals, apple picking, and a dazzling display of thousands of chrysanthemums in bloom.

Fairs usually are scheduled in late September and early October for the towns of Durham, Berlin, Harwinton, and Riverton. Each one offers its unique attractions. Durham may present arts and crafts and antiques along with top-name country music acts. There will probably be nail-driving, wood-chopping, and corn-husking contests; a frog jump; and a turtle race in Berlin. Harwinton has featured an early America display with demonstrations of old-time crafts and a country store, while Riverton, the smallest of the fairs, offers competitions in sawing and chopping, as well as a pie-eating contest. Exact events may change, but the general pattern does not.

Whichever fair you choose you'll see fine specimens of sheep, goats, poultry, rabbits, pigs, and other livestock competing for blue ribbons; as well as prize crops, cooking, and baking, and such down-home competitions as horse, oxen, and tractor pulls. All the fairs offer entertainment as well.

And wherever you attend, you'll be within a short drive of Bristol, where Bristol Nurseries, which has been described as the Disneyworld of the plant world, puts on an eye-boggling show each year during chrysanthemum season, with more than 80,000 specimens of mums, button-size to giant pompons, in an autumn rainbow of golds, bronzes, yellows, whites, and purples of every hue. Bring plenty of color film.

The whole town gets into the spirit of things with a chrysanthemum festival in late September, featuring an art show, a parade, and a Mum Ball crowning each season's queen.

While you're in Bristol have a look at the American Clock and Watch Museum, one of a few of its kind in the country. There are more than 1,600 time-keeping exhibits, some dating as far back as 1680, many of the pieces manufactured in Connecticut.

Not far away in Terryville, you can sample another kind of fall country tradition, a hayride. Just climb aboard with Ken Wood of Wood Acres, and you'll go lumbering off for an hour's drive through the woods, ensconced in a wagon piled high with sweet-smelling hay and pulled by a picture-book pair of giant dapple gray Percheron horses.

A few miles farther west is Litchfield, one of the state's oldest and loveliest towns, with a wide stately main street of 1700s Colonial mansions that rightfully ranks as one of the region's most beautiful. It's at its best in fall dress and definitely rates a detour. You can also visit the nation's first law school, the Tapping Reeve House, here.

If the Riverton Fair is your destination, be sure to stop at the Hitchcock Museum to see examples of the famous nineteenth-century chairs. The present Hitchcock factory here maintains many of the old handmade procedures and has a showroom and gift shop open to the public. Note that museum and factory are both closed on Sundays. There's also a Seth Thomas clock outlet store here, and other pleasant shops.

Fair or not, foliage watchers will want to head to Riverton for a drive through the People's State Forest nearby, a ride made even more beautiful by the reflected colors in the sparkling reservoir running beside the road. There are several scenic stopoffs on the forest road, many of them with picnic areas.

Finally, if your outing includes the first two weekends of October, you'll find the annual Apple Harvest Festival in full swing around the village green in Southington, an easy stopoff on your way home.

Pie-eating contests and apple-bobbing competitions are the order of the day along with a "Just Mutts" dog show, an old-time parade, and all kinds of races, including the wild and woolly "bed race," in which cribs, four-posters, and brass bedsteads come careening down hill to the delight of cheering spectators.

All through the festival an arts and crafts fair is open, and foodstands will offer pies, fritters, fried apple rings, caramel apples, cider, and just about everything having to do with fall's favorite crop.

If all the festivities inspire you to want to do some apple picking on your own, there are orchards in Cheshire, not far south on Route 10; Wallingford, off Route 91; and Middlefield, north of Durham on Route 157, where you are invited to do just that. A call ahead of time to the orchards is advisable, just to make sure the pick-them-yourself policy is still in effect.

As for the apple festival, it's all authentic small-town Americana, unsophisticated fun for everyone, and as traditional as—you guessed it—apple pie.

Connecticut Area Code: 203

DRIVING DIRECTIONS   Take I-95 New England Thruway. For Durham, get off at exit 48, I-91 connection at New Haven, then follow I-91 to exit 15, Route 68 east. For Berlin, from I-91 take Routes 5 and 15, Berlin Turnpike, at Meriden. For Harwinton and Riverton, get off I-95 at Route 8 (exit 27), just past Bridgeport. Harwinton is east of 8 on Route 118; Riverton is farther north and also east on Route 20.
Total distance: about 110 miles.

ACCOMMODATIONS   *Holiday Inn,* 900 East Main Street, Meriden (at junction Ct. 15 and I-91, I-91 exits 16 or 17; convenient for Durham or Southington); 238-1211; $$ • *Hawthorne Motor Inn,* 2837 Wilbur Cross Highway (Ct. 15), Berlin, 828-4181; $$ • *Jay's,* 51 E. Main Street, Terryville, 583-5417; $ • *Old Riverton Inn,* Ct. 20, Riverton, 379-8678; $ with breakfast • *Yankee Pedlar Inn,* 93 Main Street, Torrington (off Ct. 8, convenient for Harwinton), 489-9226; $$–$$$.

DINING   *Yankee Pedlar Inn* (see above); $–$$ • *Old Riverton Inn* (see above); $–$$ • *Hawthorne Inn* (see above); $–$$.

SIGHTSEEING   *Country Fairs.* For free listing of fairs, dates, events, and admission fees, call the Connecticut Department of Economic Development toll-free at (800) 243-1685 for the current address of the Association of Connecticut Fairs (the chairman changes annually). Enclose a self-addressed stamped legal size envelope • *American Clock and Watch Museum,* 100 Maple Street off Route 6, Bristol, 583-6070. Hours: daily, 11 A.M. to 5 P.M. Adults $2, children age 8–15 $1, under 8 free • *Tapping Reeve House and Law School,* South Street (Route 63), Litchfield, 567-8919. Hours: Tuesday to Saturday, 11 A.M. to 5 P.M. Adults $1.50, children 50¢ • *Hitchcock Museum,* Route 20, Riverton. Hours: June to October, Tuesday to Saturday, 10 A.M. to 5 P.M.; November through May, Saturdays only • *Hayrides,* Ken Wood, Wood Acres, Terryville, 583-8670. Admission $1 per person, $2 minimum for a one-hour ride. Phone in advance for reservations and driving directions • *Apple Orchards,* Phone to confirm information before you go: Drazen Orchards, 241 Wallingford Road, Cheshire, 272-7985; Hickory Hill Orchard, 351 S. Meriden Road, Cheshire, 272-3824; Lyman Farms, junction Routes 147 and 157, Middlefield, 349-9337; Ives Orchards, end of Tankwood Road, Wallingford, 634-0825; Young and Sons, Inc., 22 South Branford Road, Wallingford, 269-3865 • *Southington Apple Harvest Festival,* contact

Greater Southington Chamber of Commerce, 7 North Main Street, Southington, CT 06489, 628-8036, for current festival information and dates ● *Bristol Chrysanthemum Festival,* call 589-3434 for information and dates.

Family Foliage Parade to West Point and Museum Village

The thing that takes many first-time visitors to West Point by surprise is the sheer beauty of the place. The same perch high above the Hudson that once allowed Colonial troops to watch out for British ships up and down river now serves as a peaceful outlook over river and plains, with a remarkable perspective on the glorious fall foliage of the Hudson Valley.

For many who don't consider themselves promilitary, there is a second surprise in the impressiveness of the stone buildings and the contagious pride you sense in the young cadets who are continuing the "long gray line" of patriots who marched here before them.

As a result, lots of parents who come to the U.S. Military Academy primarily for the kids wind up loving the place themselves, particularly if they are able to make it on a football weekend, when the cadets are out for a full-dress parade.

Football or not, a day at West Point combined with a Sunday visit to the old-time craftsmen at Orange County's excellent Museum Village at Monroe is an ideal itinerary for fall family foliage watching— maximum scenery for the front seat, with minimum driving to inspire complaints from the back.

A phone call to the Academy Information Center of Public Affairs office will give you an up-to-date schedule of games, ticket information, and news of any other special events around the time you plan to visit. Even if you are able to get tickets to a game, you may have a problem finding a motel room nearby. But since the drive is short and scenic, it is easy enough to start from home Saturday morning and move out of the area for the night. You can see the cadet parade whether you see the game or not, and if you bring along a picnic lunch the day at West Point won't cost you a cent. All the sights are free to visitors.

First stop at the Academy is the Visitor Information Office just inside Thayer Gate. A movie on West Point is shown here hourly, and they'll give you a self-guided tour map, schedule of the day, and any other data you might like before you set out.

The tour takes you toward Michie (pronounced *my*-key) Stadium and the parking fields nearest to Fort Putnam. It's an uphill path to the fort, so wear your best walking shoes. The fortress includes a small museum and gives you some idea of a soldier's living conditions during the time of the American Revolution, as well as a splendid view of West Point and the river.

Mill Road leads on past the magnificent Gothic Cadet Chapel, which has outstanding stained-glass windows and the largest church organ in the world (18,000 pipes), and farther on past the gracious nineteenth-century homes of the superintendent and the commandant, facing the parade grounds known as The Plain.

Among the roster of cadets who have marched here are presidents Ulysses S. Grant and Dwight D. Eisenhower; Jefferson Davis; General George Armstrong Custer; and Edward White, the first astronaut to walk in space. Major General George W. Goethals, who designed the Panama Canal, was another West Point alumnus, as was Abner Doubleday, a Union commander in the Civil War who is far better known as the inventor of baseball.

A hint: If you plan to see a parade, arrive at The Plain early for good viewing or a parking space in the lots nearby.

Trophy Point is a special favorite spot for most young children, who love clambering over the cannons. Among the many relics on display at the point overlooking the river are links from the giant chain that was once stretched across the Hudson from West Point to Constitution Island to block the progress of the British fleet. The links weigh 300 pounds apiece.

A statue of the Polish soldier, Thaddeus Kosciuszko, who master-minded this blockade strategy, is elsewhere on the grounds. The battle monument at Trophy Point is dedicated to the men who were killed in the Civil War.

The West Point Museum in Thayer Academic Hall is one of the largest collections of military history in the Western hemisphere. It is a two-story panorama of the art of war from prehistory through Vietnam, and includes models of famous battles and a re-creation of the Civil War Shenandoah Valley campaign of 1862, spearheaded by another West Point graduate, Thomas J. "Stonewall" Jackson.

There's even more to see at the Academy. In the Post Cemetery is the Old Cadet Chapel, with walls lined with battle flags, and marble shields commemorating the American generals of the Revolutionary War. One shield bears only a date and no name; it belonged to Benedict Arnold, who tried to betray the fort to the British when he was in command of this post in 1780. Some other remaining sights are the Chapel of the Most Holy Trinity, a Catholic church in Norman Gothic style patterned after an abbey church in England, and Fort Clinton, another Revolutionary War station. And you might enjoy dropping into Grant Hall, where the cadets gather in their free time.

There are designated picnic sites overlooking the river, just north of the public dock where the Hudson Dayliner pulls in. The only other place to eat on the grounds is the Hotel Thayer, which is used by visiting families of cadets. It's a fine place to stay if you can get in, as well as a reasonable choice for a family dinner. If you want fast-food establishments, you'll find them in Highland Falls outside the gate, and there are also places here that will prepare a picnic for you if you haven't brought one from home.

If you can't get a room at the Thayer or in Highland Falls, the pleasant rustic Bear Mountain Inn is just a few miles away. Otherwise your best bet is in Newburgh, which itself is a historic town with many Revolutionary War sites. Two of the principal ones are the Jonathan Hasbrouck house on Liberty Street, Washington's final headquarters during the war, and the New Windsor Cantonment off Route 32, a reconstruction of the last American encampment, which also has the only surviving log structure actually built by the troops.

Both are free and open at 9 A.M. if you want to stop in before you drive farther south on Route 87 and turn west on Route 17 to exit 129 and the Museum Village of Orange County. This is one of the country's largest outdoor museums, with more than 30 buildings telling the story of the making of crafts in nineteenth-century America, from handwork to the beginnings of modern technology. It offers an interesting and entertaining bit of history with demonstrations of pottery and broom-making, weaving, blacksmithing, printing, and other trades and crafts. Among the buildings you can tour are a one-room school, a general store, a blacksmith's shop, an apothecary, and a log cabin. On October weekends you'll see special demonstrations of "putting by for winter," autumn chores such as grinding and drying corn, preserving, cidering, and other typical activities on a farm in the fall season 150 years ago. There is a snack bar on the museum grounds and once again, picnic facilities.

From here it's a short drive to county Route 13 and Sugar Loaf, a village full of crafts shops where you can watch latter-day artisans at work and possibly pick up an original souvenir of your trip.

Sugar Loaf makes for a pleasant transition back to the present, and you may still have enough light to get in some last foliage watching as you connect back to Route 17 and an easy drive home.

West Point Area Code: 914

DRIVING DIRECTIONS   George Washington Bridge to Palisades Interstate Parkway to Bear Mountain Circle (end of parkway); then Route 9W north, following signs to Highland Falls and West Point. *Total distance:* 50 miles.

ACCOMMODATIONS   *Hotel Thayer,* U.S. Military Academy grounds, West Point, 446-4731; $ ● *Palisades Motel,* Route 218 off 9W, Highland Falls, 446-9400; $ ● *West Point Motel,* 361 Main Street, Highland Falls, 446-8726; $–$$ ● *Howard Johnson's Motor Lodge,* Route 17K at Thruway, Newburgh, 565-4100; $ ● *Holiday Inn,* Route 17K at Thruway, Newburgh, 565-2100; $$ ● *Bear Mountain Inn,* Bear Mountain State Park, 786-2731; $$.

DINING   *Hotel Thayer* (see above); $–$$ ● *Bear Mountain Inn* (see above); $$; Sunday buffet $ ● *Beau Rivage,* 538 River Road, Newburgh, 561-9799, Colonial home, continental menu; $–$$.

SIGHTSEEING   *U.S. Military Academy,* Information Center just inside Thayer Gate, 938-2638. Hours: daily, April to November, 8:30 A.M. to 4:30 P.M. Phone for parade schedules and other information, or call Public Affairs office, 938-3507. All West Point buildings except cadet barracks and academic halls are open to visitors and are free ● *Museum Village in Orange County,* Museum Village Road, NY 17M, US 6. (New York 17, exit 129). Hours: daily, May to October, 10 A.M. to 5 P.M. Adults $3.50, children age 6–15 $2.75.

A Taste for History in the Tobacco Valley

The oldest house in the oldest town in Connecticut has a colorful gallery of ghosts in its past—and a guide who delights in telling about them.

"Here's the happy couple," she began, pointing to dour-faced portraits of Lieutenant and Mrs. Fyler, the home's original owners. "And here's the cupboard where they hid the booze when the parson came to call."

The woman's lively commentary proved an appropriate introduction to Windsor and to Connecticut's "Tobacco Valley," an area that seems to relish its history. Named for its best-known farm crop, this area just north of Hartford has the look of old New England and more than its share of sightseeing variety. In the peaceful little towns within the valley you can prowl the passages of a notorious underground prison or stroll through three centuries of a town's history collected into one compact historical center. A bonus is a ride through the scenic woodlands of the state-maintained People's Forest.

A good place to begin your tour is Windsor, a town that was already 140 years old when the Declaration of Independence was signed in 1776. Windsor's historic district still boasts its village green, a 1630 white-steepled church, the original town burying ground, and about three dozen houses built before the Revolutionary War. Six of the houses date back to the 1600s. Almost all are still occupied.

Open to visitors is the Oliver Ellsworth Homestead, the elegant Colonial home of the nation's third chief justice. Fyler House, the oldest of the houses, has been meticulously cared for and filled with furnishings that reflect its rich history as a home, a shop, and the town post office. Adjacent Wilson Museum displays more mementos of the town's past. If you're lucky you'll get the guide who'll fill you in on the juicier details.

Windsor is also the heart of the tobacco-farming area that gives the valley its name. Connecticut Shade Grown Tobacco is known through the world as the finest wrapper leaves available for quality cigars. At Kendrick Brothers Farm off Poquonock Road, you can see the tobacco growing under netting on a family-run farm that has been in continuous operation since 1635.

Head north on Palisado Avenue, Windsor's main street, and you'll get yourself right back to US 91. Head north and take the exit for Route 20 to East Granby, where you'll come upon one of the most unusual of our national historic landmarks, the old New Gate Prison and Copper Mine. First chartered as a mine in 1707, it was converted into a prison in 1773, designated as a place of confinement for burglars, horse thieves, robbers, and counterfeiters. During the Revolution it was used for Tories and prisoners of war. During its forty-two-year history as a prison, more than 800 prisoners were committed to New Gate's underground cells.

Today you can go down into the mine for a well-lit, self-guided tour of the winding passages where the prisoners lived in total darkness. Bring a sweater; mine temperatures can be in the mid-forties even on a sunny day.

Plane buffs will want to detour here on Route 75 near Bradley

Airport in Windsor Locks, where the Bradley Air Museum has once again come to life after a 1979 tornado that all but destroyed the place. On display are 25 historic aircraft, including a 1909 Bleriot, a Laird 1930 national air race winner, and a Republic F-105B Thunderchief, a 1950s-vintage fighter aircraft.

Some of the earliest coins minted in the original Granby mines are on display at Massacoh Plantation in nearby Simsbury, to the south on Route 202. This 22-acre site traces three centuries of Simsbury history. On the grounds are a Victorian carriagehouse, manufacturing exhibits, a sleigh shed, a one-room schoolhouse, an icehouse, and a seventeenth-century meetinghouse. One of the favorite exhibits is a Yankee peddler's wagon, loaded with geegaws and knickknacks.

Massacoh's Phelps House is one of the finest remaining examples of an old Connecticut tavern. Be sure to note the narrow lighted cupboard over the mantel. It is a rarity that is believed to have been built by a retired shipwright since it is reminiscent of forecastles of sailing ships. Look carefully and you'll see that the paneling in the tavern room includes witches' crosses meant to keep evil spirits away while the men enjoyed their liquid spirits.

Simsbury, with its wide, tree-shaded main street, is one of the valley's most charming villages. It's also an ideal place for browsing. Simsburytown Shops is a complex of boutiques featuring everything from cookery to Indian jewelry to homemade pâté. The Ellsworth Art Gallery at Massacoh Plantation has contemporary art of high quality.

While you're in Simsbury, make a stop at the One-Way Fare, an atmospheric restaurant quartered in a restored railroad station right behind the plantation. Sunday brunch is particularly recommended.

A few miles south in Avon, the Farmington Valley Arts Center on Route 44 is another pleasant browsing spot, a collection of artists' studios, gallery, bookstore, and shops housed in a historic stone building that was once an explosives plant.

Finally, for fall foliage watching, take Route 44 west out of Avon, turn right at Route 318 past New Hartford and watch for the road that takes you through the People's State Forest to Riverton. It's a drive made even more beautiful by the reflections in the sparkling reservoir that runs beside the road, and there are several scenic stopoffs along the way to let you enjoy the view, many with picnic areas.

To end the day with a last look at the colorful Connecticut hills, take Route 20 west out of Riverton and connect with Route 8 south. You'll enjoy panoramic vistas almost all the way back to the junction of the Merritt Parkway before Bridgeport.

Windsor Area Code: 203

DRIVING DIRECTIONS Hutchinson River Parkway to the Merritt Parkway to I-91. Take exit 37, Route 305 to Windsor. Bear left onto Route 159 across the Farmington River into the historic district.
Total distance: about 123 miles.

ACCOMMODATIONS *Sheraton Tobacco Valley Inn,* 450 Bloomfield Avenue at I-91, exit ·37, Route 305, 688-5221; $$, weekend package available • *Ramada Inn,* 5 Turnpike Road at junction of routes 20 and 75 off I-91 at Bradley International Airport exit, 622-9494; $$ • *Executive Inn,* 969 Hopmeadow Street, Simsbury, 658-2216; $$ • *Avon Old Farms Inn,* routes 44 and 10, Avon, 677-2818, five Colonial rooms in 1757 inn, another 44 motel units; $$.

DINING *Dunfey's Tavern,* Sheraton-Tobacco Valley Inn, Windsor (see above), Colonial, new, but with charm; $$ • *One-Way Fare,* 4 Railroad Street, Simsbury, 658-4422; $ • *Chart House,* 4 Hartford Road, Simsbury, 658-1118, former 1780 tavern; $–$$ • *Avon Old Farms Inn* (see above); $$ • *Chez Serge,* Avon Park North, 678-0175, elegant French restaurant in a rustic carriagehouse; $$$.

SIGHTSEEING *Bradley Air Museum,* Route 75 at Bradley International Airport, Windsor Locks, 623-3305. Hours: daily, 10 A.M. to 6 P.M. Adults $3, children age 6–11 $1.50 • *Fyler House and Wilson Museum,* 96 Palisado Avenue, Windsor, 688-3813. Hours: Tuesday to Saturday, 10 A.M. to noon, 1 to 4 P.M., April to November. Adults $1, children under 13 25¢ • *Oliver Ellsworth Homestead,* 778 Palisado Avenue, Windsor, 688-8717. Hours: Tuesday to Saturday, 1 to 5 P.M. April to September. Adults $1, children under 12 free • *Old New Gate Prison,* Newgate Road, East Granby, 653-3563. Hours: daily, 10 A.M. to 4:30 P.M. April to October. Adults $1.50, children age 6–17 50¢, under 6 free.

Year-round Color in Pennsylvania Dutch Country

It may be at its scenic best against a backdrop of autumn foliage, but there's plenty of color left even after the leaves fall in Pennsylvania Dutch country.

Picture-book farms, bright hex signs, windmills, and covered bridges dot the landscape. You'll still find yourself sharing the roads with black-frocked men and bonneted women driving shiny horse-and-buggy rigs into town. And the auctions, the farmers' markets, and the colorful shops await anytime you visit this unique corner of America.

The large number of people who do want to visit, however, have spawned a bit of a paradox. The area is filled with touristy gift shops and tourist-oriented recreations of Amish villages and farms when the most interesting sights by far are the real thing. Don't waste your time, which will seem short enough anyway; pick the most authentic of the attractions vying for your attention.

A good start might be a reservation for a room on a Mennonite farm. Or you could stay at the only real inn in the region, the 1767 General Sutter in Lititz (accent on the first syllable), seven miles north of Lancaster. It puts you right on the square of one of the most carefully preserved towns in Lancaster County, one with a special flavor from its Moravian origins. A walk down Main Street in Lititz takes you past more than a dozen homes dating to the mid-1700s and the brick and stucco buildings of the Moravian Church Square, which include the church itself and the old Brethren's and Sisters' Houses.

At 221 Main Street you can visit the Pretzel House where owner Julius Sturgis made the first commercial pretzels in the United States in an adjoining bakery. (You'll have a chance to try your own hand at fancy twisting.) The Museum-House of Johannes Mueller at 137 Main is practically unchanged since Mr. Mueller lived there in 1792.

The delicious aroma that lingers over Lititz is from Wilbur's Chocolate Factory, where you are invited in to see displays of historical candymaking equipment.

Having savored the peaceful small-town flavor of Lititz, move on to the city of Lancaster and one of its famous farmer's markets—potpourris of fresh fruits and vegetables; savory homemade bolognas, sausages, and scrapple; and homebaked pies, cakes, and cookies, as delicious to the eye and nose as to the tummy, await you there.

Lancaster, the oldest inland city in the United States, could easily fill up a day on its own. Among the many things to do and see in town are the historic walking tour led by costumed guides; Wheatlands, the beautifully preserved home of President James Buchanan; the Heritage Center of Lancaster County in the Old City Hall; Rock Ford and the Kaufman Museum (home of a Revolutionary War commander and a barn containing collections of rifles and folk artifacts), and the Community Art Gallery. Nearby, too, are the largest collection of timepieces anywhere at the National Association of Watch and Clock

Collectors Museum in Columbia and a Railroad Museum plus rides on a huffy-puffy old-fashioned steam train at the Strasburg Railroad.

But if you have just a two-day weekend, you might do better to settle for the market and concentrate on the small towns and the countryside that are the real heart of Pennsylvania Dutch country.

Begin at the visitors' center outside of Lancaster on Route 30, where you can arm yourself with maps and information and see a 27-minute film to prepare you for the sights ahead. You'll learn that the people of the region are not Dutch at all, but German ("Deutsch" became "Dutch" to the American ear), and that the Amish are only one sect among the "Plain People."

The bearded men you'll spot along the road are all Amish married men, obliged to mark their status by this very visible sign.

It is a firm belief among the "Old Order" of the Amish that duty to God means living simply and tilling the soil. Cars, phones, and electricity are forbidden not because they are considered evil in themselves but because they are temptations to a more worldly life. A more liberal sect, called "Church Amish," because they hold services in a church rather than at home, does allow electricity and cars, but only in plain black models. Mennonites are similar to the Old Order; you can spot their buggies because they are flat-roofed and black, while the Amish vehicles have rounded roofs and are painted grey.

In spite of warnings about some of those tourist attractions, you may well want to make time at this point for one, the Amish Farm and House, a bit farther east on Route 30, simply because it is a chance you might not get otherwise to see the inside of a typical Amish home and a close-up look at a working farm in operation. You'll discover that while their clothes and furnishings are plain, the Amish show their love of beauty indoors through the artistic decorations on the old dower chests, the gaily painted china, and the embroidered towels inside the home.

Finally it's time to get out into the real countryside again, following busy Route 30 through Paradise and wandering along any of the lush, peaceful backroads between routes 30 and 340 to see the farms. You'll recognize the Amish homesteads by their windmills and lack of electric wires; note also the distinctive additions on some of the farms. Known as "Gross Dawdis," they are an Amish solution to the generation gap. When a farmer reaches retirement age, an annex to the main house is built, allowing him to enjoy the fruits of his labor and still be part of the family group without getting in the way of the younger generation coming up. Sometimes you'll see double additions, marking a three-generation home.

Continue back west on 340 through Intercourse and Bird-in-Hand.

You'll need no guide on any of the main roads to find shops full of hex signs and fudge and every gift imaginable with Pennsylvania Dutch motifs. Some more interesting stops, however, are clustered around Intercourse. The People's Place is a center for Amish and Mennonite arts and crafts, The Quilt Room in the Old Country Store on Main Street has quilts made by local craftswomen, and one-of-a-kind handmade furniture is still turned out at Ebersol's Chair Shop.

There is a regular Saturday Farmer's Market in Bird-in-Hand, and with luck you could also find yourself here for one of the auctions that take place on some Saturdays behind Zimmerman's Store. One of the special pleasures of an auction is the possibility of seeing the Amish at close range and hearing their quaint dialects; another is the chance to garner one of those decorated dower chests. Don't expect huge bargains, but you may well pay less than you would outside this area. Auction dates change, so ask at your farm or inn or motel to find out where you are likely to find one in action during your visit.

One last attraction well worth a stop is the excellent state-operated Pennsylvania Farm Museum. More than 30 buildings here filled with 250,000 items portray rural life and the role of agriculture in Pennsylvania history. Four of the buildings are period homes of 150 years ago; others are shops, farms, a school and a tavern. The annual Harvest Days held here the first weekend of October portray old-fashioned crafts and activities of the season such as apple drying, apple-butter making, drying and grinding corn.

On Sunday wend your way through the countryside west on Route 772 to 272 to Mennonite country and one of its most interesting settlements, the Cloister, a restored community of a monastic sect founded in 1730. You'll have to duck your head to enter the low doorways (a reminder of humility) and go single-file down the narrow halls (symbols of the straight and narrow path) to see where these dedicated people lived and the narrow wooden ledges where they slept—with eight-inch wooden blocks for pillows. There are eight surviving buildings, evoking an unusually vivid sense of the austere way of life practiced here.

From spartan Ephrata, drive north toward Reading and you're on your way to Gay Dutch country, famous for its enormous banked barns decorated with giant versions of those brightly painted geometrical designs known as hex signs. Contrary to the name, the signs have nothing to do with warding off evil, but are there only for their color and beauty, or as the Dutch say, "chust for nice." These are so delightful you may be inspired to buy some miniatures as souvenirs after all.

Old Route 22, which parallels Route 78, is known as Hex Highway for the large numbers of barns it passes by. Contact the Berks County Travel Association, and they will send you a free map showing the best side roads for barn watching. Route 183 from Reading to Bernville and Shartlesville has a few barns along the way, and Shartlesville is your last chance for a real Pennsylvania Dutch meal at Haag's Hotel, which has been serving up groaning tables to tourists for four generations.

An average meal here includes chicken, ham, and beef (all you can eat), lima beans, ceci (chick peas), dried corn, garden peas, the Dutch "seven sweets and seven sours," which might include pickled beets, pepper cabbage, olives, pickles, piccalilli, apple sauce, dried apricots, and all manner of desserts including homebaked pies such as lemon sponge and that molasses-flavored local delicacy, Shoo-Fly Pie. If it isn't the best meal you've ever had, it will certainly be one of the biggest.

Continuing west on the Hex Highway to Lenhartsville, you can turn south on 143 and watch for the covered bridge on the left, then make a right to one side road boasting nine barns. If you drive north on 143 you'll come to a bird and nature-lover's special retreat, Hawk Mountain, the only designated sanctuary for birds of prey, a place to spy eagles and hawks on their migratory patterns in the fall as well as get spectacular views of the entire area spread below.

From either direction you can connect with Route 78 and a direct drive back to New York—which may suddenly seem much farther than a three-hour drive away from the spirit of Pennsylvania Dutch Country.

Lancaster Area Code: 717

DRIVING DIRECTIONS New Jersey Turnpike to the Pennsylvania Turnpike to Route 222 south to Route 30 into Lancaster; Lititz is 7 miles north on Route 501.
Total distance: 159 miles.

ACCOMMODATIONS *General Sutter Inn,* 14 East Main Street, Lititz, 636-2115; $–$$ • *Treadway Resort Inn,* 222 Eden Road, Lancaster, 569-6444; $–$$ • *Sheraton Conestoga Resort,* Oregon Pike, Lancaster, 393-0731; $–$$ • A new and noteworthy addition, unique in the area: *Cameron Estate Inn,* RD #1, Donegal Springs Road, Mount Joy, 653-2048, a restored Victorian mansion; rooms $$–$$$ • For extensive list of area motels, maps, and tourist information, contact the Pennsylvania Dutch Visitors Bureau, 1799 Hempstead Road, Lancaster, PA 17601, 299-8901 • For listing of Mennonite farms accepting guests, write to Mennonite Information Center, 2209 Millstream Road, Lancaster, PA 17602, 299-0954.

DINING *General Sutter Inn* (see above); $–$$ • *Cameron Estate Inn* (see above); $$ • *Groff's Farm,* Pinkerton Road, Mount Joy, 653-2048, Pennsylvania Dutch specialties in a farmhouse; $$ • *Brownstown Restaurant,* Brownstown, 656-9077, authentic Pennsylvania Dutch; $ • *Lemon Tree,* 1766 Columbia Avenue, Lancaster, 394-0441, elegant and excellent; $–$$ • *Jethro's,* First and Ruby streets, Lancaster, 299-1700, simple setting, sophisticated menu; $$ • *Haag's Hotel,* Main Street, Shartlesville, 488-6692; $.

SIGHTSEEING *Farmer's markets:* Southern Market, 102 South Queen Street, Lancaster. Hours: Saturday, 5:30 A. M. to 3 P.M. Central Market, Penn Square, Lancaster. Hours: Tuesday, Friday, 6 A.M. to 5 P.M. Meadowbrook Market, Route 23, Leola. Hours: Saturday, 8 A.M. to 4 P.M. • *Pennsylvania Farm Museum,* off Route 272, Landis Valley, 569-0401. Hours: Tuesday to Saturday, 10 A.M. to 5 P.M.; 4:30 P.M. May to October; Sunday, noon to 4:30 P.M. Adults $2, children under 12 free • *Amish Farm and House,* Route 30 east of Lancaster, 394-6185. Hours: daily, 8:30 A.M. to 5:00 P.M.; May to October, 4:30 P.M. Adults $3, children age 6–11 $1 • *Sturgis Pretzel House,* 219 East Main, Lititz, 626-4354. Hours: Monday to Saturday, 9 A.M. to 5 P.M. Adults 50¢, children age 4–12 35¢ • *Ephrata Cloister,* 632 West Main Street, Ephrata, 733-6600. Hours: Tuesday to Saturday, 9 A.M. to 5 P.M.; May to October, 4:30 P.M.; Sunday, noon to 5 P.M. Adults $1.50, under 12 free • *Hawk Mountain Sanctuary,* Route 2, Kempton (approach via 143), 756-6961. Hours: daily, 8 A.M. to 5 P.M. Adults $1, children 50¢ • For map of Gay Dutch barn routes, contact Pennsylvania Dutch Travel Association, Washington Towers, 50 North Fourth Street, Reading, PA 19601, 376-3931.

Winter

Uncovering the Past
in Hartford

At the turn of the century, when upper-middle-class women were expected to stick close to their elegant hearths and homes, Theodate Pope Riddle of Farmington, Connecticut, would have none of it.

The daughter of a multimillionaire industrialist and wife of an Ambassador to Russia and Argentina, Ms. Riddle was a trailblazer, studying to become one of the first licensed women architects in the country. She designed several Connecticut schools, but her most notable achievement came at the precocious age of 16 when she helped Stanford White design a home for her parents, a mansion unique because it was deliberately planned to show off the collection of Impressionist art that astute Alfred Atmore Pope acquired before the rest of the world had recognized such talents as Manet, Degas, and Monet.

Twenty major works of art were all that Mr. Pope had room for amid the Empire sofas and four-poster beds; the porcelains, bronzes, and etchings that filled his home; and he made his choices wisely, including two of Monet's haystack paintings, Degas's famous "Dancers" and "Jockeys," and portraits by James Whistler and Mary Cassatt.

Hill-Stead, as the Mount Vernon–like hilltop mansion was called, is now a public museum, one of the few places where museum-quality art can be seen in a gracious residential setting. This little-heralded art treasure in a Hartford suburb is one of many surprises awaiting visitors to Connecticut's state capital. The nation's oldest state house, its first free public art museum, the flamboyant Victorian home of Mark Twain, and the priceless firearms collection of Sam Colt are among many unexpected finds in and around Hartford, hidden from passersby on the Connecticut Turnpike by the glass-sided mini-skyscrapers that mark America's insurance center.

The first inkling that Hartford is more than insurance companies comes with your very first stop Saturday, at the Old State House housing the city's information center. The 1796 Federal-style master-piece by Charles Bullfinch sits smack in the middle of those new office towers; it was scheduled for demolition to make way for a parking lot when Hartford's aroused citizens refused to give up this memento of the city's historic past. In the late 1970s they raised $850,000 to give their grande dame a much needed facelift, and another million to ensure its future as a museum. The landscaping was accomplished by cleverly reviving an old Colonial era "viewing tax," a tax on windows that produces an annual voluntary levy of over $8,000 from the businesses surrounding the State House, with their total of 2,753 windows.

Now the courtroom and original Senate and House chambers are restored to their former splendor, and visitors to Hartford can tour the architectural landmark where seven former U.S. presidents from Adams to Grant also once paid their respects.

At the visitors' center in the Old State House, you can pick up maps and booklets on the city as well as a self-guided walking tour that offers a quick and easy overview.

First stop, however, should be the Museum of Connecticut History, since it closes for the weekend at 1 P.M. on Saturday. The Colt collection of guns here is recognized as one of the finest collections of firearms anywhere. The 1,000 guns tell the long history of the company that Sam Colt founded in 1836 and moved to his native Hartford in 1847. By 1855 he had the world's largest private armory, and Colt revolvers were known the world over. The guns on display range from Wyatt Earp's six-shooter, to Colt's then-revolutionary Gatling machine gune, to the M2 and M3 aircraft guns. In a curious way the guns are markers of the nation's history.

This fascinating small museum also has a fine collection of timepieces by early Connecticut clockmakers; much early industrial memorabilia such as the 1877 Selden, one of the earliest automobiles; and many historical documents, including the charter once hidden in the state's fabled Charter Oak.

Across the street, on a knoll dominating the city's 41-acre Bushnell Park, is the gold-domed state capitol building. Its Moorish interior is open to the public only on weekdays, but the exterior deserves more than a passing glance. The complex architectural style offers everything from Gothic spires to classical arcades, and many fine statues decorate the facade, depicting allegorical figures as well as some of the state's early heroes.

Bushnell Park's other pride is its meticulously restored 1914 carousel, a favorite of Hartford youngsters in the summertime.

With the state museum taken care of and your walking tour firmly in hand, you're now prepared to explore the curious mix of old and new that marks downtown Hartford. You'll see, for example, the white steeple of Center Church, circa 1788, reflected in the gold-mirrored walls of the Bushnell Tower, designed by I. M. Pei in 1969. View one of the earliest successful urban renewal efforts at Constitution Plaza, as well as one of the city's oldest homes at 396 Main Street. The 1782

Butler-McCook Homestead is well worth a stop, particularly interest-ing because it was occupied by one family for four generations until 1971. Their furnishings reflect the changes in style from Windsor and Queen Anne through Empire and Victorian.

Another special shop is the Wadsworth Atheneum on Main Street. America's first free public art museum, established in 1842, is now four buildings and a sculpture court and includes major work from every period, including modern paintings by Picasso, Monet, Andrew Wyeth, and Hartford-born Frederick Church. Outside the museum, Alexander Calder's soaring stabile "Stegosaurus" straddles Burr Mall.

A more controversial outdoor sculpture is the Stone Field on Gold Street, 36 glacial boulders ranging in weight from 1,000 pounds to 11 tons. Sculptor Carl Andre received $87,000 for this rock collection, which may or may not be a work of art, depending on whom you ask.

Two other major sights of the city are Union Place, renovated by ambitious shopkeepers and the city, which helped recycle the century-old train station; and the Hartford Civic Center, a combination shopping mall, hotel, convention center, and coliseum.

Come Saturday night, you may want to visit the Hartford Stage Company, a first-rate regional theater, or see the Hartford Whalers, the city's National Hockey League entry in action at the Civic Center. You could also check the newspaper for concerts or special events at Bushnell Auditorium or on the campus of Trinity College. Some of the local spots for jazz, rock, and country music include 36 Lewis Street, The Russian Lady, The Asylum Bar and Café, and Rum Bottoms.

Sleep late on Sunday, fortify yourself with a hearty brunch, and head for Hartford's major literary landmark, Nook Farm. This Victorian enclave, settled during the second half of the nineteenth century, was a colony populated by prominent actors, editors, and celebrities of the day. Among them were Harriet Beecher Stowe and Samuel Clemens, better known as Mark Twain. The restored Clemens and Beecher homes and two former carriagehouses preserve an important portion of this unusual neighborhood. The Stowe House is a simple cottage furnished with many of its original pieces and decorated with the delicate watercolors the author produced between books.

The Clemens household, however, is quite a different affair, built in 1874 for the then-princely sum of $130,000. It is a showplace with its carved mantels, goldleaf wallpapers, inlaid mahogany furniture, and decorative work by the likes of Louis Comfort Tiffany. The Twain humor is evident, however, in touches like the optical illusion fireplace, and the cigar, pipe, and billiard cue ceiling decor of the third-floor study. The story goes that Clemens gave up his second-floor study because his children were too noisy to suit him, and retired upstairs where he wrote his masterpieces with a billiard table at his side.

The billiard room leads to two balconies, one of which the Clemens called the Texas Deck because it reminded him of the uppermost deck of a riverboat steamer. Clemens himself once described his home as part steamboat, part medieval stronghold, and part cuckoo clock.

From Nook Farm, continue west down Farmington Avenue and you'll soon arrive at Farmington and the Hill-Stead Museum. The town of Farmington contains over 100 houses built prior to 1835, and most of the original village is a state historic district. Since the charming Colonial architecure is a further reminder of Hartford's historic past, if it's open you may want to make your last stop a look at the Stanley Whitman House, a gracious seventeenth-century New England home full of furnishings and other artifacts of earlier days.

Hartford Area Code: 203

DRIVING DIRECTIONS   The quickest way is following the New England Thruway (I-95) into Connecticut to New Haven, then connect with I-91 straight to Hartford. The more scenic route follows the Hutchinson River Parkway into the Merritt Parkway, making the I-91 connection just before Wallingford. In daylight, the Merritt is well worth an extra few minutes. Take the Hartford exit marked "Capitol District."

Total distance: 113 miles.

BY PUBLIC TRANSPORTATION   Amtrak serves Hartford from New York Penn Station. Most of the city sights are walkable from downtown hotels in decent weather. Take a cab to reach Nook Farm.

ACCOMMODATIONS   Plenty of center city hotels and motels; take your pick: *Best Western Governor's House,* 440 Asylum Street, 246-6591; $ ● *Holiday Inn of Hartford,* 50 Morgan Street, 549-2400; $$ ● *Hotel Sonesta,* 5 Constitution Plaza, 278-2000; $$$–$$$$ ● *Sheraton-Hartford,* Trumbull Street at Civic Center Plaza (connected to civic center), 728-5151; $$$–$$$$ ● *Farmington Motor Inn,* 827 Farmington Avenue, 677-2871; $$ ● *Suisse Chalet Inn,* 185 Brainard Road (I-91, exit 27), 525-9306; $.

DINING   *Adajians,* 297 Asylum Street, 524-5181, Near Eastern atmosphere and food; $–$$ ● *The Brownstone,* 124 Asylum Street, 525-1171, antiques and stained glass; $–$$; Sunday brunch $ ● *Carbone's Ristorante,* 588 Franklin Avenue, 249-9646, Italian restaurant popular with politicos; $$ ● *Last National Bank,* 752 Main Street,

246-5387, dinner in a converted bank vault; $$ • *36 Lewis Street,* 247-2300, popular spot on a historic street; $–$$, Sunday brunch $ • For lunch try the *Promenade Cafés* at Hartford Civic Center, six international kitchens in a row of airy, cheerful and moderately priced cafeterias.

SIGHTSEEING *Old State House,* 800 Main Street, 522-6766. Hours: Monday to Saturday, 10 A.M. to 5 P.M.; Sunday, noon to 5 P.M. Free • *Capitol Building,* Capitol Avenue, 566-3662. Hours: free tours weekdays, 9 A.M. to 2:30 P.M., except mid-November to February 1, closed weekends • *Museum of Connecticut History,* Capitol Avenue, 566-3056. Hours: Monday to Friday, 9 A.M. to 5 P.M.; Saturday, 9 A.M. to 1 P.M. Free • *McCook-Butler Homestead,* 396 Main Street, 522-1806. Hours: October 15 to May 15, Thursday to Sunday, noon to 4 P.M.; rest of year open daily. Adults $1, senior citizens 75¢, children 25¢ • *Nook Farm,* Farmington Avenue at Forest Street (I-84, exit 46). Tours: Tuesday to Saturday, 9:30 A.M. to 4 P.M.; Sunday 1 to 4 P.M. Combined tour Twain and Stowe Houses, adults $3.50, children under 16 $1.75; single home, adults $2, children under 16 $1 • *Hill-Stead Museum,* 671 Farmington Avenue (Route 4), 677-9064, Wednesday, Thursday, Saturday, Sunday 2 to 5 P.M.; adults $1.50, children under 12 75¢ • *Stanley Whitman House,* 37 High Street, off Route 4, 677-9222. Hours: March to April, November, December, Sunday, 1 to 4 P.M.; May to October, Tuesday to Sunday, 1 to 4 P.M.; closed January, February. Adults $1, children age 6–14 75¢ • *Wadsworth Atheneum,* 600 Main Street, 278-2670. Hours: Tuesday to Friday, 11 A.M. to 3 P.M.; Thursday, 11 A.M. to 8 P.M.; Saturday, Sunday, 11 A.M. to 5 P.M. Adults $2, children $1.

FOR FURTHER INFORMATION Contact the Greater Hartford Convention and Visitors Bureau, 1 Civic Center Plaza, Hartford, CT 06103, 728-6789.

Christmas Cheer at Bear Mountain

One of the younger natives was getting restless.

She had oohed at the lighting of the 40-foot Christmas tree, listened happily to the first of the carols. But now, with frosty puffs punctuating her words in the wintry night air, she could be heard plaintively asking her Dad, "When's he coming?"

Almost as if on cue, the choral group broke into "Here Comes Santa Claus," and there was the great man himself, making a grand entrance in a flurry of "Ho, ho, ho's," singing a few carols in a belly-deep baritone, and inviting everyone to come to call in a few minutes as soon as he was settled in his quarters downstairs in the Bear Mountain Inn.

The youngster's grin was ear to ear once again.

Santa's arrival on the second Friday in December annually marks the start of the season for the kids as well as the opening of the traditional Bear Mountain Christmas Festival, a regular event since 1968 under the sponsorship of the Palisades Interstate Park Commission and the Bear Mountain Inn.

For three weeks, through the start of the New Year, the bottom floor of the inn is transformed into a world of handmade crafts and special holiday displays meant for nearby families as well as visitors from afar. With Santa in residence until he is called away on Christmas Eve, warm hospitality at the inn, plus a setting that would do credit to a Christmas card, there are few better weekend jaunts for getting into the spirit of the season.

The Bear Mountain Festival is neither huge nor slick, but it has a pleasant down-home flavor and features handmade crafts and folk art. The community is invited to get involved, by loaning crafts and creations such as gingerbread villages and candy cottages. The major displays change from year to year. Recently they have ranged from Early American quilts and antique toys to Hümmel figurines and decorated Ukrainian eggs. Working toy-train layouts are perennial favorites, as are the Christmas trees decorated in original motifs.

Santa welcomes children to his workshop, off in a wing of its own, where they find him surrounded by a retinue of bigger-than-life animated friends, including a toy soldier, a Raggedy Ann doll, a panda bear, a snowman, and a group of mechanical carolers. The kids love it.

Bear Mountain Inn is a rustic fieldstone and timber affair with big beams and a giant fireplace that stretches from floor to ceiling. Out the windows, brightly garbed families can be seen ice skating against a backdrop of mountains and evergreens. At night, when the rink is lit and a dozen trees around the perimeter also light up along with the giant tree and a 40-foot star on the mountaintop, it's fairyland time.

You can choose from rooms in the inn building or the newer Overlook Lodge, or opt for rooms in four smaller lodges on the opposite side of the lake—pleasant accommodations that surround a central lobby with a fireplace. There's dancing in the inn on Friday and Saturday nights, as well as a smorgasbord dinner including shrimp and top round. Children eat half-price at the Sunday buffet, which features a salad bar and your choice of five main dishes.

When the weather cooperates, the days fly by, filled with skating, sledding, and playful snowball fights. Should you seek further diversion, West Point is just north on Route 9W, or you can cross the bridge and head a few miles north on Route 9 to Cold Spring. Pick up a walking tour brochure in one of the shops and see the historic sights of the picturesque village; then if the kids will cooperate, you can visit some of the 50-plus antique shops that crowd each other in a three-block stretch of Main Street that runs down to a bandstand on a little spit out into the Hudson.

Late in the day, head back south on 9 to Garrison, where you can enjoy another area holiday tradition, a candlelight tour at Boscobel. This beautiful nineteenth-century mansion with its columns and porticos is an outstanding example of New York Federal architecture, and its period furnishings take on a special elegance in the candleglow. Musicians are on hand to enhance the mood, and the house smells invitingly of the warm cinnamon-flavored cider refreshments waiting at the end of the tour.

Like Cold Spring, incidentally, Garrison has an overlook with a splendid Hudson view.

Treat yourself to a special dinner in Garrison in front of the fireplace in the low-ceilinged, atmospheric dining room of the Bird and Bottle Inn, a restored eighteenth-century tavern. An even more elegant (and more expensive) dinner choice farther north in Stormville is Harralds, a five-star selection with dining room where the glow from the fireplace and the candlelight make for an ambience as pleasing as the food.

To end the weekend on a final traditional note, head home via Route 9 and stop in at the Sleepy Hollow Restorations. Each of the three buildings has a different offering: Van Cortlandt Manor in Croton-on-Hudson presents the traditional decorations of St. Nicholas Day; Sunnyside in Tarrytown displays the ways that Washington Irving entertained his family and friends at Christmas, and Philipsburg Manor in north Tarrytown is filled with the traditional trimmings for Twelfth Night or Old Christmas. Each building also offers candlelight tours; check the schedules to see if they coincide with your own.

Bear Mountain Area Code: 914

DRIVING DIRECTIONS Across George Washington Bridge to Palisades Interstate Parkway to Park.

Total distance: about 50 miles.

ACCOMMODATIONS   *Bear Mountain Inn,* Bear Mountain 10911, 786-2731; $$.

DINING   *Bird & Bottle Inn,* just off Route 9, Garrison, 424-3000; prix fixe dinner $25.50, $$$$ ● *Harralds,* Route 52, Stormville 12482; 878-6595; prix fixe dinner $35, $$$$ ● *Bear Mountain Inn* (see above); $$, Sunday buffet, $.

SIGHTSEEING   *Bear Mountain Christmas Festival,* Bear Mountain Inn, 786-2731. Hours: Mid-December to January 1, 10 A.M. to 9 P.M.; Santa's arrival (with tree lighting, caroling, and lighting of yule log), second Friday in December beginning at 6 P.M., Santa around 7:15 P.M.; Santa's house, to December 24, Monday to Friday, 10 A.M. to noon, 1 to 5 P.M.; Saturday, Sunday, 11 A.M. to noon, 1 to 6 P.M.; exterior light displays, to January 1, Monday to Friday, 5 to 9 P.M.; Saturday, Sunday, 5 to 11 P.M. Free ● *Boscobel,* Route 9D, Garrison, 265-3638; daily except Tuesday, April to October, 9:30 A.M. to 5 P.M.; March, November, and December, 9:30 A.M. to 4 P.M. Phone for current schedule and fees for tours ● *Sleepy Hollow Restorations,* 150 White Plains Road, Tarrytown 10591, 631-8200. Phone or write for holiday exhibits, tour dates, and hours. Adults $4, children and senior citizens $2.50.

FOR FURTHER INFORMATION   Contact Palisades Interstate Park Commission, Bear Mountain, NY 10911, 786-2701.

Catching the Brandywine Spirit

The ghost of Christmas past is alive and well in the Brandywine Valley.

Teddy bears and toys that delighted children a century ago, trees festooned with nature's own ornaments, a new England winter scene populated by antique dolls, the foods and feasts of early America, Victorian garlands and wreaths, candlelight, carols, and cascades of red poinsettias light up this rural area where Delaware and Pennsylvania meet, creating a contagious, noncommercial spirit that even old Ebenezer Scrooge would have found hard to resist. If you're feeling a bit cynical about the season, there's no better antidote than a dose of Brandywine cheer.

Both the du Pont and Radisson hotels in Wilmington are decked out for the season, and both offer special weekend package rates that make them ideal holiday headquarters. Planning an itinerary is more of a challenge, since the list of annual events runs into the dozens. One practical approach is to work around the major attractions, starting with the ones closest to Wilmington.

The Delaware Art Museum delights visitors young and old with the display that seems to be becoming a tradition, the antique toys of Pennsylvania collector Richard Wright. Called "Remembrances of Holidays Past: Dolls, Toys and Teddy Bears," it includes European and American dolls in porcelain, wood, wax, cloth, china, and bisque; early Disney characters and Steiff bears; miniature furniture and a choice dollhouse.

The Museum's Christmas crèche is another area favorite, an elaborate eighteenth-century Nativity scene with more than 40 handcarved and amazingly lifelike figures.

Children love the downstairs White Whale gallery, where participatory exhibits allow them to express their own creativity. Parents, meanwhile, will be free to visit the museum shop, with its array of unusual gifts, and the gallery where contemporary art is for sale.

The works of Howard Pyle, the Wyeths, and other noted American artists remain on display during the Christmas season.

Rockwood, the second Wilmington high spot, is a total change of scene, a rural Gothic home and garden with Victorian decorations to match the decor in its period rooms and conservatory. A recent added display of miniature rooms was so popular it seems destined to become a regular feature for the holidays. The settings varied from a tiny rendition of Santa's workshop to a perfect replica of Winterthur's famous Readbourne Parlor.

Follow Route 52 out of town to Winterthur itself, and you'll find that the antique-filled rooms of one of the nation's greatest collections of early American furnishings have been filled for the season with holiday fare that might have been appropriate for each room's period. Dessert parties, musicales, punch parties, yuletide balls, and a Pennsylvania-German supper, with foods ranging from suckling pigs to syllabub to homemade cakes and cookies, are all so lifelike you'll want to dig right in. All are based on documented evidence of early yuletide customs. Six period Christmas trees, a conservatory banked with poinsettias, and a formal boxwood-edged garden room are part of the tour.

If it leaves you feeling starved, there's a perfect lunch stop nearby on Route 52 at the Greenery Too in Greenville Center, with excellent salads, hot sandwiches, and a local favorite, oyster stew. It's a good bet for Sunday brunch, as well.

Hagley Museum, located right on the Brandywine River, was created to show how the river's water power built early industries that helped industrialize the nation, including du Pont's black powder mills. The exhibits tracing industry from the 1600s into this century are interesting, as are the restored mills and shops, but at this time of year it's the 1803 Georgian home of E.I. du Pont, Eleutherian Mills, that is a tribute to the season. It is decorated upstairs and down with original creations using fruit and greenery and other natural materials that may well give you lots of new ideas for your own home holiday decor. A little booklet on sale at the museum shop will teach you how to make the apple and pineapple door fans, pine roping, ivy wreaths, cranberry trees, and Victorian natural tree ornaments that make this house so full of good cheer.

If you've chosen the second weekend of December for your visit, you'll want to get back in time to attend the annual candlelight house tour in Colonial New Castle, six miles south of Wilmington on Route 202. Time seems to have stood still in Delaware's onetime capital, leaving the red-brick Georgian and Federal homes of the town looking much as they did back in the 1700s. They are a real delight decked out for the holidays, with candles in every window and lighting the paths outside, and carolers add even more atmosphere with their songs of the season.

Other kinds of evening Christmas festivities can be found at the Grand Opera House on Wilmington's Market Street Mall, where Christmas pops concerts, Hans Christian Anderson, and Peter Pan are among the attractions scheduled each December. The Delaware Theater Company presents classics like Dickens's *A Christmas Carol,* and a check of local papers will show a choice of performances such as *The Messiah, Amahl and the Night Visitors,* Baroque, Renaissance, choral music, and other music traditional for the season.

On Sunday you'll be heading across the Pennsylvania border for two of the valley's prime attractions. It's hard to imagine a cheerier scene than the Brandywine River Museum, where tiny fingers can be seen pointing in all directions as children urge parents to "look, look" at the wondrous sights. The December features have become a local tradition, repeated year after year, and always eagerly anticipated. On the third floor of this museum that displays so many works by the Wyeth family, Ann Wyeth McCoy offers an annual gift to the children of the community, an exhibit featuring her magnificent collection of antique porcelain dolls. A doll's Christmas tree is one of the scenes put together by Mrs. McCoy and her artist husband, John, and each year there is a special scene such as a winter landscape of dolls congregating in front of a New England church, each quite literally "dolled up" in Victorian finery. It's so realistic that there's even a crying youngster who slipped trying to cut across the frozen river.

The second-floor gallery here whizzes and hums with five toy trains winding their way along thousands of feet of track, through mountains and valleys, past houses and factories, on their way to a huge railroad yard. Grown-ups love it just as much as the small fry. The model *O*-gauge railroad is a serious year-round interest of the museum, which employs a special full-time "engineer" to restore and maintain the antiques and other toy trains and the extensive scenery.

The first-floor galleries, as always, feature the artistic efforts of Brandywine artists, including the Wyeths and Howard Pyle, but they take second place in December to the five giant trees in the hallway, festooned with munchkins, mice, beguiling angels, and other totally wonderful whimsical "critters" made by museum volunteers each year from natural materials found in abundance in the woods outside. Once again a little booklet is available to show you how to make these tiny treasures for your own tree, and there are other unique gift ideas in the shop, as well as Wyeth prints.

Things become even merrier in the museum when choral groups appear during the day to put the festivities to music. Outside the rustic converted mill, vendors in the courtyard offer roasted chestnuts and handmade gifts—dolls, quilts, and tree ornaments among them.

It's hard to leave the good cheer at the Brandywine, but you'll find ample compensation when you proceed on Route 1 to Kennett Square and Longwood Gardens. Santa's figure in an antique sleigh pulled by sparkling reindeer greets you from the main terrace, and inside the conservatory is resplendent with thousands of poinsettias, begonias, primroses, coleus, and spring bulbs, a breathtaking red and white holiday display.

Prize-winning trees decorated by local garden clubs are just a prelude for Longwood's own 16-foot beauty, and to put you further in a Christmas mood, organ recitals and choral concerts are offered in the adjacent ballroom at 2, 4, and 7 P.M. on weekends.

Visit the Reception Suite beneath the conservatory, where a model home will give you further ideas for decorating your own quarters, and if you stay until the sun goes down, 3,500 lights will twinkle outside, bedecking dozens of trees near the parking area and the walkways.

And these are just the major sights in the valley. Every weekend there are more—open houses in historic homes, traditional Swedish and Colonial celebrations, tree displays, fairs featuring homemade gifts and fresh baked goodies, more candlelight tours, caroling, tree-trimming parties, and many other classic holiday delights. And as a bonus along the way, the winter landscape of the valley is a typical Andrew Wyeth scene come to life.

It's an extraordinary Christmas celebration here in the Brandywine Valley—one you may well decide to make a tradition of your own.

Delaware Area Code: 302; Pennsylvania Area Code: 215

DRIVING DIRECTIONS   Take New Jersey Turnpike to its end and across the Delaware Memorial Bridge, then 295 to I-95 north into Wilmington.
Total distance: 121 miles.

ACCOMMODATIONS   *Hotel du Pont,* 11 and Market Streets, Wilmington, 656-8121; $$$; ask about weekend packages • *Hotel Radisson,* 700 King Street, Wilmington, 655-0400; $$$; special weekend rates.

DINING   See page 31.

SIGHTSEEING   *Delaware Art Museum,* 2301 Kentmere Parkway, 571-9590. Hours: Monday to Saturday, 10 A.M. to 5 P.M.; Sunday, 1 to 5 P.M. Free • *Hagley Museum,* Route 141, Greenville, 658-2400. Hours: Tuesday to Saturday, 9:30 A.M. to 4:30 P.M.; Sunday, 1 to 5 P.M. Adults $2, senior citizens $1.25, students $1, under 14 free. Call for schedule of candlelight tours • *Rockwood Museum,* Shipley Road, Wilmington, 571-7776. Hours: Tuesday to Saturday, 11 A.M. to 5 P.M. Adults $1, family $2 • *Winterthur Museum,* Route 52, Centerville, 654-1548. Tours: one-hour yuletide tours by reservation only, every half-hour Tuesday to Saturday, 10 A.M. to 3:30 P.M.; Sunday, 1 to 6:30 P.M. Adults $4, children age 12–16 $2, under age 12 not admitted • *Brandywine River Museum,* Route 1, Chadds Ford, Pennsylvania, 459-1900. Hours: daily, 9:30 A.M. to 4:30 P.M. Adults $1.75, senior citizens and children $1 • *Longwood Gardens,* Route 1, Kennett Square, Pennsylvania, 388-6741. Hours: daily, 10 A.M. to 9 P.M. Adults $3, children $1. • *Historic New Castle Candlelight Tour.* For current dates and fees phone 322-8411.

FOR FURTHER INFORMATION   Contact Greater Wilmington Convention and Visitors Bureau, Box 111, Wilmington, DE 19800, 571-4088, or Delaware State Travel Service, 630 State College Road, Dover, DE 19901, toll-free (800) 441-8846, for a complete listing of Brandywine Valley Christmas activities.

All Aboard for a
Connecticut Christmas

The conductor looks familiar. There's something about the pudgy build, the bright red suit. And why is he handing out goodies instead of punching tickets?

The reason, of course, is that Santa Claus himself presides aboard Connecticut's *North Pole Express,* a huffing, puffing steam train that rides the rails every holiday season between the towns of Essex and Chester.

The *Express* is one of many happy traditions that make Christmas special for children in Connecticut. Take a weekend off with the family and you can share that ride with Santa, visit with his reindeer and toymakers, mail your cards from a picture-postcard village called Bethlehem, go caroling, see a magnificent eighteenth-century Italian crèche, load down the trunk with one-of-a-kind gifts, and maybe even head home with a tree you've chosen and chopped down yourself.

This is a rambling trip, but it isn't difficult since no two points in this compact state are more than two hours apart. And there are so many interesting stops along the way, it's doubtful whether you'll hear many complaints coming from the backseat.

For your first stop, drive north past New Milford, past gracious white clapboard homes and kids skating on ponds, to a unique shop where the children may actually let you get some shopping done because they'll be so intrigued with the giant tree that is a holiday tradition at The Silo. This converted stable, silo, and barn are chock full of gifts made by local craftspeople—everything from baskets and batiks to quilts and statues. Even the ornaments on the eye-boggling 18-foot tree are handmade. The gingerbread, dough, blown-glass, and stained-glass creations can be purchased right off the tree.

From New Milford, drive east on 109 through the handsome Colonial village of Washington, continuing on to Route 61, then south to Bethlehem, where the post office on intersecting Route 132 will not only postmark your cards but offer an assortment of 24 rubber stamps dating back over the years to personalize your envelopes. It's a good idea to bring extra paper for the kids, most of whom seem determined to try out every stamp design at least twice.

About a mile south of the Bethlehem village green, in a weathered barn on the grounds of the Regina Laudis Priory, is an eighteenth-century Neapolitan crèche of museum quality. It is, in fact, the gift of a wealthy collector of religious art whose other endowments now rest with New York's Metropolitan Museum.

The crèche is 16-feet long by four-feet high by five-feet deep. The setting is a blend of a scene from an eighteenth-century Italian hillside village and a classical Nativity, and the detail in the 60 carved figures is fascinating. All the clothes are of silks, satins, and brocades in rich muted shades; each figure is a lifelike recreation of a townsperson going about his or her daily tasks. It is a rare work of art in a remarkable rural setting.

Continuing north to Torrington, you'll find another kind of creation, the town's annual Christmas Village. Santa Claus has been in residence here the week before Christmas for more than 30 years, receiving young guests in a comfortable, oak-beamed living room with logs crackling in the fireplace. After a chat and a small gift from Santa, the children can go across the corridor to the toy shop, where local "elves" are busily working on toys for youngsters in the town hospital.

On the grounds near the rear of the building is a Nativity scene with almost life-size figures. And nearby is Santa's sleigh, a favorite spot for photographers with pint-size models along. Eight reindeer are waiting in a pen close at hand, as is Rudolph, a red-nosed reindeer with his own gingerbread house. There's also Snowflake, a baby deer who's a favorite with the youngest visitors. There is no admission charge to the village and nothing is for sale here. It is a Christmas gift from Torrington residents for the enjoyment of children.

You can stay the night in Torrington if you've had enough driving for one day, but it's worth trying for the less-than-an-hour's trip to Hartford via 202 and 44 eastbound and the eye-popping annual Festival of Lights in that city's Constitution Plaza. In the midst of the 250,000-bulb spectacular are sculptured angels with brass trumpets, reindeer, a Nativity scene, a 75-foot Christmas tree decked with hundreds of tiny lights and a six-foot starburst, the South Plaza Fountain, a cascade of shimmering light.

Check the papers to see if the Hartford Ballet is doing its holiday run of *The Nutcracker,* just in case you couldn't get tickets at Lincoln Center.

Sunday morning you'll set out on I-91 to Route 9 for Essex, but if the dates are right, you may want to make a shopping stop along the way at Wesleyan Potters. The work of more than 200 fine craftsmen is for sale here from late November through mid-December—pottery, jewelry, weaving, wood, leather, glass, and pewter—all one of a kind and all high quality.

The *North Pole Express* leaves the Essex depot afternoons and evenings every Friday, Saturday, and Sunday in December. The cars are lit with toy-shaped Christmas lights, the caroling begins as soon as the train whistle blows, and the Connecticut countryside outside the window is bedecked with special Christmas lights and decorations supplied by friendly residents along the train's route. The ride has a special charm at night when the decorations are aglow.

Since the first train rides of the day aren't until noon, you'll have time to take a stroll through Essex, a lovely old seaport town whose beautifully preserved homes are a delight any time of year, but especially with Christmas decorations decking the doors and windows. After a snowfall, Essex is a Christmas card come true.

Have your lunch—or the big late Sunday hunt breakfast—or at least a look inside the Griswold Inn on Main Street. A village landmark since 1776, the inn is a must, not only for its Colonial ambience but also for the many collections that make it almost a mini-museum of nautical lore.

After you ride the train, you can head east on I-95 to Mystic Seaport, which is transformed every December into a nineteenth-century celebration of Christmas. Evergreens sprout from the masts of historic ships, doorways are festooned, homes are decorated for the holiday, and carolers stroll the grounds, inviting visitors to join in the chorus. Costumed guides lead groups to selected exhibits of Christmas past, and lanternlight tours are held late in the afternoon. There are also special hands-on activities for children kindergarten through third-grade age, reliving pastimes of the nineteenth century—roasting chestnuts, making pomanders, and decorating a shell tree. Advance reservations are needed for tours and children's festivities.

You may want to stay for the romantic lanternlight strolls or the wassail and plum pudding that is available at the Seaman's Inne. Or you may want to get an earlier start back onto 95, where any of several easy detours will bring you to farms where you can pick out your Christmas tree and chop it down yourself. Just don't forget to come prepared with enough rope to anchor the tree to the car roof.

Properly laden with memories and your tree, you should be set to keep up the holiday spirit after you get home.

Connecticut Area Code: 203

DRIVING DIRECTIONS   Take the Hutchinson Parkway to 684 to 84 east, take exit 4, US 202 to Brookfield and New Milford; then 202 north, 109 east, 61 south to Bethlehem. Then 61 north to Litchfield and 202 north to Torrington, 202 and 44 west into Hartford. Middletown

and Essex are on Route 9 east of Hartford, Mystic is east on Route 95.
   Total distance: to Torrington 109 miles; to Hartford 113 miles; to
Essex about 100 miles.

ACCOMMODATIONS   *Yankee Pedlar Inn,* 93 Main Street, Tor-
rington, 489-9226; $$ • For numerous hotel-motels in Hartford, see
page 174 • *Griswold Inn,* Main Street, Essex, 767-1812; $ with
breakfast • For Mystic Seaport accommodations, see page 27.

DINING   *Yankee Pedlar Inn* (see above); $–$$ • *Griswold Inn* (see
above); $–$$; Sunday hunt breakfast $ • *The Gull,* Essex Harbor, 767-
0916; $–$$.

Winter Pleasures around Williamstown

He's a diehard skier, one of the first on the slopes no matter what the
weather.

She's ambivalent. If the sun isn't bright, the snow powdery, and the
temperature above 20 degrees, she'd just as soon be inside a good
museum.

Can they find happiness together on a winter weekend?

If there is any area equipped to handle both athletes and esthetes, it
is the northern Berkshires of Massachusetts. For skiers there is a choice
of Brodie Mountain or Jiminy Peak, both challenging enough for all
but the most expert, and Vermont areas like Haystack and Bromley are
within an hour's drive for the really determined.

This is also good territory for cross-country skiers. A new center
opened recently at Brodie, with five miles of packed trails and 50 acres
of rolling fields, plus a network of 25 miles of unplowed roads adjacent
to the magnificent 11,000 acres of Mt. Greylock State Reservation.

But for those who want no part of wintry winds, here's an area with
more sophisticated pleasures than most destinations farther north,
beginning with one of the most inviting and impressive small museums
to be found anywhere, Williamstown's Sterling and Francine Clark Art
Institute.

Sterling Clark had the good fortune to be heir to the fortune his
grandfather amassed as a partner to Isaac Singer, the sewing machine
king. Clark began using his inheritance to collect fine art around 1912,
beginning with works of the Old Masters. But with the encouragement

of his French-born wife, he shifted emphasis in the 1920s and 1930s to concentrate on nineteenth-century French painting, with some attention also to American artists like Sargent, Remington, and Winslow Homer, who is represented by seven choice oils.

In the 1950s, when the Clarks decided to build a structure to house their collection, they chose Williamstown for the beauty of its pastoral setting and had a building designed to make the most of it. Tall windows in the corridors look out on natural scenes that are works of art in themselves and that add to the pleasure of visiting the museum.

The fact that the galleries are done to drawing-room scale and furnished in many cases with fine antiques also makes a visit to the museum more rewarding.

You'll see excellent examples of some of the world's greatest painters here, dating from the Renaissance and later, including Van Ruisdael, Hals, Gainsborough, Tiepolo, Goya, Turner, and Mary Cassatt. There is also a remarkable silver collection, five centuries of the most exquisite pieces of the silversmith's art.

The French works include Géricault, Courbet, Daumier, Corot, and Millet, but the real heart of the museum, the paintings that may remain in your mind's eye long after you've left the galleries, are those exceptional ones found in gallery two—by Rubens, Monet, Degas, and Renoir. Among the most memorable works are Monet's "Tulip Fields at Sassenheim" and one of his Rouen Cathedral series, and Renoir's "At the Concert" and "Sleeping Girl with Cat."

At the center of the stately room is a fountain that was never put into operation for fear of damaging the paintings with excess humidity. Instead, its center is Degas's "The Ballet Dancer." This sculpture has so fascinated viewers who cannot resist touching the skirt's net hem that the costume has shortened considerably from wear over the years.

There are grander and more famous museums than the Clark Art Institute, but few that offer a more satisfying visual experience.

All of Williamstown, in fact, is a visual delight. It is a beautiful old New England town with a college dating back to 1793 at its center. Williams is so much a part of its home town that it is hard to distinguish where the campus begins and ends, and it offers other interesting places to visit. The Chapin Library on the second floor of Stetson Hall has an extensive collection of rare books—some 17,000 of them—and changing exhibits on English and American literature. The Williams Art Museum also has a notable collection of art, with sculpture and painting dating from ancient Egypt to the present. There is a whole room of Spanish art and a section of Early American paintings and furnishings.

If you've absorbed your artistic limit for the day, walk over to Water

Street (Route 43) and poke through half a dozen shops that include custom leather goods; gold and silver jewelry; two gift shops with a mix of wares; and The Potter's Wheel, a gallery of high quality stoneware, glass, metal sculpture, and jewelry. The work of a dozen or so talented artisans is on display, as well as contributions from the Rochester Folk Art Guild. The view of the frozen brook behind the gallery is one of its prize exhibits.

If you choose to stay at the Williams Inn, all of this is within easy walking distance. In spite of its Colonial furnishings the inn is disappointingly new and sterile for such a special town, but it does offer comfortable rooms, a sauna, and an indoor pool. The Berkshire Hilton in Pittsfield offers these same amenities, but if you want a country inn you'll have to settle for the six rooms over Le Jardin, just outside Williamstown, or move into New York State to the Milhof, an alpine-style inn about 12 miles west of Williamstown. (Lenox, of course, is only 20 miles to the south.)

If the weather remains willful on Sunday, some driving is required to see the remaining sights in the area. About 20 minutes to the north is Bennington, Vermont. Old Bennington with its green, monument, colonial homes, and church is worth quite a few snapshots, and you can stop in at Bennington Potters to see (and buy) some of the well-known stoneware produced here. Hawkins House in nearby Shaftsbury is another crafts gallery of working studios and shops set in a landmark Colonial home and barns on the property. Quilts, carvings, glass and pottery, sculpture, wrought-iron pieces, jewelry in gold and silver, candles, and drawings are some of the works you'll find being turned out in the studios.

Back into Massachusetts, Pittsfield has the Berkshire Museum, a place to see paintings from Old Masters to the Hudson River School. And if you are a lover of Herman Melville and Moby Dick, phone ahead for an appointment to visit Arrowhead, where Melville lived while he wrote his epic. The home is now headquarters of the Berkshire County Historical Society.

If there is still time to spare while one partner is up on the slopes, there is West Stockbridge, with another dozen shops and galleries to explore. Or you'll find the lodge at Brodie a very congenial place to pass the time—Irish decor, good company, and good Irish coffee.

By now you should be back together again and ready to enjoy dinner in one of the many good Berkshire inns farther south on your way home, a happy end to an exhilarating winter weekend.

Williamstown Area Code: 413

DRIVING DIRECTIONS Saw Mill River Parkway north to the Taconic Parkway to the New York Thruway Berkshire spur (Route 90) east to exit 2, then follow Route 102 to US 20 past Lenox and Pittsfield into Route 7 into Williamstown.
Total distance: 175 miles.

ACCOMMODATIONS *The Williams Inn,* on the green, Williamstown, 458-9371; $$ ● *Berkshire Hilton Inn,* Berkshire Common at West Street on Route 7, Pittsfield, 499-2000; $$ ● *Milhof Inn,* Route 43, Stephentown, New York, (518) 733-5606; $$ ● *Le Jardin Inn,* Route 7 and Cold Spring Road, Williamstown, 458-8032; $–$$ ● *1896 Motel,* Route 7, Williamstown, 458-8125; $ with continental breakfast ● *The Springs Motor Inn,* Route 7, New Ashford, 458-5945; $$ ● For Lenox accommodations and dining, see page 84.

DINING *Le Jardin* (see above), converted estate, French menu; $$–$$$ ● *River House,* Water Street (Route 43), Williamstown, 458-4829, varied menu, also lunch and late night snacks; $–$$ ● *The Springs* (see above), continental cuisine, attractive decor; $–$$$ ● *British Maid,* Route 2, Williamstown, 458-4961, converted barn, continental menu; $–$$.

SKIING *Jiminy Peak,* Corey Road, Hancock, 458-5771; daily and night skiing. Phone for current rates ● *Brodie,* Route 7, New Ashford, 443-4752, daily and night skiing ● For details on vertical drops, number of trails, lift ticket prices, and special ski packages available at local lodgings, write for "Ski and Stay the Berkshires" brochures, Berkshire Vacation Bureau, 20 Elm Street, Pittsfield 01201, 443-9186 ● Berkshire ski reports toll-free, (800) 628-5030.

SIGHTSEEING *Sterling and Francine Clark Art Institute,* South Street, Williamstown, 458-8109. Hours: daily, except Monday, 10 A.M. to 5 P.M. Free ● *Williams College Art Museum,* Lawrence Hall, 597-3131. Hours: Monday to Friday, 9 A.M. to 5 P.M.; Saturday, Sunday, 1 to 5 P.M. ● *Chapin Library,* Stetson Hall. Hours: Monday to Friday 9 A.M. to noon, 1 to 5 P.M.; Saturday 9 A.M. to noon. Free ● *Berkshire Museum,* 39 South Street (Route 7), Pittsfield, 442-6373. Hours: Tuesday to Saturday, 10 A.M. to 5 P.M.; Sunday 2 to 5 P.M. Free ● *Arrowhead,* 780 Holmes Road, Pittsfield, 442-1793. Phone for appointment and current fees.

FOR FURTHER INFORMATION Contact Berkshire Conference, 205 West Street, Pittsfield, MA 01201, 443-9186.

Philadelphia for All Seasons

The old joke was always good for a laugh: First prize, one week in Philadelphia. Second prize, two weeks in Philadelphia."

But things have changed drastically in the City of Brotherly Love. The town once known mostly for its dullness has done a remarkable turnaround in the past two decades, returning by its tricentennial in 1982 to what it was in the first place—a vibrant, varied, and interesting city.

Staid William Penn still presides atop the block-square City Hall at Broad and Market streets, but he has been joined by Claes Oldenberg's giant "Clothespin" across the way, one of the visible symbols of the new contemporary beat throughout the city.

It all began in the late 1960s when the National Park Service rescued beautiful Independence Hall and the rest of the city's pre-Revolution buildings, razing the warehouses and urban blight that had all but hidden them, and transforming the area into a handsome historic urban park.

While the park was taking form, neighboring Society Hill also began to revive with restorations of its cobbled streets and charming red-brick Colonial townhouses. NewMarket, a lively modern complex of shops and restaurants, grew up between Society Hill and the Delaware River. The waterfront itself was refurbished for the 1976 Bicentennial, old piers and ramshackle buildings giving way to a park and sculpture garden with a floating nautical museum of three permanently moored historic ships at the pier.

And good things just keep happening. Four hundred fifty new restaurants have opened in Philadelphia since 1976—and a thriving new local Restaurant School produces fine chefs to serve them. Gleaming new office buildings and high-rise hotels have transformed the city's skyline. Even Philadelphia's sports teams suddenly came to life, and a new sports complex was built to house their happy fans.

With all of the new, plus the best of the old—more than 100 museums, the fine Philadelphia Orchestra, the bustling Italian market and historic Germantown, the cheese-steak shops and pretzel vendors, the world's largest city park—a weekend is hardly enough time to take it all in. But a winter weekend, when many of the better hotels offer tempting bargain packages, is a perfect time to begin to get acquainted.

The logical place to start is where our nation started—in the recently created Independence National Historic Park. Make a first stop at the city's excellent midtown convention and Visitors Bureau near Town Hall for free walking tours and maps, then either a pleasant 15-minute walk or the Market Street bus will take you to the oldest part of the city.

There are few places that can re-create so vividly the charged atmosphere of a new colony daring to challenge the powerful English crown. A film at the park visitors center sets the stage, and the enthusiastic park guides help to make the past events come alive with colorful stories about the eventful days that saw the nation declare its independence. In Independence Hall you'll stand in the room where it all happened, just a few strides from the chair where Benjamin Franklin sat and the rostrum where John Hancock presided over the signing of the Declaration of Independence. The square just outside is where the Declaration was first read to the citizens of Philadelphia— and to the world.

The many visitors who take the 25-minute tour of Independence Hall and only glance at the other buildings making up the park are missing out on interesting sights. Flanking Independence Hall are Congress Hall, where the first American Congress met, and the Old City Hall, which housed the first Supreme Court. In Congress Hall you'll learn that the Senate became known as the Upper House quite literally because it was quartered on the second floor.

Carpenter's Hall has been restored to the way it was when the first Constitutional Convention met there, the Second National Bank has become a portrait gallery of the nation's founders, and down the block is the house where Dolley Payne lived when she met her future husband, James Madison, a delegate to the Constitutional Convention.

Don't overlook Franklin Court, tucked away in an alleyway between 3rd and 4th Streets off Market. Only a steel frame remains as a symbol of Franklin's home, but the museum underground would almost certainly have pleased the ingenious Mr. Franklin. The entry is history, disco-style—a mirrored hall with flashing signs citing Franklin's many roles as statesman, inventor, wit, and much more. There is a bank of telephones and a listing of numbers to dial to talk to people like John Adams, George Washington, and John F. Kennedy about Franklin's importance to the country. A dial-it computer produces Franklin witticisms on almost any subject, his many inventions (including library steps hidden in a chair and the first pair of bifocals) are on display, and a changing marionette gallery depicts his adventures as ambassador for his country. It's an altogether delightful way to learn about a remarkable man.

And then of course there is the Liberty Bell, housed in a glass pavilion, accessible to the throngs who want to gaze at the famous crack and touch the bell for luck. The bell, you'll learn, was actually ordered in 1751, the fiftieth anniversary of the democratic constitution granted by William Penn to his colony, but its motto, "Proclaim Liberty," became prophetic for the new nation. It had been recast before, but the final crack that put it out of service came in 1812 as the bell tolled the death of Chief Justice John Marshall, according to local lore.

If you do it justice Independence Park will take the entire morning, finishing just in time for a historic lunch in the 1773 City Tavern, once called "the most genteel tavern in America" by John Adams. The menu still includes old English favorites, and your waitress will be dressed as she might have been in Adams's day.

After lunch there are many nearby sights for exploring. Society Hill, south of the park, roughly between South and Spruce and 2nd and 5th streets, has become a prototype for urban restoration with its many blocks of Colonial townhouses lovingly restored within the past two decades. A walk through the area also takes you past several historic churches, all clearly labeled with informative signs, and past some intriguing shopping areas to get you out of the cold, including Head House Square, a red-brick restored marketplace, and NewMarket and South Street, a mix of funky shops and nightlife a bit reminiscent of Greenwich Village.

Another quite elegant shopping complex nearer to Independence Park is the Bourse, once a Victorian merchant's exchange, now a series of couturier boutiques and other lavish shops and eateries around a 10-story atrium. While you're in the neighborhood, look into the Curtis Publishing Company building, which houses the Norman Rockwell Museum including many of the artist's famous *Saturday Evening Post* covers, as well as an unexpected art treasure in the lobby, a magnificent wall-to-wall Tiffany glass tile mosaic called "The Dream Garden," the only one of its kind in this country.

North of Market Street is the Old City, the old commercial district that is still a bit run down. Do walk over however, to see Elfreth Alley, the perfectly charming cobbled avenue lined with 33 houses built between 1713 and 1811, the oldest continually occupied street in America. Not far away is historic Christ Church, where Washington and many members of the Continental Congress worshiped, and the tiny Betsy Ross House where the nation's first flag was made.

If the weather is conducive and there is time, you may also want to tour the tall ships and the submarine at Penn's Landing.

When it comes to dinner, the choices are endless. La Bec Fin is considered the city's finest—and most expensive—restaurant. Both the Bookbinder restaurants are landmarks and full of atmosphere. And there are over 100 restaurants in the area around NewMarket and South Street. The shops at NewMarket also stay open until 9:30 P.M., in case you missed them during the day.

As for city nightlife, Ripley's Music Hall, Brick's Café, or Borgia's are the places for jazz; flamenco dancers tap up a storm at the Maison Don Quijote; Elan in the Warwick Hotel is the "in" disco at the moment; and at the Middle East you'll find belly dancers gyrating downstairs and a lineup of comedians hoping to be discovered upstairs at the Comedy Works.

If you want to hear the Philadelphia Orchestra at bargain prices and you don't mind sitting in the peanut gallery, join the long line of locals waiting for the gallery tickets that go on sale before each performance at the Academy of Music.

For Sunday brunches two recommended spots are O'Brien's at the Bellevue Stratford and Wildflowers, where the bountiful buffet may well hold you all day. If you want to sample a cheese steak, try Jim's Steaks at 4th and South streets.

Sunday is the day to board the Victorian trolleys that leave the convention and Visitors Bureau regularly for tours through Fairmount Park. It will take you past lush meadowland and rustic trails, restored mansions, outdoor theaters, a zoo, and even a Japanese teahouse. In spring and summer regattas are a regular sight on the river adjoining the park, rowing out from the boathouses along the edge.

During the warmer seasons the trolley runs every 20 minutes all day and you can make unlimited stopoffs along the 90-minute tour, just catching up with the next bus that comes along. In winter they sometimes eliminate stops since so many attractions are closed, making it a warm motor tour with one stop to see whichever mansion may still be open to the public.

Philadelphia's best-known museums, located at the entry to Fairmount Park on broad Benjamin Franklin Parkway, know no seasons. The Philadelphia Museum of Art takes you anywhere from an Amish farmhouse to a Peking palace. The art collections are large, the American wing outstanding, and the Oriental section is a knockout, with a Buddhist temple, a palace reception room, a Chinese scholar's study, and many magnificent pieces of rosewood furniture from the Ming dynasty. If you climb the banks of steps outside that *Rocky* made famous, you'll be rewarded with a striking vista of the city.

Across the Parkway in the Rodin Museum is the largest collection of the sculptor's works to be found outside of France, including such masterpieces as "The Thinker," "The Burghers of Calais," and "Gates

of Hell," all a gift to his fellow citizens from a little-known Philadelphian named Jules E. Mastbaum.

The Franklin Institute Science Museum on the other side of the
boulevard is a change of pace and one of the most innovative
institutions of its kind, with participatory exhibits that let you pilot a
plane, steer a ship, ride a 350-ton locomotive, and walk through a giant
human heart.

With the park and the museums, the day will be gone before you
know it and you still won't have been to Germantown or the Italian
Market or the Mummer's Museum, or seen the excellent American art
collection at the Pennsylvania Academy of Fine Arts or the famous
Mummy Room at the University Museum, which has shared many
archaeological expeditions with the British Museum. And then there is
the U.S. Mint and the "Please Touch" Museums and the gardens . . .
and later in the year the outdoor activity at NewMarket and in
Fairmount Park . . . and the antique stores on Pine Street . . . and on
and on.

W. C. Fields might not have enjoyed spending time in the native city
he used to joke about, but nowadays most first-time visitors to
Philadelphia leave town calculating how soon they can come back.

Philadelphia Area Code: 215

DRIVING DIRECTIONS Take the New Jersey Turnpike to exit 7.
Follow signs to Route 202 southbound. Continue to Route 295, then to
exit 34, Route 70 west, which leads to Route 30 west and the Benjamin
Franklin Bridge into the city.
Total distance: 98 miles.

BY PUBLIC TRANSPORTATION Amtrak has frequent service
to Philadelphia and the city's sights are easily accessible on foot or via
public transportation.

ACCOMMODATIONS Many Philadelphia hotels, including the
elegant Bellevue Stratford, offer excellent weekend package deals. The
Visitors Bureau has a complete current list. The hotels following are
just a small sampling of the dozens available in the city: *Latham Hotel,*
17th at Walnut, LO 3-7474, small, elegant, European; $$$ ● *Bellevue
Stratford,* Broad at Walnut, 893-1776, large, grand after a $25 million
renovation; $$$–$$$$ ● *Society Hill Hotel,* 301 Chestnut Street,
925-1394, tiny, atmospheric; $$ with breakfast ● *Holiday Inn-Indepen-
dence Mall,* 4th and Arch, 923-8660; $$ ● *Barclay Hotel,* Rittenhouse

Square, 545-0300, old standby; $$$–$$$$ ● *Franklin Motor Inn,* 22nd at Benjamin Franklin Parkway, 568-8300, convenient for museums; $ ● *Warwick Hotel,* 1701 Locust, 735-6000, another super-elegant, small hotel; $$$–$$$$ ● Also note there is an association called Bed-and-Breakfast of Philadelphia, which advises on rooms in private homes and small hotels, approximately $18 double. For directory, write P. O. Box 101, Oreland, Pennsylvania 19075.

DINING *Wildflowers,* 516 South 5th Street, 923-6708, oak and stained glass, bountiful salad bar; $–$$, Sunday brunch, $$ ● *Dickens Inn, NewMarket,* 421 South 2nd Street, 928-9307, pub atmosphere; $$–$$$ ● *Frog,* 1524 Locust, 735-8882, varied fare, very popular locally; $–$$ ● *The Garden,* 1617 Spruce Street, 546-4455, elegant townhouse, French; $–$$ ● *Le Bec Fin,* 1312 Spruce Street, 732-3000, the city's best; $$$$ ● *Le Beau Lieu,* Barclay Hotel (see above); $$–$$$ ● *Versailles Restaurant,* Bellevue Stratford (see above), continental, elegant; $$$ ● *Siva's,* 34 South Front Street, 925-2700, Indian; $–$$ ● *Le Famiglia,* 8 South Front Street, 922-2803, Italian; $–$$ ● *Middle East,* 126 Chestnut Street, Lebanese, Greek, Armenian; $ ● *Cafe Lisboa,* NewMarket at 2nd and Pine, 928-0844, Portuguese; $$–$$$ ● *Bookbinder's Old Original,* 125 Walnut Street, 925-7027, landmark; $$–$$$$ (higher prices are for lobster) ● *Bookbinder's Seafood House,* 215 South 15th Street, 545-1137, landmark; $$–$$$$ (higher prices are for lobster) ● *City Tavern,* 2nd and Walnut, 923-6059, very special; $$–$$$, lunch, $ ● *Caraway,* 714 South Street, 925-4950, natural foods; $$ ● *O'Brien's,* Bellevue Stratford (see above); Sunday brunch $ ● Again, this is just a sampling—the restaurants could fill a book.

SIGHTSEEING *Independence National Historical Park,* 3rd and Chestnut, 597-8974. Hours: daily, 9 A.M. to 5 P.M. Free ● *Betsy Ross House,* 239 Arch Street, 627-5343. Hours: 9 A.M. to 5 P.M. Free ● *Christ Church,* 2nd Street above Market Street, 922-1695. Hours: Monday to Saturday, 9 A.M. to 5 P.M.; Sunday, 1 to 5 P.M. Free ● *Fairmount Park Trolley Bus,* from visitors' bureau, 16th and JFK Boulevard, 879-4044. Check for current rates and schedules at time of visit ● *Franklin Institute Science Museum,* 20th Street and Benjamin Franklin Parkway, 488-1000. Hours: Monday to Saturday, 10 A.M. to 5 P.M.; Sunday noon to 5 P.M. Adults $3.50, children under 12 and college students with ID $2.50, children age 4–11, $2 ● *Norman Rockwell Museum,* Curtis Building, 6th and Walnut, 922-4345. Hours: daily 10 A.M. to 4 P.M. Adults $1.50, under 12 free. (No charge to see mosaic in building lobby.) ● *Rodin Museum,* 22nd and Benjamin Franklin Parkway, 763-8100. Hours: Wednesday to Sunday, 10 A.M. to

5 p.m. Donation ● *Philadelphia Museum of Art,* 26th and Benjamin Franklin Parkway, 763-8100. Hours: Wednesday to Sunday, 10 a.m. to 5 p.m. Adults $2, children $1, free on Sunday between 10 a.m. and 1 p.m.

FOR FURTHER INFORMATION   Write or phone Philadelphia Convention and Visitors Bureau, 1525 JFK Boulevard, Philadelphia, PA 19102, 568-1976. Bureau is open daily 9 a.m. to 5 p.m.

Snow and Snuggling in the Berkshire Hills

It's just as the song pictures it. Outside the inn there's a one-horse open sleigh waiting to jingle you through the snow. Unless, of course, you'd rather skate on the pond, or practice your cross-country strides, or head for a ski area where snowmaking guarantees that 65 percent of the slopes are always ready for action.

If it's too cold or too warm for all that, how about antiquing or sightseeing, or snapping photos of white-steepled churches and picture-book village greens? Or you could always just join that contented tabby cuddled in front of the inn fireplace.

Weekends are all but weatherproof in the Berkshire Hills of Connecticut, where winter sports share billing with New England villages, interesting shops, and old-fashioned inns where hospitality is warm, whatever the weather.

For skiers, the major attraction here is Mohawk Mountain, a small, friendly area with many of the amenities of a larger complex. Mohawk is unusually attractive, set in the middle of a state forest, reached via an arching bridge over a surrounding brook, with lakes that are sometimes used for ice skating. The chalet-style cedar lodge has a wall-size picture window and a large deck for enjoying the view. And this is one of few lodges that worries about creating inviting indoor atmosphere, with potted trees and green plants, rafters hung with sleighs, wagon wheels, and old wooden skis, and even a wall of books next to the fireplace for those who aren't skiing for the day.

Mohawk is an ideal place to learn to ski. There are special day rates for novices and even a separate, slower chairlift for beginners. Cross-country lessons and rentals are also available, and there are miles of beautiful trails in the adjacent Mohawk State Forest. If Mohawk's 20 downhill trails are not as steep as those farther north in Vermont, there's the compensation of lift lines that seldom call for more than a 5 to 10 minutes wait.

At day's end welcoming fires and refreshments await in a number of inns in the area. A few are particularly noteworthy, making for a pleasant winter weekend with or without skiing.

For a small, secluded spot away from it all, head for the Under Mountain Inn, north of Mohawk in the charming village of Salisbury. Owners Al and Lorraine Bard, former Californians, took well to their new environs and have created a gracious Colonial atmosphere in their inn. Each of the seven rooms is decorated differently, all using striking reproductions of Early American wallpapers, often with bedspreads and drapes to match, and with furnishings that vary from formal to country in mood.

Downstairs, handsome Oriental rugs grace the wide-board floors, and there's a fireplace glowing in each of the three intimate dining rooms as well as in the cozy parlor. Al will serve your drinks in the candlelit tap room, while Lorraine prepares some of the dishes that have made the inn a favorite area dining spot. Among her specialties are crisp duckling with plum sauce and juicy leg of lamb.

While in Salisbury, stop in at the White Hart, the venerable inn on the village green, for a meal or some of the home-baked goodies or the inn's own blend of Sarum tea, for sale in the lobby gift shop. And be sure to pay a visit to Undermountain Weavers on Route 41 to watch fine wools being woven by hand on a century-old Scottish loom.

In neighboring Lakeville, the home of the Hotchkiss School, there are Lily Pulitzer, Jaeger, and other elite shops to explore, and the Interlaken Inn, a modern resort that lacks Colonial charm but does offer lots to do—tobogganing and ice skating, a sauna, game room, evening entertainment, and sleigh rides Sunday from 1 to 4 P.M.

On a knoll overlooking lake and hills is The Inn at Lake Waramaug, just west of New Preston. There, in addition to a warm welcome from the resident Coombs family, you'll find plenty to do indoors and out.

The inn has an indoor pool and sauna, there's ping-pong and a pool table for the kids, you can ice-skate or cross-country ski over the snow-covered lake, and on Sunday afternoon a one-horse sleigh will be waiting outside to take you for a free ride around the grounds.

The handsome white inn building (circa 1791) still has its original paneled chestnut walls and old fireplaces. The wide-windowed dining rooms are filled with heirloom collections of silver, copper, and pewter. They're particularly attractive this time of year, dressed up in holiday red cloths with matching poinsettias on every table. Owner Richard Coombs predicts they'll stay in bloom at least until Valentine's Day. Specialty of the house is the Saturday night prime-rib buffet, and the

Sunday brunch is generous enough to see you through Sunday dinner as well.

There are a few rooms in the inn, but most of Waramaug's 23 accommodations are in motel-type lodges on the grounds. Many units have fireplaces.

From the inn it's just a few miles to Litchfield, one of the area's most historic and photogenic towns. In Litchfield, drive to Bantam Lake off Route 209 and you can watch the ice skaters in action on winter afternoons.

Or you may just decide to forget it all and return to the most traditional winter activity in northwest Connecticut—sitting by the fire alongside that contented cat.

Berkshire Hills Area Code: 203

DRIVING DIRECTIONS   Take I-684 north to exit 9E, I-84 east to exit 7, US 202 north to New Preston. From New Preston follow signs and lakeside road to Inn at Lake Waramaug. For Salisbury use above route but continue on I-684 north (it becomes NY 22) to the end, then take U.S. 44 east. For Lakeville, follow 41 south from Salisbury. For Mohawk Mountain, follow Route 7 north to Route 4 east at Cornwall Bridge and follow signs.

Total distance: to New Preston 83 miles; to Salisbury 103; to Lakeville 106.

ACCOMMODATIONS AND DINING   *The Inn at Lake Waramaug,* Lake Waramaug Road, Lake Waramaug, New Preston, 868-2168; $$$–$$$$ MAP; dinner $$ ● *Under Mountain Inn,* Undermountain Road (Route 41), Salisbury, 435-0242; $$ with continental breakfast; dinner entrées $$ ● *Interlaken Inn,* Route 112, Lakeville, 435-9678; $$; dinner entrées $$.

SKIING   *Mohawk Mountain Ski Area,* Cornwall, 672-6100. Call for current prices.

Yankee Winter Weekends in Sturbridge

Open fires and roasting chesnuts set the scene. Your welcoming drink is a steaming eighteenth-century concoction. The hostesses are in Yankee costumes, and Friday dinner is served to the tunes of a strolling minstrel singing Colonial songs. Another Sturbridge Yankee Weekend is underway.

The weekends, held throughout January, February, and March, were initiated by the Publick House Inn, no doubt as a way to drum up winter business, but they've proven so popular that they are now a town tradition, joined by several of the other inns and motels in town in cooperation with Old Sturbridge Village. The notion is to revive early American winter pleasures to make our twentieth century winters a little more bearable, concentrating on the many facilities at Sturbridge Village and a luscious menu that was obviously concocted in less calorie-conscious times.

Saturday, for example, begins with a breakfast of fried corn mush, sausages, and hot deep-dish apple pie. To work it off, you bundle up and take a stroll around Old Sturbridge Village, the 40-building reconstruction of a typical Colonial town. Even if you've been here before, the village takes on a new dimension in the winter as it concentrates on cold weather activities of its time. After lunch you'll even get to see how they used to make maple sugar candy by hardening the syrup in the snow.

The usual crafts demonstrations—weaving, printing, tinsmithing, and the like—also are in order in the winter, and you finally may have time to take a look at some of the indoor exhibits that usually are forgotten in the summer. There are seven galleries to be seen, filled with firearms, clocks, lighting devices, folk art, textiles, blown and molded glass, mirrors, scientific instruments, handsewn and knitted garments, weaving and quilts, and much more.

A buffet lunch is served right at the Village Tavern, and after you watch the maple candy in the making, you'll be treated to a rollicking sleigh ride through the snow.

Wild boar and roast venison are the kinds of things you can expect on the dinner menu; afterward it's back to Sturbridge Village for an evening of nineteenth-century entertainment at the Tavern.

All the meals are served at the village or at the Publick House Inn, no matter where you are staying. The inn itself is most people's first choice for lodging as well (the price for the weekend is standard whether you are in an inn or a motel). It is a onetime coaching tavern opened in 1771, and the atmosphere probably hasn't changed a lot since then. Period furniture, low ceilings, and tilty floors and door frames remain, though the carpeting and TV sets upstairs are strictly twentieth century.

One almost equally appealing alternative is the Ebenezer Crafts Inn, under the same management, a restored 1786 Colonial home with 10 airy bedrooms furnished in Colonial style and with sweeping views of the snow-covered hills from the windows.

Wherever you stay, you'll be back to the inn on Sunday for yet another glorious breakfast—hearty portions of homemade sausage and country eggs with pumpkin and blueberry muffins, porridge with maple syrup and cream, and hot apple pandowdy. Figuring that half the guests probably can't move anyway, the rest of the day is unplanned. You can return to Sturbridge or visit some of the area shops on Route 20 such as Sturbridge Yankee Workshop or the Seraph for reproductions of Early American furniture, or Basketville, or the Quilter's Quarters, or a variety of other shops, any of which can supply excellent souvenirs of the weekend.

One other possibility is to take less than half an hour's drive farther east on 86 to Route 90 and discover a little-known New England town. Worcester, Massachusetts, is mainly thought of (and accurately) as a factory town, but it is much more. New England's second largest city, it has a Colonial heritage that dates back to 1673, an attractively hilly terrain, and lovely residential areas. It is the home of 12 colleges and two fine museums.

The most special of the two is the Worcester Science Center, where the building's self-sufficient energy system is actually displayed for the public's edification in an exhibit. There are some clever demonstrations of scientific principles—a push-pull device to show how a fulcrum works, a hot air compressor that shows what makes balloons go up—as well as more traditional natural science exhibits, including a giant stuffed Indian tiger. The live animals outside feature a couple particularly appropriate for winter visitors—Ursa Major and Ursa Minor, a pair of polar bears known affectionately as the Major and Ursa. A special window lets you watch the bears swimming underwater.

Worcester's Art Museum may surprise you. The traditional stone building contains some fine exhibits, including a thirteenth-century French chapel rebuilt here stone by stone. The brochure describes the collection as "the development of man as seen through 50 centuries of his art," and they've shown just that through displays from Greek and Roman vases to Persian and Indian miniatures to Rembrandts, Goyas,

Matisses, and Picassos. The painting galleries are separated by schools, including Dutch, French, Spanish, and Italian.

The two Worcester museums are easy to find, as signs are posted pointing the way no matter how you enter the city. The contrasting exhibits make for a rewarding afternoon, and when you're done you'll discover that some of those dull factories associated with the city are now converted into very lively places for food and drink. One good choice right around the corner from the art museum is Northworks on Grove Street—casual, congenial, and inexpensive with a menu of burgers, fried zucchini, and other light foods that may be welcome after all that Colonial feasting in Sturbridge. (Also check out the Factory Flea in the basement of the building for possible bargains.)

If you have a more elegant dinner in mind, head toward Lincoln Square and Union Place and Maxwell Silverman's Tool House, another restored factory, this time done with real flair.

If you're ever in Worcester on a day other than Sunday, by the way, keep in mind that the Town Center, a shopping mall, contains a large, bargain-packed, and uncrowded edition of Filene's basement, inexplicably located on the second floor. The Worcester Crafts Center also has beautiful original pieces for sale.

Reliving the past and discovering a promising small city of the present—it's a winning combination for a winter weekend.

Worcester Area Code: 617

DRIVING DIRECTIONS Hutchinson River and Merritt parkways or I-95 north to I-91 to Hartford; from Hartford take I-84 toward Boston, which becomes I-86. Sturbridge is exit 3. Publick House Inn is on Route 131 in the center of Sturbridge, south of Route 20.

Total distance: 160 miles.

ACCOMMODATIONS *Sturbridge Yankee Winter Weekends,* lodging, 2 dinners, 2 breakfasts, Saturday lunch, and all admissions, $139.95 per person double occupancy. Weekends run January through March; choice of six accommodations: The Publick House, Chamberlain House, Colonial Crafts Inn, Treadway Motor Inn, Old Sturbridge Village Motor Lodge, Sturbridge Coach Motor Lodge. For information, contact Publick House Inn, Sturbridge, MA 01566, 347-3313.

DINING *Northworks,* 106 Grove Street, Worcester, 755-9657; $
• *Maxwell Silverman's Tool House,* 25 Union Street, Worcester, 755-1200; $–$$.

SIGHTSEEING *Worcester Art Museum,* 55 Salisbury Street, 799-4406. Hours: Tuesday to Saturday, 10 A.M. to 5 P.M.; Sunday 2 to 5 P.M. Adults $1; senior citizens, children age 5–14 50¢ ● *Worcester Science Center,* 222 Harrington Way, 791-9211. Hours: Monday to Saturday, 10 A.M. to 5 P.M.; Sunday, noon to 5 P.M. Adults $2.50, senior citizens, children age 3–16 $1.50.

Snowtime in the Poconos

Invigorating days out-of-doors and a welcoming fire at a cozy inn at day's end: For many people that's the perfect formula for a winter weekend. But it's not an easy order to fill in Pennsylvania's Pocono Mountains. Though there is plenty of scenery and an abundance of outdoor activity in this area so easy to reach from the city, Poconos lodgings run to large resorts, honeymoon havens, or bland motels. Until you get to Canadensis, that is.

Remember that name, Canadensis. This tiny town—hardly more than a crossroads, really—somehow has garnered the only three country inns in the Poconos. And once you've found them you've found the best of both worlds. You can be snug and secluded when you want, but when you don't feel like sitting home by the fire, not only are the major ski areas at your disposal but also the facilities at many of those big resort hotels as well. Many of them are ideal if you are a cross-country skier or even just beginning at downhill.

First then, pick an inn. The most sophisticated is Overlook Inn, which you might guess when you note that the chairs in the living room bear family college seals from Williams and Harvard. The Tuppers are one of those couples who decided to get away from it all by establishing a warm and welcoming inn, and they've done a fine job with this century-old home. Walk past the wide, railed porch into the entry, and you'll find a comfortable living room with the obligatory fireplace on the right, a booklined, paneled, and inviting library-game room-den on the left. Afternoon tea is served every day.

Upstairs the rooms are furnished simply with old-fashioned pieces—iron bedsteads, Victorian chests, and the like.

Dinner at the Overlook is fine—homebaked bread, tender filet de boeuf, fresh-caught brook trout, moist rice pilaf, vegetables cooked just right to retain their crunch.

Pine Knob, which has been accommodating visitors since the 1880s, is more like a visit to Grandma's house. Redoing the old house was another labor of love, this time by Jim and June Belfie, expatriate suburban Philadelphians. It has homey touches like hobnail bed-spreads, sheer ruffled curtains, and African violets on the bedside tables. The living room-parlor is Victorian, dominated by a grand piano, an immense breakfront, and an ancient stone fireplace. Cotton chintz tablecloths, bentwood chairs, and arrangements of evergreens and dried flowers brighten the dining room, which is also highly recommended in the area. Hot corn muffins or popovers, homemade soups and chowders, and desserts like praline cheesecake keep people coming back for more.

It's really the dining room that distinguishes the third inn, the Pump House. Many people rate it as the best restaurant in the Poconos. The story goes that the Pump House started as an inn with a small restaurant but turned out to be a restaurant with five pleasant rooms upstairs. In addition to the formal French dining room that has won the inn its acclaim, there is the Garden Grill with an English menu and a come-as-you-are informal wine cellar serving nothing but hors d'oeuvres for snacks, or enough for a meal as you prefer. You won't have a parlor to come home to here, but you will have a continental breakfast included in the price of the room and those three dining rooms to choose from without venturing any farther on a wintry night than right downstairs.

Now, having made your choice, enjoyed your breakfast, and resisted the lure of the fire, you have the pleasant prospect of planning an outdoors day in the Poconos. Skiing is gentle here, but there are compensations since even Camelback, the closest and largest of the ski areas, is able to offer snowmaking over the entire mountain. There is also night skiing, if you are so inclined. Between Camelback and other areas such as Big Boulder, Jack Frost, or Shawnee, there should be enough to suit all but the really expert skier. Write ahead to the Pocono Mountains Vacation Bureau and they'll send you a free guide to all the areas so you can choose your slope in advance.

If you are a beginner, you may be happier heading for Buck Hill, a resort that is even closer to Canadensis and where the two slopes and J-lifts are open to the public for a fee. Fifteen miles of cross-country trails are also available at no charge if you have your own skis, but they do ask that skiers register at the desk prior to setting out. And if you want to try out a snowmobile, you can rent one by the half hour or the hour, with the Buck Hills golf course at hand to provide plenty of room for safe maneuvering.

Pocono Manor also allows skiing on its baby slopes and trails served by a J- and T-bar. This is also where you will find the Rossignol Nordic Touring Center, with rentals and lessons and 40 miles of groomed and marked trails for all abilities.

Buck Hill and the Manor are two of the grand old timber and stone mountaintop hotels that were once the pride of the Poconos, with 6,000 and 3,000 acres of spectacular grounds, respectively. Their locations, views, and grounds are as grand as ever, though the hotels themselves are struggling to maintain themselves in a new resort era. If they're not quite what they used to be, they're still quite something and you should see them while you're in the area. If you like to do winter hiking, trails at either hotel are simply magnificent.

Skytop is the one grand manor that has retained its elegance, and it is worth a drive to see its fine building and setting. You can visit or dine if you like, but you won't be invited to use the facilities.

At Mount Airy, however, a far livelier and much different kind of resort, you'll find not only downhill, cross-country, and snowmobile trails available to you, but guaranteed snow for all three. They actually make snow for cross-country and snowmobile trails, taking no chances on disappointing their guests. If the weather is hopeless, you can also use Mount Airy's Indoor Sports Palace for a fee, complete with tennis, ice skating, a health club, heated pool, basketball, and handball courts.

The Poconos area is not one for quaint villages, but if shopping is your favorite outdoor sport, there is enough to keep you occupied for a pleasant couple of hours. The Other Woman on Route 390 in Mountainhome is probably the pick of the shops, an eight-room house filled with all kinds of nice things like fabrics, dried flowers, custom pillows, antiques, lamps and even baked goods. Also in Mountainhome, the brittle, fudge, Pocono crunch, and other temptations at Callie's Candy Kitchen are a treat, and the Queen's Treasures is a collector's haven of plates, spoons, thimbles, figurines, and music boxes.

Memorytown U.S.A. is a village of shops and museums in pseudo–Early American style, but there is a variety of wares, and you can have an old-fashioned sepia souvenir photograph made at Lucky Ned Pepper's Picture Parlor. Visitors here are invited to ice skate on the pond, weather permitting.

Two other crafts shops to visit on Route 611 are Stone Ware Potters in Tannersville and The Woodworker in Bartonsville, where you'll find unusual handmade furniture.

One other kind of recreation widely available in the Poconos is horseback riding. A number of stables offer horses and/or guided trail rides, and on the right day there's really nothing like the beauty of moving past untouched snow through the winter stillness.

"Pocono People Love Winter" says the slogan from the local vacation bureau, and considering the many ways they have to enjoy the season, it's no wonder.

Poconos Area Code: 717

DRIVING DIRECTIONS Take the George Washington Bridge to I-80 west to exit 52 in Pennsylvania. Follow 447 north to Canadensis. Ask your inn for more specific directions to their door.
Total distance: 109 miles.

ACCOMMODATIONS AND DINING *Overlook Inn,* Dutch Hill Road, Canadensis, 595-7519; $$$ MAP ● *Pine Knob Inn,* Route 447, Canadensis, 595-2532; $$–$$$ MAP ● *Pump House Inn,* Skytop Road, Route 390, Canadensis, 595-7501; $ with continental breakfast; $; dinner entrées, $$–$$$.

SKIING For information and prices for all Pocono ski resorts, plus the "Ski the Poconos" brochure, write Pocono Mountains Vacation Bureau, 1004 Main Street, Stroudsburg, PA 18360.

Ringing Sleighbells in Southbury

A one-horse sleigh may sound like fun, but Glen Morris says a pair of horses is even better—not to mention a three-horse troika.

Morris is one of a handful of Connecticut traditionalists devoted to preserving the old-fashioned pleasures of a sleigh ride through the snow, jingling bells and all—a treat he will provide for you any weekend when Mother Nature cooperates with the necessary white ground cover.

He has been dashing off across the scenic golf course behind Harrison Inn in Southbury for more than a decade now in a bright red ten-seater sleigh he built himself with sturdy runners once used by the Roxbury Fire Department. Half-hour rides are available any weekend when snow is on the ground, but advance reservations are a must. If only one couple reserves for a particular day, he'll pull out his two-seater sleigh.

A schoolteacher by profession, Morris uses the proceeds he brings in from winter sleigh rides and fall and spring hayrides to help support the Morgan horses he breeds and trains. He'll tell you fondly about his two-time Morgan national champion, Townsend Challenge, as well as about the father-mother-son trio that forms the three-horse hitch for his sleigh. That family was raised and trained by another father, mother, and son, he notes with pride, referring to his own family.

The Morrises also own two antique sleighs that they show at winter sleigh rallies, an almost vanished tradition that has managed to survive in this part of Connecticut. Rallies are a Currier & Ives scene come to life. Judging categories go from teams of ponies to giant draft horses like Percherons, and driver categories range from juniors and ladies to old-timers over age 64. The final judging, the Currier & Ives class, is the one that brings out the gleaming antiques and passengers swathed in Victorian cloaks and greatcoats, bonnets and muffs and stovepipe hats. These unusual events are held regularly during the winter and are listed in local newspapers but are never widely promoted outside the immediate area since they are usually held on a local farmer's land with no facilities for large crowds of spectators. One regular event open to the public is sponsored by the Newtown Parks and Recreation Department in mid-February; Glen Morris can probably tell you about others. Rallies, too, are subject to the whims of the weather.

Morris is not the only person who offers sleigh rides, but he's the safest driver to aim for since you could spend a happy winter weekend in this area even if there's a snow drought.

The Harrison Inn itself is an excellent choice for lodging. It's an unusual building for this locale, a contemporary complex of rough-hewn wood with super-modern rooms, but the welcome is no less warm for its modern architecture. There are wide stone fireplaces aglow downstairs, a billiards room, a sauna and whirlpool for guests, a busy bar, a lavish Sunday brunch and—adjoining the inn—a multilevel shopping complex where you can while away the hours without ever having to go outdoors.

If Colonial is more your style, drive north on US 6 to Woodbury, a typical New England town of white-steepled churches and a Main Street lined with antique shops. Curtis Inn here is the oldest hostelry in the state. It's an unpretentious place, moderately priced, where you can sleep in a canopy bed and dine in authentic Early American atmosphere.

Another Colonial-style inn in one of the prettiest New England villages in this or any other state is the Mayflower Inn in Washington. Here's a picture-perfect green, dominated by the tall-spired Congregational church and surrounded with magnificent white clapboard homes set off with dark shutters. This is a very private town—old wealth, old homes, two prestigious prep schools—but it still offers pleasures for visitors. The Hickory Stick Bookstore, makes for perfect browsing on a cold winter's day; the Gunn Historical Museum is small but packed with interesting mementos of the past; and the Washington

Art Association is an attractive gallery with an interesting schedule of shows.

A more unusual place to visit is the American Indian Archaelogical Institute, dedicated to showing the life of the first inhabitants of the northeastern woodlands. The exhibits include a reconstructed long-house, a mammoth mastodon, and other artifacts portraying 12,000 years of Indian history. In addition to the baskets and crafts on display, there are special collector's pieces for sale in the museum shop.

The Mayflower Inn is a handsome building set on 32 acres, but it has changed owners and chefs in the past couple of years so it's difficult to know how you'll find it at the present.

Any one of these inns is convenient to the Woodbury Ski and Racquet Club, where you can make your own tracks in the snow. This small, uncrowded slope is an ideal place for learning or practicing downhill skiing, and the 50-mile network of cross-country trails offers challenge for every level of skill. Lessons and rentals are available for both kinds of skiers. Woodbury makes its own snow for downhillers, but should the weather prove totally uncooperative, there are indoor tennis and paddle tennis facilities.

A mix of a morning of antiquing, a ride through the snow, an afternoon in Washington, and a Sunday out-of-doors makes for a near-perfect winter weekend recipe. And if you can manage to end things with a visit to an old-time sleigh rally, you'll have Currier & Ives icing for dessert.

Southbury Area Code: 203

DRIVING DIRECTIONS Hutchinson River Parkway to I-684 north to exit 9E, I-84 east to exit 15, US 6 north to Southbury 83 miles. Follow Route 6 north to Woodbury, then 47 northwest to Washington.
Total distance: about 100 miles.

ACCOMMODATIONS AND DINING *Harrison Inn,* Village Green, Heritage Village, Southbury, 264-8255; $$$. Dinner $$ ● *Curtis Inn,* Main Street, Woodbury, 263-2101; $. Dinner $–$$ ● *Mayflower Inn,* Route 47, Washington, 868-0515; $$. Dinner, $$.

SIGHTSEEING For a sleigh rides listing and up-to-date information about rallies, write Connecticut Department of Economic Development, 210 Washington Street, Hartford, CT 06106, or call toll-free (800) 243-1685 ● *Sleigh rides:* Write or phone Glen Morris, Poverty Road, Southbury, CT 06106, 264-6196, for reservations, current rates, and driving directions to stables ● *Newtown Sleigh Rally*, Newtown Parks and Recreation Department, phone 426-8131 for dates ● *Woodbury Ski and Racquet Club*, Route 47 north of town, Woodbury, 263-2203. Phone for current rates ● *American Indian Archaeological Institute*, off Route 199, Washington, 868-0518. Hours: Monday to Saturday, 10 A.M. to 4:30 P.M.; Sunday 1 to 4:30 P.M. Adults $2, children $1 ● *Gunn Historical Museum*, on the green (Route 47), Washington, 868-7756. Hours: Tuesday, Thursday, 2 to 5 P.M.; Saturday 1 to 4 P.M. Free.

Newport: Snug Harbor in the Off Season

The winter waves were whipping against the cliff. A couple, knitted hats pulled down against the wind, arms wound around each other's ski parkas, were standing on the Cliff Walk, mesmerized by the sight.

Newport, Rhode Island, summer haven for the socialite, the sailor, and the sightseer, has a fascination of its own in the winter's chill. The Ocean Drive looking out to sea is even more spectacular, the Cliff Walk along the bluffs more dramatic, and the harbor takes on a special serenity in its unaccustomed stillness.

The boats may have taken cover until spring, but with the fabled mansions still receiving visitors, the sights still worth seeing, and dozens of shops and restaurants still open for business, Newport remains a snug harbor for a weekend by the sea.

Top choice for a romantic outlook is the Inn at Castle Hill on Ocean Drive. The old Victorian house with huge rooms has an unmatched view of rocky coast and a crackling fire downstairs to ward off winter chills. The Inntowne Inne, an elegant Colonial on a block of equally stylish renovations, lacks a view but offers more sophisticated charm. Two other standards in town are the Sheraton Islander Inn (with indoor pool), a five-minute drive away on Goat Island, and the Treadway Inn in the middle of the action in the wharf area.

To get a sense of the city, begin by taking the well-marked 10-mile Ocean Drive past all the mansions and out along the bluffs looking out to sea. If the weather is kind, stop off along Bellevue Avenue and follow some of the 3½-mile Cliff Walk, a path along the bluffs giving you views of lawns and mansions on one side and an eagle's-eye ocean view on the other.

To warm up you can take a tour of the mansions. If you think we had no royalty in this country, you may well change your mind when you see the massive scale, the marble floors, chandeliers, the ballrooms, and priceless brocades of these summer cottages of America's nineteenth-century industrial magnates, some with as many as 70 rooms. Three of the homes are open during the winter months: Marble House, designed by Richard Morris Hunt for William K. Vanderbilt and named for the many kinds and colors of marble used in its construction and decoration; the Elms, a summer residence of Philadelphia coal magnate Edward Berwind, modeled after the Château d'Asnieres near Paris, and Château Sur Mer, one of the most lavish examples of Victorian architecture in America and the site of Newport's first French ballroom. Less opulent but also interesting is Hunter House, a mansion that once served as headquarters for the French naval forces during the Revolution.

Back in town everything centers around the harbor. Sailboats and yachts have replaced the clipper ships that once dropped anchor here with treasures from around the world. The first American navy was established in Newport in 1775 to protect against the British ship H.M.S. *Rose*. As a result the town was burned by the British not only during the Revolutionary War but again during the War of 1812. A rebuilt version of the *Rose* now occupies a berth of honor in the harbor, though on far friendlier terms than the original.

Newport kept her navy ties and was home to a large fleet of ships up until 1973. It was after the Navy destroyers moved out that the yachts and America's Cuppers moved in, and shops began to spring up along the restored wharf areas. The two principal centers are Bowen's and Bannister's wharves right on the waterfront and the Brick Market Place across the way.

Along the wharves, in old restored warehouses and new structures with Colonial-modern lines you'll find shops with clothing from the Greek isles, original gold and silver jewelry designs, handcrafted leather goods, children's clothing and toys, a candy store noted for its homemade fudge, and a shop specializing in distinctive printed fabrics.

The Brick Market Place is a cobbled maze of condominiums and 30 shops with a wide variety of wares—Eskimo art, Irish fabrics and handknits, and Scandinavian imports, to name a few.

Nostalgia Factory contains every kind of collectible that has to do with old advertising, from movie posters to Coca-Cola signs, as well as old political campaign buttons and early postcards. At Kitchen Pot Pourri you'll find rack upon rack of utensils and gourmet cookbooks and tea balls in the shapes of spoons, bells, and miniature teapots. Fortify yourself for more shopping here with a hot cup of the house blend or special-of-the-day coffee, or a choice of teas and pastries.

If antiquing is your goal, you'll find shops on lower Thames, on parallel Spring Street, and on many of the side streets tucked in between. Note that Newport shop hours can be irregular in the off-season, but most are open sometime over the weekend. If you miss one or two, there are plenty to take their place.

On Sunday you can sample some of the city's other numerous and varied attractions. Drive or walk the narrow streets near the town center, where scores of sixteenth- and seventeenth-century Colonial homes have been lovingly restored, painted rainbow hues, and occupied by proud residents. Stop at the lovely Colonial-style Touro Synagogue, the nation's oldest, and the Trinity Church designed by Christopher Wren. The Tennis Hall of Fame on Bellevue Avenue offers aficionados a look at early racquets and quaint costumes, while the nearby Newport Automobile Museum not only displays classic cars but sells them.

There are more than enough things to do in Newport. But who could blame you if you were to decide to forget them all and just return to the Cliff Walk to memorize that mesmerizing vista of the wintry sea.

Newport Area Code: 401

DRIVING DIRECTIONS   Take I-95 east to exit 3 in Rhode Island, then Route 138 east to Newport.
Total distance: about 185 miles.

ACCOMMODATIONS   *Inn at Castle Hill,* Ocean Drive, 849-3800; $–$$$$ with continental breakfast • *The Inntowne,* 6 Mary Street, 846-9200; $$$ • *Sheraton Islander Inn,* Goat Island, 849-2600; $$–$$$$ • *Treadway Inn,* America's Cup Avenue, 847-9000; $$$$.

DINING   *La Petite Auberge,* 19 Charles Street, 849-7778, renowned French chef; $$–$$$ • *Le Bistro,* 250 Thames Street, 849-7778, French café, one flight up; $$–$$$ • *Clark Cooke House,* Bannister's Wharf, 849-2900, elegant eighteenth-century dining room; $$–$$$ • *Black Pearl,* Bannister's Wharf, 846-3000, converted wharf warehouse; $–$$$ • *White Horse Tavern,* Marlborough and Farewell Streets, 849-3600, nation's oldest continuously operating tavern; place to try Rhode Island johnnycakes; $$–$$$.

SIGHTSEEING   *Newport Mansions,* Preservation Society of Newport County, 118 Mill Street, 847-1000. Hours: For Marble House, The Elms, Château sur Mer, November to March, Saturday, Sunday, 11

A.M. to 4 P.M.; Hunter House by appointment only. All 6 mansions open after April 1, 10 A.M. to 5 P.M.; later in summer. Admission $3 to $3.50 at each house ● *International Tennis Hall of Fame and Tennis Museum,* Newport Casino, Bellevue Avenue, 846-4567. Hours: November to April, daily, 11 A.M. to 4 P.M.; rest of year, 10 A.M. to 5 P.M. Adults $3; children age 6–12 $1.25 ● *Newport Automobile Museum,* 1 Casino Terrace at Bellevue Terrace, 846-6688. Hours: daily, 10 A.M. to 7 P.M. Adults $3, children age 6–12 $2 ● *Touro Synagogue,* 72 Touro Street, 847-4794. Hours: Sunday only through spring, 2 to 4 P.M. Free ● *Trinity Church,* Church and Spring streets, 846-0660. By appointment except in summer. Free.

FOR FURTHER INFORMATION   Contact the Newport Chamber of Commerce, 10 America's Cup Avenue, Newport, RI 847-1600.

Tapping the Maples in Stamford

The calendar says winter, but the crackling fires and the boiling syrup kettles tell you not for long. Maple-sugaring is the first sure sign we've made it through another winter, and it's a perfect reason for an early March Connecticut weekend not too far from home.

Though maple-sugaring is largely associated with the farms of Vermont, New Hampshire, and upstate New York, a pleasant sampling is available just 40 miles away at the Stamford Museum and Nature Center. The museum puts up its sugar shed as soon as the sap starts to rise and taps the sugar maple trees that dot its 100-acre grounds.

You'll spy the collection buckets on the trees as soon as you arrive, but you may be surprised to see that the sap running is as thin and clear as water. The filled buckets are taken to the shed, where the sap is emptied into an evaporator to simmer slowly over a wood fire until it thickens into golden, gooey delicious syrup. Staff members tending the fire are generous with free tastes and will allow you to chop a log or two for the fire if the outdoor spirit moves you.

Maple-sugaring is a time-honored occupation, and you'll also see demonstrations of how the Indians did it—in a hollowed tree trunk using heat from stones that had been baked in the fire—as well as the way the colonists used to boil down their syrup in giant black kettles.

Maple-sugaring usually takes place the first two or three weekends in

March, but the museum warns visitors to call ahead to be sure the sap is running and the weather cooperating before you plan to come.

By far the most charming accommodations in the Stamford-Greenwich area are the elegant Victorian rooms at the Homestead Inn in Greenwich, a recently refurbished 1724 farmhouse. If this is a family outing and you prefer motel accommodations, there are many of them in the vicinity. Since you are only an hour or so from New York, if the stars are shining Friday night you can take advantage of the weekly free open house at the Stamford Museum Observatory from 8 to 10 P.M. It's exciting to look through a professional telescope and discover that the stars are really round and that you can clearly see the rings around Saturn.

Come Saturday your first stop should be United Housewrecking Company, off exit 6 on the Connecticut Turnpike. It's hard to imagine anyone who wouldn't have fun at this one-of-a-kind, five-acre junkyard. As the name suggests the company began by selling off the contents of homes and buildings that had been torn down. It was a place where locals came to browse among surplus phone booths, gasoline pumps, soda fountains, and church pews, or to search for bargains in secondhand storm windows, doors, fireplace tools, or furniture.

When it was discovered by decorators and out-of-town shoppers, the variety of wares grew even wackier to meet the new demand. Today you might find a canopied wicker beach chair on wheels for $350 or an old New York City subway sign for $10. Or a statue of a World War I doughboy, an airplane nosecone, surplus army mailbags, parachutes, barstools, old records and postcards, china, bric-a-brac—and heaven knows what else. The surprises are part of the fun.

One of United Housewrecking's prime attractions is the possibility of finding old things to convert into nostalgic new ones. Some possibilities are ships' wheels, portholes, and hatch covers for tabletops; old-fashioned sewing machine heads for lamps; and wooden type cases whose many small compartments are ideal for showing off knickknacks and collections. Since the tourists started coming, many new versions of these old favorites are available, and there are dozens of sizes and shapes of new wrought-iron pieces.

The scene changes dramatically when you drive into downtown Stamford, where you'll note all manner of modern architecture in the apartments, office buildings, corporate headquarters, and department stores that make up this city's urban renewal area. The sloped sides of Landmark Plaza, the round glass buildings of St. Johns Towers, and the inverted pyramid of the GTE headquarters are some of the more unusual designs.

One of the city's longtime architectural attractions is the First Presbyterian Church, a few blocks north of downtown on Bedford Street, one of the two main shopping streets. Known as the Fish Church for its shingled contemporary shape, the building has extraordinary windows made of more than 20,000 pieces of inch-thick colored glass imported from Chartres, France. The glass is set in an abstract depiction of the Crucifixion and the Resurrection, and the panes are a glorious sight as the jewel-hued light varies with changes in the sun and clouds outside.

Continue north straight up Bedford Street until it becomes High Ridge Road and you are on your way to the Stamford Museum. In addition to watching the maple-sugaring, you'll be able to see a growing reconstruction on the museum grounds of an old-fashioned Connecticut farm.

One of the last remaining eighteenth-century barns in the state was rescued, brought down from Cheshire, Connecticut, plank by weathered plank, and painstakingly reassembled here as the centerpiece of a model farm. Half a dozen kinds of seventeenth- and eighteenth-century fencing have been re-created by hand to enclose the fields, and an exhibit in a second barn shows how the early farmer accomplished so much with so little in the way of tools. The entire crop cycle is depicted, from plowing, harrowing, and sowing to cultivating, harvesting, and preserving, with displays of the authentic pre-machine age implements that were used for each task.

Maple-sugaring is just one of the many seasonal demonstrations of farm activities here, such as apple cidering, ice harvesting, and sheep shearing. All year round you'll see a barnyard full of the tamest and most appealing farm animals to be found anywhere outside of Mother Goose. They are longtime residents of the museum's Hecksher Farm for Children, which has been incorporated into the new displays.

There is also a small zoo of native Connecticut wildlife, a pond inhabited by dozens of varieties of ducks and geese, miles of nature trails, and an imposing Tudor mansion up the hill, once the home of retail magnate Henri Bendel and now housing nature and art exhibits.

In the evening you will find excellent live theater at Stamford's Hartman Theater and lighted outdoor ice skating at the Landmark Plaza rink.

Greenwich provides a variety of Sunday diversions for visitors. On pleasant days its Audubon Center offers 485 acres of beautiful woodland with many walking trails. The Bruce Museum has fine and decorative arts, as well as natural science and history exhibits and a salt-water aquarium. More unusual is the U.S. Tobacco Company Museum, which traces the history of tobacco on five continents in a collection of pipes, snuffboxes, and other tobacco-related artifacts. There are also a few cigar-store Indians and advertising graphics around for nostalgia buffs.

Bush-Holley House in Cos Cob, home of the Greenwich Historical Society, traces another kind of history. It is a seventeenth-century saltbox home restored and authentically furnished with impressive Jacobean fireplaces, as well as fine paneling and many rare early furniture pieces.

Greenwich, incidentally, is one of those towns like Southampton and Newport where you can pass a pleasant hour just driving and gazing wistfully at the mansions. Northbound roads like Lake Avenue, North Street, and Round Hill Road and their environs offer ample opportunities for scenery- and estate-watching.

Finally, with or without the kids, you can detour on the way home to Rye, New York, for the Museum of Cartoon Art. It's crammed with original cartoon drawings from "The Yellow Kid," the first color comic, to "Peanuts." Though it may date you to admit that you remember, you can find some of the classic old-timers like "Buster Brown," "Oaky Doakes," and "The Katzenjammer Kids." Comic book heroes like Superman, Dr. Strange, and Captain Marvel are also part of the collection, along with political cartoons and satiric drawings dating all the way back to Hogarth and Goya.

There are continuous showings of old cartoons. Depending on what is being shown on the day you come, you may see some of the early silents, the first Disneys, vintage "Popeye" and "Betty Boop," the beginning of "Tom and Jerry" back in 1931, and the original "Tweetie Pie" from 1947.

It was interesting to see that grown-ups seem to outnumber the kids at the cartoon exhibits.

Connecticut Area Code: 203

DRIVING DIRECTIONS   Take the New England Thruway (I-95), which becomes the Connecticut Turnpike. Greenwich exits are 3 to 5, Stamford exits 6 to 8 are just beyond. If you are going directly to the museum, take the Hutchinson River Parkway onto the Merritt Parkway, turn left at Exit 35, High Ridge Road, and proceed 1¼ miles. Museum is on the left.
Total distances: 40 miles.

ACCOMMODATIONS   *Homestead Inn,* 420 Field Point Road, off exit 3, Greenwich, 869-7500; $$$ • *Showboat Motor Inn,* 500 Steam-

boat Road off exit 3 on the riverfront, Greenwich, 661-9800; $$
• *Sheraton New Englander Motor Inn*, 1114 Post Road, off exit 5,
Greenwich, 637-3691; $$ • *Howard Johnson's Motor Inn*, 135 Harvard
Avenue off exit 6, Stamford, 357-7100; with heated indoor pool and
sauna, $$ • *Marriott Hotel*, 2 Stamford Plaza, off exit 7, Stamford,
357-9555, indoor pool and game and exercise room; $$$$; weekend
packages often available.

DINING *Homestead Inn* (see above); $$ • *Boodles*, 21 Field Point
Road, Greenwich, 661-3553, varied menu, hanging plants and what-
nots; $$ • *Greenstreet*, 253 Greenwich Avenue, Greenwich, 461-4459,
varied menu, another "in" local spot; $$ • *Cinquante Cinq*, 55 Arch,
Greenwich, 869-5641, elegant French; $$$ • *Le Cremaillaire*, North
Street between Greenwich and Bedford, Banksville, New York, (914)
234-3306, just north of Greenwich, best restaurant in this area, up to
New York gourmet standards in food as well as price; $$$$ • *Pellici's*,
98 Stillwater Avenue, Stamford, 323-2542, no atmosphere, but reason-
able and good Italian home cooking; $ • *The Country Tavern*, north of
the Merritt Parkway on Long Ridge Road (Route 34), North Stamford,
322-5316; atmospheric Colonial; $$–$$$.

SIGHTSEEING *Stamford Museum and Nature Center*, 39 Scofield-
town Road, 322-1646. Hours: Monday to Saturday, 9 A.M. to 5 P.M.;
Sunday, holidays, 1 to 5 P.M. Admission for nonresidents, adults $2,
children and senior citizens 50¢, not to exceed $5 per car • *United
Housewrecking Co.*, 326 Selleck Street, Stamford, 348-5371. Hours:
Tuesday to Saturday, 9 A.M. to 5 P.M. (Connecticut Turnpike exit 6,
right on Harvard Avenue and follow signs) • *First Presbyterian Church*,
1101 Bedford Street, Stamford, 324-9522 • *Greenwich Audubon
Society*, 613 Riversville Road, 869-5272. Hours: Tuesday to Sunday, 9
A.M. to 5 P.M. Adults $1, children 50¢ • *Bruce Museum*, Museum
Drive, Greenwich, 869-0376. Hours: Tuesday to Saturday, 10 A.M. to 5
P.M.; Sunday 2 to 5 P.M. Donation • *Bush Holley House*, Strickland
Road, Cos Cob, 622-9686. Tuesday to Saturday, 10 A.M. to noon, 2 to 4
P.M.; Sunday, 2 to 4 P.M. Adults $2, children $1, under 12 50¢ • *U.S.
Tobacco Company Museum*, 96 West Putnam Avenue, Greenwich,
869-5531. Hours: Tuesday to Sunday, noon to 5 P.M. Free • *Museum of
Cartoon Art*, Comly Avenue, Rye, (914) 939-0234. Tuesday to Friday,
10 A.M. to 4 P.M.; Sunday 1 to 5 P.M. Adults $1, children 50¢.

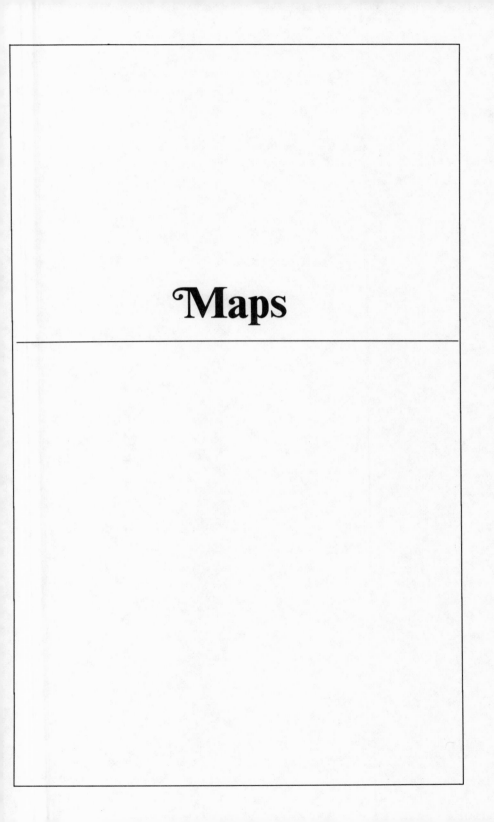

Maps

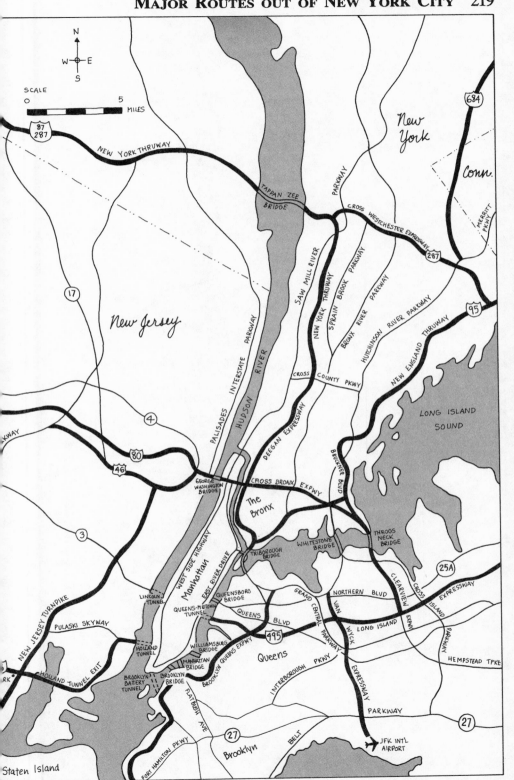

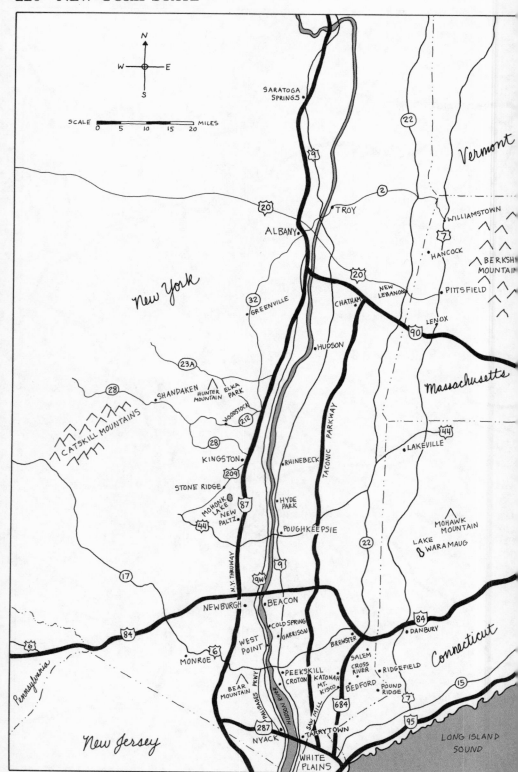

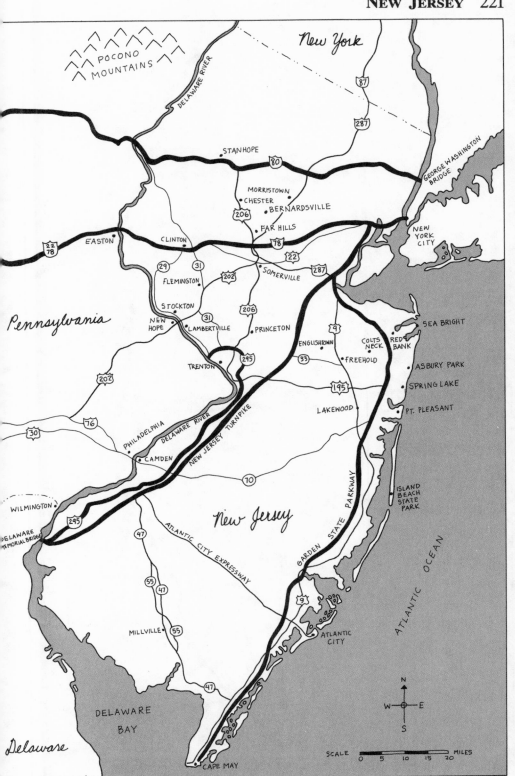

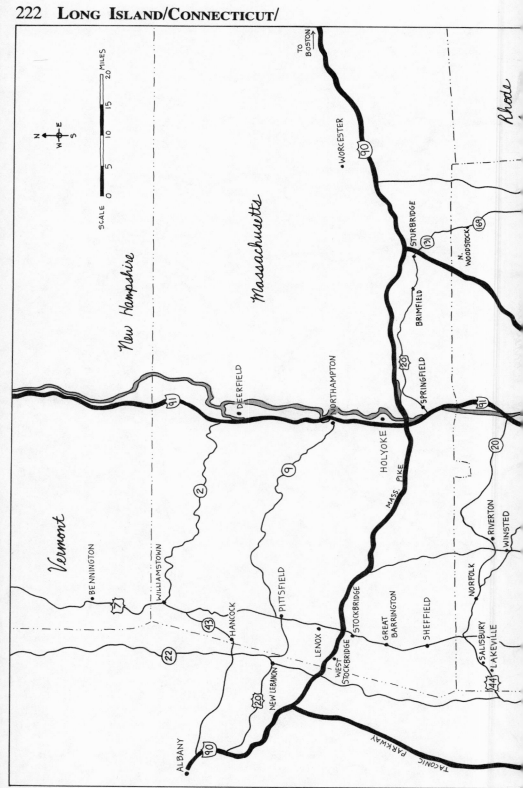

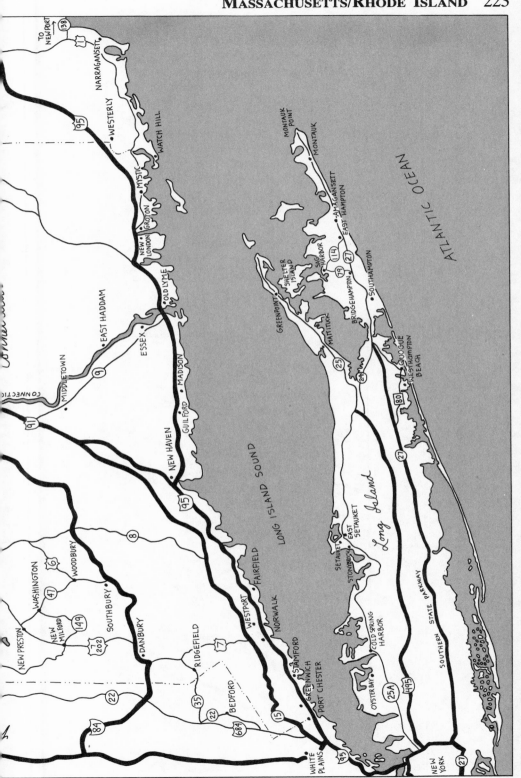

General Index

Category Index

Museums and Galleries